TEACH YOURSELF

Arabic

A.S. Tritton, D.Litt.
Professor Emeritus of Arabic, School of Oriental and African Studies,
University of London,

KITAB BHAVAN
NEW DELHI-110 002

KITAB BHAVAN
Publishers, Distributors, Exporters & Importers
1784, Kalan Mahal, Darya Ganj,
New Delhi - 1100 02 (India)

Phones : (91-11) 23277392/, 23274686
Fax : (91-11) 23263383
Online Store: www.kitabbavan.net
Email : info@kitabbhavan.net
: nasri@vsnl.com

ISBN: 81-7151-359-X
Book Code: T00164

First Indian Edition 1943
Reprint 2017

Printed & Published in India by :
Nusrat Ali Nasri for KITAB BHAVAN
Moonis Ali Nasri for KITAB BHAVAN
1784, Kalan Mahal, Darya Ganj,
New Delhi - 1100 02 [India]

TEACH YOURSELF BOOKS

ARABIC

The would-be student of Arabic is not faced with an easy task. He has to master a strange script and a structure which is quite unlike that of any of the European languages, and thus has none of the familiar landmarks to guide him. This book, however, reduces his difficulties to a minimum. It is a carefully graded course of lessons specially prepared for students working on their own by an Oriental scholar who has many years' experience of teaching Arabic. Both the script and the grammar are explained clearly and in detail, with many examples and exercises. The reader should find that he is able to make good progress.

You really can teach yourself Arabic from this little book. It is well printed, very cheap, pocket size and just over 300 pages. I am aware, from an experience of a number of years in teaching languages of this group, that Dr. Tritton's method of attack is sound and productive of good results.

Professor Norman Snaith

INTRODUCTION

Arabic is a Semitic language and so different from those usually studied in Europe; this is perhaps the main difficulty, there are none of the familiar landmarks. The verbs 'have' and 'be' do not exist; when 'be' is indispensable, 'become' is used as a substitute and it does not take the same case after it as it does before it. The verb has no tenses, only two forms indicating completed and incomplete action. Normally the 'finished' form is used to describe past events but it is also used to express wishes and prayers where the action is only ideally finished. To make up for this poverty the verb is developed in other ways, thus 'be good', 'do well', 'approve' are all expressed by modifications of the same verb.

Most words are derived from roots which consist of three consonants called radicals; it is obvious that these roots are not words. The addition of vowels, prefixes, suffixes to the root makes words. In this way some seventy word patterns are made, each with its own meaning. In English 'man', 'ran', 'fat' are all of the same pattern, a short vowel between two consonants but one is a noun, one a verb, and one an adjective; this is impossible in Arabic. As there are so few word patterns the language sounds rather monotonous; a poem must have the same rhyme throughout and it is common to find nearly one hundred lines with a complicated rhyme like *a:muha:*.

An illustration will make the next point clear. *KaTaBa* has a vowel between the first and the second radical, *yaKTuBu* has not. The beginner, especially in trying to hear the language, finds it hard to believe that the syllable *yak*, which ends in *k*, has anything to do with words which begin with *k*.

The Arab grammarians used the root *fʕl*, a real root, with its derivatives, as the type of all words; they called *ka:tibu* the *fa:ʕilu* of *ktb* not the active participle and *maktu:bu* the *mafʕu:lu* instead of the passive participle.

maktabu and *maka:nu* are the *maf*ʕ*alu* of *ktb* and *kwn* respectively; we should call them nouns of place. In *maka:nu* the *w* of the root has combined with the short vowel to form a long one.

They recognized only three parts of speech, noun, verb, and particle. This classification is useful because, (1) it is not often needful to distinguish the noun from the adjective, what is true of the first is usually true of the second; and (2) there are some words which have no equivalents in English and are lumped together with prepositions and conjunctions as particles. In most languages the commonest words are irregular; this is also true of Arabic, but it has fewer irregularities than most languages. The structure of sentences is simple; elaborate periods are few; clause is joined to clause by 'and' while it is left to the imagination of the reader to supply a more precise link. Effects are obtained by the combination of simple words; 'what is in me' may mean 'my abilities' or 'my feelings' according to the context.

The primary sense of the root usually develops derived meanings. To push money to someone is to pay him; to try to push his enemy from him is to defend him. 'Total' and 'eloquence' both come from 'arrive'; by the addition of small sums you arrive at a total, by persuasive words your ideas arrive at the minds of your hearers. It is obvious that the primary meaning of the root must be picked out from the mass of derivatives.

Print and handwriting are essentially the same. The script unites at least two stages of history. At first only the consonants were written, though in the earliest known inscriptions three of them, *alif* (which was then the glottal stop), *w*, and *y* were also used to indicate the long vowels. The first book to be written was the Koran and this fixed the spelling of the language because the text was too sacred to be tampered with. Unfortunately, Muhammad spoke the dialect of Mecca which did not use the glottal stop, replacing it near *u* and *i* by the consonants *w* and *y*. Other dialects kept the glottal stop and were considered more elegant. So a special sign for the glottal stop was invented, written like the new vowel signs outside the consonantal framework. It was introduced into the Koran and now appears in all Arabic sometimes alone and sometimes in conjunction with *alif* or *w* or *y* but representing only one sound.

Apart from school books all vowels are written only in the Koran ; elsewhere they are used sparingly.

The Arabic of a newspaper is in essentials that of the Koran ; the main difference is the large new vocabulary, partly old words with new meanings, partly loan words. The syntax is slightly simplified. The spoken tongue varies from place to place and differs from the written by the loss or degeneration of inflections and a different vocabulary. It is written only in jokes in comic papers, dialogue in novels, and sometimes in short stories.

Formerly the Arab sat on the floor, ate with his fingers and at meal or bed times his food or bed was brought to him. The result is that many words, indispensable in English, scarcely occur in accounts of native life. For 'table' Syria uses an Italian, Egypt a Greek, and Mesopotamia a Persian word.

This book is an introduction to written Arabic which is understood from the Atlantic to the frontiers of Persia. It will not help a man to talk to a crossing-sweeper the day of his arrival but it will quicken his progress in talking after the first month or so.

Words, which have been fully explained in the lessons, are left out of the vocabularies.

Proper names, which come in the examples, have not been transliterated in the phonetic alphabet.

In the transcription *j* and *y* have their English sounds.

Owing to the nature of the type in this book many of the vowels are to the left of the consonants instead of being directly above them.

ACKNOWLEDGMENT

The author and publishers gratefully acknowledge the assistance given by Mr. J. R. Firth, M.A., in connection with the sections on the sounds of the language.

CONTENTS

THE ALPHABET

Writing runs from right to left and the letters consist of strokes or strokes and dots. Vowels are not counted letters. At the end of a word or when standing alone many letters end with a flourish (compare the figures in a doctor's prescription 11ȷ). There are two classes of letters; those which can be joined on both sides and those which can only be joined to the preceding letter. The first class has four forms, initial, medial, final, and independent; the second has two, final and independent. The essential part of the letter remains unchanged as is shown here :—

independent	final	medial	initial
ب	ـب	ـبـ	بـ

when there is a final flourish the dot or dots are often put in the middle of it.

Name.	Independent.	Final.	Medial.	Initial.	Equivalent.
alif	ا	ـا			ʼ
bā	ب	ـب	ـبـ	بـ	b
tā	ت	ـت	ـتـ	تـ	t
thā	ث	ـث	ـثـ	ثـ	θ
jīm	ج	ـج	ـجـ	جـ	j
ḥā	ح	ـح	ـحـ	حـ	ḥ
khā	خ	ـخ	ـخـ	خـ	x
dāl	د	ـد			d
dhāl	ذ	ـذ			ð
rā	ر	ـر			r
zā	ز	ـز			z

Name.	Independent.	Final.	Medial.	Initial.	Equivalent.
sīn	س	ـس	ـسـ	سـ	s
shīn	ش	ـش	ـشـ	شـ	ʃ
ṣād	ص	ـص	ـصـ	صـ	ꞩ
ḍād	ض	ـض	ـضـ	ضـ	đ
ṭā	ط	ـط	ـطـ	طـ	ŧ
ẓā	ظ	ـظ	ـظـ	ظـ	ð̄
'ain	ع	ـع	ـعـ	عـ	ʕ
ghain	غ	ـغ	ـغـ	غـ	ɣ
fā	ف	ـف	ـفـ	فـ	f
ḳāf	ق	ـق	ـقـ	قـ	q
kāf	ك	ـك	ـكـ	كـ	k
lām	ل	ـل	ـلـ	لـ	l
mīm	م	ـم	ـمـ	مـ	m
nūn	ن	ـن	ـنـ	نـ	n
hā	ه	ـه	ـهـ ـهـ	هـ	h
waw	و	ـو			w
yā	ى	ـي ـى	ـيـ	يـ	y

Even in old Arabic the feminine termination *at* was often pronounced *ah* and written with *h*. When they began to study their own grammar they rectified the existing spelling by putting the two dots of *t* over the *h* ة or ـة —and this hybrid must be pronounced *t*.

In writing it is often convenient to put one consonant above another:—

بح *bḥ*; لمح *lmḥ*; لجم *ljm*; حجج *ḥjj*. In a book printed in Europe this last might appear as حجج.

CONSONANTS

Twelve of the consonants form correlative pairs.

	Tip of Tongue				Back of tongue towards soft palate	Throat and larynx
	Between teeth	Touching upper teeth	Behind lower teeth (see below)	Behind upper teeth		
Breathed unsingable .	θ	t	ŧ	s	x	ħ
Voiced singable .	ð	d	đ	z	ɣ	ʕ

The rest, including liquids and semivowels, stand in the next table in the order of their articulation, beginning with the lips and ending with the glottis, i.e. the space between the vocal cords, which may close the glottis completely in a stop *ʔ* or remain apart allowing the passage of breath in *h*.

	Labial	Labio-dental	Dental	Gums	Palatal	Velar	Uvular	Glottal
Voiced .	b		ð		j			h
Breathed .		f		ʃ ṡ		k	q	ʔ (h)
Liquids and semi vowels (voiced)	m w		l	r n	y		ʻ	

The six pairs :—

θ as English ' th ' in ' think '.

ð as ' th ' in ' this '.

t as ' t ' in ' eighth '.

d as ' d ' in ' width '.

ŧ voiceless, đ voiced ; counterparts of ' t ' and ' d '.

Emphatics.—Tip of tongue behind lower teeth, blade behind upper teeth touching gums. There is a depression or hollowing of the tongue just behind this and a raising of the back of the tongue. The sides of the tongue make a sort of inverted lid for the upper jaw, overflowing the back teeth and just touching the inside of the cheeks. The back of the tongue is raised in the same way for the other two emphatics ꞩ and ð̵.

s breathed, **z** voiced.

s is a strong clear sound as in ' hissing ' to be sharply differentiated from the emphatic ꞩ ; the tip of the tongue is behind the upper teeth.

z is a clear buzzing sound as in whizzing.

x breathed, **ɣ** voiced.

x is like the ' ch ' in the Scottish ' loch ' or the German ' ach ' but more scrapy. The difficulty is not so much in the sound as in the positions in which it can occur —e.g. initially. Pronounce ' loch ' and then try to pronounce it backwards.

ɣ bears a similar relation to **x** as **z** does to **s**. Try to voice **x**, that is, make it a singable sound, put the buzz of voice into it. Make it a little further back than **x** ; do not roll it, thus making it a back **r**.

ħ breathed, ʕ voiced.

ħ differs from **h**, which is frequently voiced, and has a sharper friction of an entirely different resonance caused by the forced depression of the back of the tongue and the tightening of the throat, the larynx being raised at the same time. The back of the tongue is as low as when the doctor presses it down with a spoon. With **a** it is very like the stage whisper 'ha!' It must not be produced with scrapy friction which confuses it with **x**.

ʕ is the voiced correlative of **ħ** pronounced with more tightening of the throat and forcing up of the larynx. The feeling in the throat is suggestive of slight retching. If you pronounce English vowels with a tightened throat and squeezed larynx, producing a metallic, rather low-pitched voice, they will be near to Arabic vowels in the neighbourhood of this consonant.

The two remaining emphatics :—

ṣ is the counterpart of **s** and is made with the blade of the tongue against the teeth ridge, the tip being behind the lower teeth.

ð̣ is the counterpart of **ð**; it is interdental but the tip of the tongue points upwards to the upper lip.

The four emphatics and **q** give to the vowel 'a', when it precedes or follows them, special dark qualities like the vowel in 'not'.

q is the furthest back **k** sound you can make, with the back of the tongue closing the arches of the back of the mouth, which are laterally squeezed nearer together to make the closure easier.

ʃ as in 'ship'. In Arabic **s** and **h** can come together without producing the ʃ sound.

ʔ the glottal stop. This sound is commonly used in Cockney instead of 't' in words like 'better', 'bottle' and also in standard English when a word which begins with a vowel is strongly emphasized, ʔ absolutely ʔ awful.

r is rolled as in Scotland; never fricative as in southern England.

The other consonants need no remark.

VOWELS

Three, which occur both short and long, are recognised in writing. Doubtless there were many variations in speech but only one is mentioned here. The consonants *alif*, 'w,' and 'y' were used to indicate the long 'a', 'u', and 'i'. The signs are put above or below the consonant which precedes the vowel.

NAME.	SIGN.	SOUND.	SYMBOL.
i, short	ـِ	as in 'sin'	*i*
long	ـِي	as in 'yeast'	*i:*
u, short	ـُ	much as in south English 'foot'	*u*
long	ـُو	much as in 'food' . . .	*u:*
a, short	ـَ	as in south English 'bat' .	*a*
long	ـَا	as in south English 'man' (drawled)	*a:*

There are two diphthongs:

ai	ـَي	much as in south English 'fight'	*ay*
au	ـَو	much as in south English 'shout'	*aw*

Near an emphatic consonant 'a' short is like the vowel in 'not', 'a' long is like that in 'was' (drawled); represented by *ɒ* and *ɒ:*; and *ay* becomes more like the sound in 'boy'. There is no English equivalent of *aw* under these circumstances; the 'a' component becomes *ɒ*.

OTHER CONVENTIONAL SIGNS

Sukûn.—Every consonant, which has no vowel immediately following it, is marked by sukûn ْ. This of course does not apply when the consonant is a letter of prolongation, only indicates a long vowel, as in سُو *su:*, contrasted with سَوْ *saw*, or when it is written but not pronounced, as اَلدَّارُ *adda:ru*, where the 'l' is assimilated to the 'd'.

Shadda.—If the same consonant is repeated and no vowel comes between the two, it is written once and the sign shadda ّ put over it. This may be due to assimilation, as in *adda:ru* above, or it may be part of the word form; thus كَسَرَ *kasara*, 'he broke,' but كَسَّرَ *kassara*, 'he smashed,' when the first syllable ends with 's' and the second begins with 's'. Apparent exceptions are due to the fact that the two consonants belong to different words as اَللَّيْلُ *allaylu*. The first 'l' belongs to the article and the second to the noun. The first 'l' does not take sukûn because it has been assimilated to the second and is indicated by shadda.

Nunation.—The word nunation is formed from the Arabic name of the letter 'n'. In one class of nouns the final vowel, which is the case ending, is written twice to indicate the pronunciations *un, an, in* respectively. With 'u' the upper sign is usually reversed ٌ or ٌ is used instead.

مَدِينَةٌ *madi:natun* ; مَدِينَةً *madi:natan* ; مَدِينَةٍ *madi:natin.*

Hamza.—This is the glottal stop (see Introduction). The sign ء is usually written with one of the three consonants *alif, w*, or *y*, which is called its bearer. *y*, when written with hamza, always loses its dots.

Hamza always has *alif* at the beginning of a word and, after the vowel 'a', at the end.

After a long vowel it has no bearer except in the sequence *a:ʔi* when it usually has 'y'.

After sukûn it may be written over a line connecting two letters.

أَقْرَأُ *ʔaqraʔu* ; إِبِلٌ *ʔibilun* ; أُذُنٌ *ʔudunun*

كِسَاءٌ *kisa:ʔun* ; سَاءَلَ *sa:ʔala* ; مَسْـؤُولٌ *masʔu:lun*

أَبْنَائِهِ *ʔabna:ʔihi* ; سُؤَالٌ *suʔa:lun* ; أَسْئِلَةٌ *ʔasʔilatun*

To find out how to write hamza.—Pronounce the word as if the hamza were not there, write the result, and add hamza. Take the word *fuʔa:dun*. Without hamza it becomes *fuwa:dun*, which is the correct way to write it, فُوَادٌ then add hamza فُؤَادٌ . The plural of this word is *ʔafʔidatun* ; without hamza it becomes *ʔafi:datun*. This is أَفِيدَةٌ remove the dots from the 'y' and add hamza, and remove 'i' one step to the left, أَفْئِدَةٌ is the right spelling.

Madda.—This takes the place of hamza when *a:* follows the glottal stop. This sound group may be original or it may be derived from the group *ʔaʔ*, which to Arabs is unpronounceable. In both cases it is written آ . So آكَلَ *ʔa:kala* may stand for *ʔa:kala* 'he ate with' and *ʔaʔkala* 'he fed' (transitive).

Syllable.—Every syllable must begin with one consonant ; the glottal stop is a consonant. A syllable may consist of consonant and vowel or of consonant vowel consonant.

Liaison.—Some words should begin with two consonants. From what has been said about the syllable it is clear that this is impossible so a helping vowel is put before the first consonant when the word stands alone. This vowel is indicated by *alif* always. If such a word stands alone the helping vowel is ushered in by the glottal stop. In connected speech the helping vowel is dropped and the final vowel of the preceding word takes its place. If there is no final vowel, a short one, usually 'i', is inserted.

In connected speech the sign ʼ is written over the *alif*.

In liaison a final long vowel is shortened in pronunciation and a diphthong is resolved into its component parts.

The best manner is never to write hamza over the liaison *alif* and that is followed in this book.

The words

اِبْتِدَاءِ *ibtida:ʔi* اِنْهِزَامِ *inhiza:mi* اَلْعَدُوِّ *alʕaduwwi*

when connected, read

فِي ٱبْتِدَاءِ ٱنْهِزَامِ ٱلْعَدُوِّ

fibtida:ʔinhiza:milʕaduwwi (note that *fi:* is shortened).

يَدَيْ *yaday* becomes *yadayi*

يَدَيِ ٱلْكَلْبِ *yadayilkalbi*

رَمَوْا *ramaw* (*alif* is purely graphic) becomes *ramawu*

رَمَوُا ٱلْعَدُوَّ *ramawulʕaduwwa*

The Arabs call this هَمْزَةُ ٱلْوَصْلِ *hamzatulwasli.*

ACCENT

The accent rests on—

(1) The penultimate syllable when it is long; i.e. has a long vowel or two consonants. *ki'ta:bun, ya'ku:nu.*

(2) On the antepenultimate when it is long and the penultimate short; when a word has three short syllables. *'ka:tibun, 'kataba.*

(3) On the long syllable before the antepenultimate when the penultimate and the antepenultimate are both short *mu'ka:tabatun*; on the first syllable if there is no such long vowel *'katabatuhuma:.*

Note that monosyllables and the definite article which are joined in writing to the following word do not affect the accent.

wa-'kataba ; al-'madadu

NUMBERS

The figures are read from left to right and are combined as in English :—

1	2	3	4	5	6	7	8	9	10
١	۲ ٢	۳ ٣	۴ ٤	٥	٦	٧	٨	٩	١٠

١٧٨٩ = 1789

Letters, when used as numbers, follow the order of the Hebrew alphabet, those peculiar to Arabic coming last, they represent the units, tens, hundreds, and a thousand. They are divided into these barbarous words :—

ابجد هوز حطي كلمن سعفص قرشت ثخذ ضظغ

Usually a line is drawn over the number.

غضعد = 1874

EXERCISE IN READING

كَانَ خَمَّارٌ يُسَافِرُ بِخَمْرٍ لَهُ وَمَعَهُ قِرْدٌ وَكَانَ يَمْزُجُ
ٱلْخَمْرَ بِٱلْمَاءِ نِصْفَيْنِ وَيَبِيعُهُ بِسِعْرِ ٱلْخَمْرِ وَٱلْقِرْدُ
يُشِيرُ إِلَيْهِ أَنْ لَا تَفْعَلْ فَيَضْرِبُهُ فَلَمَّا فَرَغَ مِنْ بَيْعِ
ٱلْخَمْرِ وَأَرَادَ ٱلرُّجُوعَ إِلَى بَلَدِهِ رَكِبَ ٱلْبَحْرَ وَقِرْدُهُ
مَعَهُ وَخُرْجٌ فِيهِ ثِيَابُهُ وَٱلْكِيسُ ٱلَّذِي جَمَعَهُ مِنْ ثَمَنِ
ٱلْخَمْرِ فَلَمَّا سَارَ فِي ٱلْبَحْرِ ٱسْتَخْرَجَ ٱلْقِرْدُ ٱلْكِيسَ
مِنْ مَوْضِعِهِ وَرَقِيَ ٱلدَّقَلَ وَهُوَ مَعَهُ حَتَّى صَارَ فِي
أَعْلَاهُ وَرَمَى إِلَى ٱلْمَرْكَبِ بِدِرْهَمٍ وَإِلَى ٱلْبَحْرِ
بِدِرْهَمٍ فَلَمْ يَزَلْ ذٰلِكَ دَأْبَهُ حَتَّى قَسَمَ ٱلدَّرَاهِمَ
نِصْفَيْنِ.

Phonetic Transcription

ka:na xamma:run yusa:firu bixamrin lahu wamaˁahu qirdun waka:na yamzuju͡ lxamra bilma:i nisfayni wayabi:ˁuhu bisiˁri͡ lxamri walqirdu yuʃi:ru ʔilayhi ʔan la: tafˁal fayadribuhu falamma: faraɣa min bayˁi͡ lxamri waʔara:da͡ rruju:ˁa ʔila: baladihi rakiba͡ lbaħra waqirduhu maˁahu waxurjun fi:hi θiya:buhu walki:su͡ llaði jamaˁahu

min θamani͡ lxamri falamma: sa:ra fi͡ lbaħri͡ staxraja͡ lqirdu͡ lki:sa min mawđiʕihi waraqiya͡ ddɑqɒla wahuwa maʕahu ħatta: sɒ:ra fi: ʔaʕla:hu warama: ʔila͡ lmarkabi bidirhamin waʔila͡ lbaħri bidirhamin falam yazal ða:lika daʔbahu ħatta: qɒsama͡ ddara:hima nisfayni.

Translation

a wine merchant used to travel in wine he had and a monkey was with him. He mixed the wine with water half and half and sold it at the price of wine. The monkey signed to him: don't do that, so he beat it. When he had finished selling the wine and wanted to go back to his town, he rode on the sea having with him the monkey and saddle-bags in which were his clothes and the purse which he had collected from the price of the wine. When he was well at sea, the monkey pulled the purse from its place and climbed the mast, it being with him, till he reached the top. He threw one dirham into the ship and one into the sea and that continued to be his practice till he had divided the dirhams into two halves.

LESSON I

NOUN AND ARTICLES

The distinction between a definite and an indefinite noun is fundamental.

The indefinite article *n* is put at the end of the noun, is not expressed by a consonant, but is indicated in one class of nouns by nunation. For inflection the noun falls into four classes but, as two of them are indeclinable, they cannot be called declensions. This lesson deals with one class only.

نَهْرٌ *nahrun* a river ; مَلِكٌ *malikun* a king

The *u* is the nominative inflection.

One way of making a noun definite is to give it the definite article اَلْ *al*, which is written in front of the noun and joined to it. The vowel of the article is only a helping vowel, liaison, so in connected speech it is replaced by the final vowel of the preceding word. If the noun begins with a dental, sibilant, *r*, *l*, or *n*

ت ث د ذ ر ز س ش ص ض ط ظ ل ن

that letter assimilates to itself the *l* of the article in pronunciation though the *l* is still written. The assimilating consonant takes *shadda*. No noun can be both definite and indefinite at the same time, so nunation must be dropped when the definite article is present. اَلْبَيْتُ *albaytu* the house ; اَلشَّمْسُ *aʃʃamsu* the sun. Arabic uses the definite article where English does not ; abstract nouns usually have it ; and it also indicates the class. ' Man is a reasoning animal ' must be translated ' The man '.

An adjective, which qualifies a noun, follows it, agrees with it in gender (if it is singular), in case, and in definiteness.

بُسْتَانٌ كَبِيرٌ *busta:nun kabi:run* a big garden.

اَلْبَحْرُ الْوَاسِعُ *albaħrulwa:siʕu* the spacious sea.

The verbs ' is ' and ' are ' are not expressed ; so ' the man is handsome ' is literally ' the man handsome '. Arabic grammar took its technical terms from logic, so ' the man ' is subject and ' handsome ' (the complement of the verb to be, as we call it) is the predicate. The subject must be definite, unless the sentence is negative or interrogative, and the predicate must be indefinite.

اَلرَّجُلُ حَسَنٌ *arrajulu ħasanun* the man is handsome.

اَلْبَحْرُ وَاسِعٌ *albaħru wa:siʕun* the sea is spacious.

Questions are asked by prefixing one of the particles أَ *ʔa* or هَلْ *hal* to the sentence; *ʔa* is connected with the word it precedes.

أَرَجُلٌ *ʔarajulun* . . . is a man . . . ?

هَلِ ٱلْبَحْرُ وَاسِعٌ *halilbaħru wa:siʕun* is the sea spacious?

ʔa drives out the *alif* of the definite article;

أَلرَّجُلُ حَسَنٌ *ʔarrajulu ħasanun* is the man handsome?

Personal Pronouns

	Singular.	*Dual.*	*Plural.*
3. Masc.	هُوَ *huwa*	هُمَا *huma:*	هُمْ — هُمُ *hum, humu*
Fem.	هِيَ *hiya*		هُنَّ *hunna*
2. Masc.	أَنْتَ *ʔanta*	أَنْتُمَا *ʔantuma:*	أَنْتُمْ *ʔantum* أَنْتُمُ *ʔantumu*
Fem.	أَنْتِ *ʔanti*		أَنْتُنَّ *ʔantunna*
1. Com.	أَنَا *ʔana.*		نَحْنُ *naħnu*

Note.—أَنَا has two short syllables, in spite of the spelling. Arabic uses the second person singular. هُمُ *humu* and أَنْتُمُ *ʔantumu* are used before liaison.

Vocabulary 1

The words in brackets are the customary plurals which are all feminine. Five of the commonest plurals are indicated by letters from the second vocabulary onwards ; they are :

أَفْعَالٌ a — فُعُولٌ b — فِعَالٌ c — فُعُلٌ d — أَفْعُلٌ e

نَهْرٌ (أَنْهَارٌ) river, canal.

بَيْتٌ (بُيُوتٌ) house.

مَلِكٌ (مُلُوكٌ) king.

بَحْرٌ (بِحَارٌ) sea.

بُسْتَانٌ (بَسَاتِينُ) garden.

رَجُلٌ (رِجَالٌ) man.

خُبْزٌ bread.

لَحْمٌ flesh, meat.

شَارِعٌ (شَوَارِعُ) street.

قَصْرٌ (قُصُورٌ) castle, palace.

إِنْسَانٌ (نَاسٌ) human being.

وَلَدٌ (أَوْلَادٌ) child, boy.

كَبِيرٌ big.

صَغِيرٌ little.

نَظِيفٌ clean.

وَسِخٌ dirty.

فَقِيرٌ poor.

غَنِيٌّ rich.

حَسَنٌ good, beautiful.

قَبِيحٌ ugly, bad.

عَرِيضٌ wide.

حَبِيبٌ beloved, friend.

وَاسِعٌ spacious.

صَادِقٌ truthful.

طَيِّبٌ good. لَطِيفٌ gracious.

قَدِيمٌ old (of things).

Exercise 1

نَهْرٌ كَبِيرٌ ـ اَلْمَلِكُ اللَّطِيفُ ـ اَلْبَيْتُ نَظِيفٌ ـ بُسْتَانٌ
حَسَنٌ ـ خُبْزٌ طَيِّبٌ ـ اَلرَّجُلُ الْفَقِيرُ ـ إِنْسَانٌ قَبِيحٌ ـ
اَللَّحْمُ طَيِّبٌ ـ اَلشَّارِعُ عَرِيضٌ ـ أَنَا غَنِيٌّ ـ وَلَدٌ
وَسِخٌ ـ أَهُوَ حَبِيبٌ ـ قَصْرٌ قَدِيمٌ ـ هَلْ أَنْتَ صَادِقٌ.

Transcription

nahrun kabi:run — almalikullαti:fu — albaytu nαði:fun — busta:nun ħasanun — xubzun ŧɒyyibun — arrajululfαqi:ru — ʔinsa:nun qɒbi:ħun — allaħmu ŧɒyyibun — aʃʃa:riʕu ʕari:đun — ʔana ɣaniyyun — waladun wasixun — ʔahuwa ħabi:bun — qɒsrun qɒdi:mun — hal ʔanta sɒ:diqun.

2

a small house — the house is small — a poor man — the friend is truthful — he is ugly — I am a man — you (masc. sing.) are gracious — the spacious garden — a wide river — the sea is beautiful — the ugly street — the little boy is dirty — the bread is good.

LESSON 2

GENDER

There are two genders, masculine and feminine, so gender is not co-extensive with sex as it is in English.

The commonest feminine ending is *at*, with case ending

and nunation, which is written with the dotted *h* ةٌ.

Some nouns and all the adjectives, which have so far been mentioned, form a feminine in this way; though most feminine nouns have no masculine correlative.

كَبِيرَةٌ *kabi:ratun* big; مَلِكَةٌ *malikatun* queen;

جَارِيَةٌ *ja:riyatun* girl; قِطْعَةٌ *qitʕatun* piece.

Two nouns have *t* as feminine ending:—

بِنْتٌ *bintun* daughter, girl; أُخْتٌ *ʔuxtun* sister.

Names of males are masculine even when they have the feminine ending. Otherwise all nouns with the feminine ending are feminine. Names of females, those of towns and countries and some collectives are feminine.

Some feminine nouns have no feminine ending: names of females:—

أُمٌّ *ʔummun* mother; عَرُوسٌ *ʕaru:sun* bride;

عَجُوزٌ *ʕaju:zun* old woman; أَتَانٌ *ʔata:nun* she ass.

Names of towns and countries:—

مِصْرُ *misru*, Egypt, Cairo (no nunation);

اَلشَّامُ *aʃʃa:mu*, Syria, Damascus.

Parts of the body which occur in pairs:—

يَدٌ *yadun* hand; عَيْنٌ *ʕaynun* eye;

قَدَمٌ *qvdamun* foot, leg ; رِجْلٌ *rijlun* foot, leg ;

سَاقٌ *sa:qun* leg.

Some everyday words though no reason can be given :—

أَرْضٌ *ʔarđun* earth ; شَمْسٌ *ʃamsun* sun ;

خَمْرٌ *xamrun* wine ; نَارٌ *na:run* fire ;

دَارٌ *da:run* house ; نَفْسٌ *nafsun* soul ;

رِيحٌ *ri:ħun* wind ; سُوقٌ *su:qun* street of shops, bazaar.

The feminine ending has other uses. From collective nouns it forms a noun of unity, a singular :—

شَجَرٌ *ʃajarun* trees ; شَجَرَةٌ *ʃajaratun* a tree.

It forms emphatic nouns :—

عَلَّامٌ *ʕalla:mun* a learned man ; عَلَّامَةٌ *ʕalla:matun* very learned ; perhaps under this head comes خَلِيفَةٌ *xali:fatun* deputy, caliph. (Other feminine forms are given in Lesson 10).

Vocative.—If the noun has the article, it is put in the nominative and أَيُّهَا *ʔayyuha:* is prefixed ; أَيُّهَا ٱلْمَلِكُ *ʔayyuhalmaliku* O king ; before a feminine noun أَيَّتُهَا

ʔayyatuha: is used. If the noun stands alone, it is put in the nominative without nunation and the exclamatory particle is يَا *ya:*.

يَا وَلَدُ *ya: waladu* O boy ; يَا جَارِيَةُ *ya: ja:riyatu* O girl. Proper names, which have the definitive article, lose it after *ya:* ; يَا شَامُ *ya: ʃa:mu* O Syria.

Vocabulary 2

جَارِيَةٌ (جَوَارٍ)[1] girl.	أُخْتٌ (أَخَوَاتٌ) sister.
مَدِينَةٌ (d) town.	دَارٌ (آدُرٌ) house.
أُمٌّ (أُمَّهَاتٌ) mother.	عَجُوزٌ (عَجَائِزُ) old woman.
رِيحٌ (c) wind.	سُوقٌ (a) market.
جَزِيرَةٌ (جَزَائِرُ) island.	نَارٌ (نِيرَانٌ) fire.
أَرْضٌ (أَرَضُونَ) earth, land.	شَمْسٌ sun.
شَجَرٌ (a) trees.	شَيْخٌ (b) old man, chief.
جَدِيدٌ new.	شَدِيدٌ strong, violent.
بَعِيدٌ far, distant.	قَرِيبٌ near.
حَارٌّ hot.	عَزِيزٌ mighty.
طَوِيلٌ long, tall.	نَفْسٌ (b) soul.
بِنْتٌ (بَنَاتٌ) daughter.	عَيْنٌ (b) eye.
رِجْلٌ (e) foot, leg.	سَاقٌ (سِيقَانٌ) leg, stalk.
قَدَمٌ (a) foot, leg.	خَلِيفَةٌ (خُلَفَاءُ) deputy, caliph.

[1] Plurals of this form are explained in Lesson 26; till then there is no need to use them.

Exercise 3

جَارِيَةٌ صَغِيرَةٌ ـ أُخْتٌ كَبِيرَةٌ ـ اَلْمَدِينَةُ نَظِيفَةٌ ـ اَلْأُمُّ
حَسَنَةٌ ـ دَارٌ جَدِيدَةٌ ـ اَلرِّيحُ شَدِيدَةٌ ـ عَجُوزٌ صَادِقَةٌ ـ
اَلشَّيْخُ اُلطَّوِيلُ ـ اَلسُّوقُ بَعِيدَةٌ ـ اَلشَّجَرَةُ صَغِيرَةٌ ـ
جَزِيرَةٌ وَاسِعَةٌ ـ هَلِ اُلْبِنْتُ حَبِيبَةٌ ـ اَلشَّمْسُ حَارَّةٌ ـ
يَا وَلَدُ ـ أَيَّتُهَا اُلْمَلِكَةُ اُلْعَزِيزَةُ ـ أَرْضٌ قَرِيبَةٌ ـ
أَأَنْتِ غَنِيَّةٌ .

Transcription

jaːriyatun ꞩɒɣiːratun — ˀuxtun kabiːratun — almadiːnatu nɑðiːfatun — alˀummu ħasanatun — daːrun jadiːdatun — arriːħu ʃadiːdatun — ˤajuːzun ꞩɒːdiqɒtun — aʃʃayxuŧŧɒwiːlu — assuːqu baˤiːdatun — aʃʃajaratu ꞩɒɣiːratun — jaziːratun waːsiˤatun — halilbintu ħabiːbatun — aʃʃamsu ħaːrratun — yaː waladu — ˀayyatuhalmalikatulˤaziːzatu — ˀarđun qɒriːbatun — ˀaˀanti ɣaniyyatun.

4

the hot sun — the island is distant — a tall mother — the big (elder) sister — the old woman is kind — the fire is hot — the powerful chief — the house is new — the ancient palace — is she poor ? — you (fem. sing.) are kind.

LESSON 3

CASE

There are three cases ; the familiar names, nominative, accusative, and genitive fit them well though the use of the accusative and genitive is wider than in English. Nouns of both genders which have nunation, have three case endings : *u* nominative, *a* accusative, and *i* genitive. Indefinite masculine nouns add *alif* to the accusative unless the word ends in *ʔ* preceded by *a:*. This *alif* is a letter of prolongation and is due to the fact that in Mecca a final *an* was often pronounced *a:*.

	Nominative.	Accusative.	Genitive.
moon	قَمَرٌ	قَمَرًا	قَمَرٍ
	qɒmarun	*qɒmaran*	*qɒmarin*
	اَلْقَمَرُ	اَلْقَمَرَ	اَلْقَمَرِ
	alqɒmaru	*alqɒmara*	*alqɒmari*
clothing	كِسَاءٌ	كِسَاءً	كِسَاءٍ
	kisa:ʔun	*kisa:ʔan*	*kisa:ʔin*
garden (now paradise)	جَنَّةٌ	جَنَّةً	جَنَّةٍ
	jannatun	*jannatan*	*jannatin*
	اَلْجَنَّةُ	اَلْجَنَّةَ	اَلْجَنَّةِ
	aljannatu	*aljannata*	*aljannati*

Construct state.—When one noun governs another in the genitive, the first is said to be in the construct state. The governing noun comes first and loses nunation :

بَيْتُ رَجُلٍ *baytu rajulin* a house of a man ;

بَيْتُ ٱلرَّجُلِ *bayturrajuli* the house of the man.

The second noun being definitive makes the first definitive also. Most Europeans find it hard to accustom themselves to this. The first noun, being definitive by position, does not need and cannot have the definitive article.

Nothing can come between the construct and its genitive ; hence the name. An adjective agreeing with the first noun must come after the second. If the construct is definite, the adjective must be definite also ; there is only one way of making an adjective definite, giving it the definite article.

شَعَرُ ٱلْبِنْتِ ٱلْجَمِيلُ

ʃaʕrulbintiljami:lu the beautiful hair of the girl.

دار البنت الجميلة is ambiguous if the vowels are not added as the feminine adjective may refer to either noun.

A sentence like ' a house of the man ' cannot be translated directly into Arabic, you must go a roundabout way :

بَيْتٌ لِلرَّجُلِ *baytun lirrajuli* a house (belonging) to the man. (Another mode of expression in Lesson 19.)

Emphasis.—' The house is big ' may be translated in two ways :—

اَلْبَيْتُ كَبِيرٌ *albaytu kabi:run.*

إِنَّ ٱلْبَيْتَ كَبِيرٌ *ʔinnalbayta kabi:run.*

To an Arab the second is slightly more emphatic than the first but it is a degree of emphasis which cannot be represented in English. *ʔinna* puts the subject into the accusative but it is best left untranslated. A degree of emphasis, which can be translated, is got by using *ʔinna* with the particle *la*. This *l* also appears in the definite article and in some demonstrative pronouns.

إِنَّ الْبَيْتَ لَكَبِيرٌ

ʔinnalbayta lakabi:run the house is indeed big.

This *la* must not be confused with the negative *la:*.

Prepositions. (For a full list see Lesson 36.)

All prepositions, with one partial exception, govern the genitive. Those, which consist of one consonant, are written as one word with the word they govern.

بِ *bi* by, with ; لِ *li* to, for ; كَ *ka* as, like.

After *li* the *alif* of the definite article is omitted and, if the noun begins with *l*, the *l* of the article also.

بِالْيَدِ *bilyadi* by the hand ; بِاللَّيْلِ *billayli* by (the) night ;

لِمَلِكٍ *limalikin* to a king ; لِلْمَلِكِ *lilmaliki* to the king ;

لِلَّبَنِ *lillabani* for the milk.

There is no verb 'have' ; the idea is expressed by a preposition. 'The man has a book' can be said in three ways with shades of meaning :—

لِلرَّجُلِ كِتَابٌ *lirrajuli kita:bun* (the fact of possession).

عِنْدَ الرَّجُلِ كتاب *ʕindarrajuli kita:bun*
مَعَ الرَّجُلِ كتاب *maʕarrajuli kita:bun*
} he has it on him.

The subject can be indefinite because the predicate is a prepositional phrase.

God. إِلَاهٌ or إِلَـهٌ *ʔila:hun god* (pl. آلِهَةٌ *ʔa:lihatun*)

أَلْإِلَاهُ *alʔila:hu* is sometimes used for *God* but usually it is shortened to أَللّٰهُ *alla:hu.* Note the spellings بِاللّٰهِ *billa:hi* and لِلّٰهِ *lilla:hi.*

مِنْ *min* of, from becomes مِنَ *mina* before the definite article and مِنِ *mini* in any other liaison.

With مِنْ *min* and عَنْ *ʕan*, the *n* is assimilated to the *m* of a following monosyllable; مِمَّنْ *mimman,* from whom; مِمَّـا *mimma:*, from what. After لِ *li,* ما *ma:* is often shortened; لِمَ — لِمَـا *lima* or *lima:*, for what, why.

Vocabulary 3

بَابٌ (a) door, chapter.

كِسَاءٌ (أَكْسِيَةٌ) clothing, covering.

مِفْتَاحٌ (مَفَاتِيحُ) key.

لِسَانٌ (أَلْسِنَةٌ) tongue.

رَفِيقٌ (رُفَقَاءُ) companion.

حِفْظٌ keeping (abstract noun).

عِزٌّ might.

حِكْمَةٌ (حِكَمٌ) wisdom, wise saying.

تَاجِرٌ (تُجَّارٌ) merchant.

كِتَابٌ (d) book.

ظِلٌّ (c) shade, shadow.

خَفِيفٌ light.

كَرِيمٌ noble, generous.

مَفْتُوحٌ opened, open.

شُبَّاكٌ (شَبَابِيكُ) window.

قُفْلٌ (a) lock.

وَجْهٌ (b) face.

جَارٌ (جِيرَانٌ) protected alien, neighbour.

طَرِيقٌ (d) road.

سَلَامَةٌ safety.

رَأْسٌ (b) head.

مَخَافَةٌ fear.

صَحْنٌ (b) courtyard, dish.

شَعْرٌ (a) hair.

جَمِيلٌ beautiful.

ثَقِيلٌ heavy.

شَرِيفٌ (a) noble.

لَا no, not.

Exercise 5

بَابُ بَيْتٍ ـ بَابُ ٱلْبُسْتَانِ ـ شُبَّاكُ ٱلدَّارِ مَفْتُوحٌ ـ
إِنَّ ٱلْأَرْضَ وَاسِعَةٌ ـ ٱلْقَبِيلَةُ غَنِيَّةٌ ـ هَلِ ٱلْكِتَابُ
لِبِنْتِ ٱلشَّيْخِ ـ لَا هُوَ لِأُخْتِ ٱلتَّاجِرِ ـ شَارِعُ
ٱلْمَدِينَةِ عَرِيضٌ ـ صَحْنُ بَيْتِ ٱلْمَلِكِ ٱلْكَبِيرُ ـ إِنَّ
مِفْتَاحَ ٱلْبَابِ فِي ٱلْقُفْلِ ـ إِنَّ كِسَاءَ ٱلشَّيْخِ
نَظِيفٌ ـ إِنَّ وَجْهَ ٱلْبِنْتِ حَسَنٌ ـ سَلَامَةُ ٱلْإِنْسَانِ
فِي حِفْظِ ٱللِّسَانِ ـ ٱلْجَارُ قَبْلَ ٱلدَّارِ وَٱلرَّفِيقُ

قَبْلَ ٱلطَّرِيقِ ـ ٱلْعِزُّ لِلّٰهِ ـ رَأْسُ ٱلْحِكْمَةِ مَخَافَةُ
ٱللّٰهِ ـ ٱلْخَلِيفَةُ ظِلُّ ٱللّٰهِ عَلَى ٱلْأَرْضِ.

Transcription

ba:bu baytin — ba:bulbusta:ni — ʃubba:kudda:ri maftu:ħun — ʔinnalʔarđa wa:siyatun — alqɒbi:latu ɣaniyyatun — halilkita:bu libintiʃʃayxi — la: huwa liʔuxtitta:jiri — ʃa:riʕulmadi:nati ʕari:đun — ꞩɒħnu baytilmalikilkabi:ru — ʔinna mifta:ħalba:bi filqufli — ʔinna kisa:ʔaʃʃayxi nɑði:fun — ʔinna wajhalbinti ħasanun — sala:mtulʔinsa:ni fi: ħafðillisa:ni — alja:ru qɒbladda:ri warrafi:qu qɒblaŧŧɒ-ri:qi — alʕizzu lilla:hi — raʔsulħikmati maxa:fatulla:hi — alxali:fatu ðillulla:hi ʕalalʔarđi.

6

a royal garden — the strength of a man is in the tongue — the beautiful face of the beautiful girl — the key of the door is heavy — the little house is in the shade of a big tree — a (the) good companion is the beginning of safety on the road — the merchant is the strength of the land — the little book is indeed light — the girl has light clothing and the old woman heavy clothing.

LESSON 4

NUMBER

There are three numbers, singular, dual, and plural.

The dual is formed by cutting off the case ending from the singular and adding اَنِ *a:ni* for the nominative and ـَيْنِ *ayni* for the accusative or genitive. There is no nunation. When a noun has only one form for these two cases, it is convenient to call it the oblique case.

عَيْنٌ *ʕaynun* eye, spring (of water) ; عَيْنَانِ *ʕayna:ni* ;

عَيْنَيْنِ *ʕaynayni.*

قِطْعَةٌ *qitʕatun* piece ; قِطْعَتَانِ *qitʕata:ni* ; قِطْعَتَيْنِ *qitʕatayni.*

The construct state is made by cutting off the *ni* :—

عَيْنَا الْبِنْتِ *ʕaynalbinti* the (two) eyes of the girl. The *a:* is shortened in liaison.

عَيْنَيِ الْبِنْتِ *ʕaynayilbinti.* The diphthong resolved in liaison.

Plural.—There are two ways of forming the plural, the sound or external and the broken or internal.

The external plural of nouns with the feminine ending is made by lengthening the *a* before the *t* which is then written as *t*, not as *h* with dots.

خَادِمَةٌ *xa:dimatun* maid servant ; خَادِمَاتٌ *xa:dima:tun*, maids. This plural has two cases, *u* for the nominative, *i* for the oblique. It takes nunation.

Masculine plural.—Most participles and a few nouns make an external plural by cutting off the case ending and adding *u:na* for the nominative and *i:na* for the oblique case. There is no nunation. Note the alternation of vowels in the dual and the masculine plural.

خَادِمٌ *xa:dimun* servant ; خَادِمُونَ *xa:dimu:na* ;

خَادِمِينَ *xa:dimi:na.*

The construct state is formed by cutting off *na*.

خَادِمُو ٱلطَّبِيبِ *xa:dimuttvbi:bi* خَادِمِي الطبيب *xa:dimittvbi:bi* the servants of the doctor. The long vowels are shortened in liaison. Adjectives agreeing with the external masculine plural usually take the external plural themselves.

Broken plural.—Nearly all masculine and many feminine nouns use the broken plural. This is made by a change in the word. No rules can be given for the simplest nouns and the plural must be learnt with the singular, it is all memory work. Many nouns have more than one plural; as a rule one form is the favourite or one form may be allotted to a special meaning.

عَبْدٌ *ʕabdun* slave, servant; عَبِيدٌ *ʕabi:dun* slaves;

عِبَادٌ *ʕiba:dun* slaves of God, worshippers, men.

All. There is no adjective meaning *all* which has to be expressed by كُلٌّ *kullun,* totality. Of course, this governs the genitive.

كُلُّ رَجُلٍ *kullu rajulin* every man;

كُلُّ ٱلرِّجَالِ *kullurrija:li* all the men.

As the accusative is the adverbial case so:—

كُلَّ يَوْمٍ *kulla yawmin,* every day, daily;

كُلَّ ٱلْيَوْمِ *kullalyawmi* all day long.

وَ *wa* 'and' is written with the following word. It was

enough for the Arabs to join two contrasting phrases by 'and' where we must use 'but'.

Vocabulary 4

قِطْعَةٌ (قِطَعٌ) piece.

خَادِمٌ (خُدَّامٌ) servant.

نَجَّارٌ carpenter.

فَرَّاشٌ domestic servant.

خَيَّاطَةٌ sempstress.

حُجْرَةٌ (حُجَرٌ) room.

فَرَسٌ (a) horse, mare.

لَاعِبٌ playing (participle).

جَالِسٌ sitting.

مُظِلٌّ giving shade, shady.

نَعَمْ yes.

كَثِيرٌ many, much.

صَاحِبٌ (a) companion, master, owner.

طَبِيبٌ (أَطِبَّاءُ) physician.

خَبَّازٌ baker.

طَبَّاخٌ cook.

خَيَّاطٌ tailor.

أُذْنٌ (a) ear.

بَقَّالٌ greengrocer.

حِمَارٌ (حَمِيرٌ) donkey.

مَشْغُولٌ busy, busied.

قَصِيرٌ short.

غَنَمٌ sheep (collective).

قَلِيلٌ few.

Exercise 7

هَلِ ٱلْخَبَّازُ غَنِيٌّ ـ لَا هُوَ فَقِيرٌ ـ ٱلْخَبَّازُونَ

وَٱلنَّجَّارُونَ مَشْغُولُونَ ـ إِنَّ فِي ٱلْمَدِينَةِ خَبَّازِينَ

وَنَجَّارِينَ كَثِيرِينَ ـ ٱلْعَيْنَانِ وَٱلْأُذْنَانِ فِي ٱلرَّأْسِ ـ

ٱلْوَلَدَانِ لَاعِبَانِ ـ بِنْتَانِ لَاعِبَتَانِ ـ يَدَا ٱلْوَلَدِ وَسِخَتَانِ ـ

اَلشَّيْخُ وَٱلْعَجُوزُ جَالِسَانِ عِنْدَ شَجَرَةٍ قَصِيرَةٍ وَمُظِلَّةٍ ـ
فَرَسَانِ وَحِمَارَانِ ـ إِنَّ أُخْتَيِ ٱلتَّاجِرِ فِي ٱلْحُجْرَةِ
ٱلصَّغِيرَةِ ـ هَلْ أَنْتُمَا صَادِقَانِ ـ نَعَمْ نَحْنُ صَادِقَانِ ـ
إِنَّ ٱلْغَنَمَ ٱلْقَلِيلَةَ لِصَاحِبِ ٱلْبَيْتِ ٱلصَّغِيرِ .

Transcription

halilxabba:zu ɣaniyyun — la: huwa faqi:run — alxabba:zu:na wannajja:ru:na maʃɣu:lu:na — ʔinna filmadi:nati xabba:zi:na wannajja:ri:na kaθi:ri:na — alʕayna:ni walʔuðuna:ni firraʔsi — alwaladà:ni la:ʕiba:ni — binta:ni la:ʕibata:ni — yadalwaladi wasixata:ni — aʃʃayxu walʕaju:zu ja:lisa:ni ʕinda ʃajaratin qɒs̶i:ratin wamuðillatin — farasa:ni waħima:ra:ni — ʔinna ʔuxtayitta:jiri filħujratis̶s̶ɒɣi:rati — hal ʔantuma: s̶ɒ:diqɒ:ni — naʕam naħnu s̶ɒ:diqɒ:ni — ʕinnalɣanamalqɒli:lata lis̶ɒ:hibilbaytis̶s̶ɒɣi:ri.

8

the two doors of the house are open — he is the owner of two horses — she is the owner of a house and a garden in the town — the donkey is the poor man's horse — there are two doctors in the town — each room in the house has two windows — are you domestic servants ? — no, we are cooks — two pieces of meat and much bread are in the house — the garden belongs to two friends of the king — they are busy sempstresses.

LESSON 5

BROKEN PLURAL

The commonest forms for the plural of short nouns are :—

أَفْعَالٌ — فُعُولٌ — فِعَالٌ — فُعُلٌ — أَفْعُلٌ — examples have been given in the vocabularies to earlier lessons.

For some forms of the plural rules can be given.

أَفْعِلَاءُ is a plural of فَعِيلٌ : صَدِيقٌ — أَصْدِقَاءُ :

غَنِيٌّ — أَغْنِيَاءُ : نَبِيٌّ prophet أَنْبِيَاءُ .

فُعَلَاءُ is plural of فَعِيلٌ when it has become a noun:

أَمِيرٌ prince, commander أُمَرَاءُ : شَرِيكٌ partner شُرَكَاءُ.

أَفْعِلَةٌ is plural of nouns with three consonants and a long vowel in the second syllable : جَنَاحٌ wing أَجْنِحَةٌ :

طَعَامٌ food أَطْعِمَةٌ — رَغِيفٌ loaf of bread أَرْغِفَةٌ —

عَمُودٌ pillar أَعْمِدَةٌ .

مَفَاعِلُ is plural of مَفْعَلٌ or مَفْعَلَةٌ whatever the vowels may be :—

مَكْتَبٌ school, office, library مَكَاتِبُ — مَدْرَسَةٌ

school مَدَارِسُ — مَسْجِدٌ mosque مَسَاجِدُ — مِنْجَلٌ

sickle مَنَاجِلُ. أَقْرَبُ relative أَقَارِبُ.

مَفَاعِيلُ is plural of nouns with four consonants, two syllables and a long vowel in the second whether they have the feminine ending or not. مِفْتَاحٌ key مَفَاتِيحُ —

صُنْدُوقٌ box صَنَادِيقُ — مَمْلُوكٌ slave مَمَالِيكُ —

تَصْوِيرٌ picture تَصَاوِيرُ.

فَوَاعِلُ is plural of فَاعِلَةٌ and sometimes of فَاعِلٌ

فَاكِهَةٌ fruit (considered as food) فَوَاكِهُ — صَاحِبَةٌ

companion صَوَاحِبُ — فَارِسٌ rider فَوَارِسُ.

فَعَائِلُ is plural of feminine nouns with three consonants and a long vowel in the second syllable.

رِسَالَةٌ letter رَسَائِلُ — فَضِيلَةٌ virtue فَضَائِلُ —

رَذِيلَةٌ vice رَذَائِلُ.

فِعَلٌ is plural of فِعْلَةٌ.

قِطْعَةٌ piece قِطَعٌ — سِيرَةٌ manner of walking, character سِيَرٌ.

فُعَلٌ is plural of فُعْلَةٌ.

رُكْبَةٌ knee رُكَبٌ — تُحْفَةٌ gift تُحَفٌ.

All broken plurals are grammatically collective nouns in the feminine singular; consequently they may be construed with feminine singular adjectives.

نِسَاءٌ حَسَنَاتٌ or نِسَاءٌ حَسَنَةٌ fair women

رِجَالٌ كَبِيرَةٌ — كَبِيرُونَ — كِبَارٌ important men

(كِبَار is a broken plural of كَبِير generally used of persons.)

Second declension.—Several of the broken plurals end in *u* without nunation. These and similar nouns form the second declension which has two case endings, *u* for the nominative and *a* for the oblique, when they are indefinite. When definite, they have the three terminations of the first declension.

Nominative.	Accusative.	Genitive.
مَدَارِسُ	مَدَارِسَ	.
اَلْمَدَارِسُ	اَلْمَدَارِسَ	اَلْمَدَارِسِ

(The second declension has *a* in the oblique case while the sound feminine plural has *i*.)

All proper nouns, which end in ةٌ, belong to the second declension.

Nouns which end in *a:*, whether written with *alif* or *y*, are indeclinable.

شَكْوَى complaint ; دُنْيَا world.

The *a:* in these words is a feminine ending which is spelt with *y*, unless the third radical is *y* when *alif* is used for variety. The same ending occurs in the 'elative adjective'.

Vocabulary 5

مَطْبَخٌ kitchen.

وَارِثٌ (وَرَثَةٌ) heir.

حَارِسٌ (حُرَّاسٌ) a guard, watchful.

دُكَّانٌ (دَكَاكِينُ) shop.

عَامٌّ general.

عَامَّةٌ (عَوَامُّ) the common herd.

حِنْطَةٌ wheat.

شَعِيرٌ barley.

صَدْرٌ (b) breast, chest.

إِصْبَعٌ (أَصَابِعُ) finger.

مِرْفَقٌ (مَرَافِقُ) elbow.

عُنُقٌ (a) neck.

قَلْبٌ (b) heart.

عَالِمٌ (عُلَمَاءُ) learned man.

عَقْرَبٌ (عَقَارِبُ) scorpion.

كَلْبٌ (c) dog.

فَلَّاحٌ peasant.

خَاصٌّ special.

خَاصَّةٌ (خَوَاصُّ) the upper ten.

قَمْحٌ wheat (ripe).

ذُرَةٌ millet, maize.

كَتِفٌ (a) shoulder.

إِبْهَامٌ (أَبَاهِيمُ) thumb.

ظُفْرٌ (a) finger nail.

بَارِدٌ cold.

Exercise 9

اَلْأَقَارِبُ عَقَارِبُ - اَلْعُلَمَاءُ وَرَثَةُ ٱلْأَنْبِيَاءِ - لِلنَّجَّارِ شُرَكَاءُ - اَلْأَطْعِمَةُ عِنْدَ ٱلطَّبَّاخِ فِي ٱلْمَطْبَخِ - شَبَابِيكُ ٱلْبَيْتِ ٱلْكَبِيرِ كَثِيرَةٌ - إِنَّ فِي ٱلْمَدِينَةِ مَدَارِسَ كَثِيرَةً - هَلْ مَفَاتِيحُ ٱلْمَدِينَةِ عِنْدَ ٱلْحَارِسِ - لَا هِيَ عِنْدَ ٱلْأَمِيرِ - اَلشُّيُوخُ وَٱلْعَجَائِزُ جَالِسُونَ [جَالِسَةٌ] فِي ظِلِّ ٱلْأَشْجَارِ - اَلْكِلَابُ كَثِيرَةٌ عِنْدَ قَبِيلَةٍ مِنْ قَبَائِلِ ٱلْعَرَبِ - إِنَّ رَذَائِلَ ٱلْخَاصَّةِ فَضَائِلُ ٱلْعَامَّةِ - إِنَّ ٱلْأَرْغِفَةَ مِنْ دَكَاكِينِ ٱلْخَبَّازِينَ - اَلْأَشْرَافُ شُرَكَاءُ ٱلْأُمَرَاءِ فِي حِفْظِ ٱلْمُدُنِ - دَكَاكِينُ ٱلْبَقَّالِينَ فِي سُوقٍ خَاصَّةٍ .

Transcription

alʔaqɒ:ribu ʕaqɒ:ribu — alʕulama:ʔu waraθatulʔanbiya:ʔi — linnaɟɟa:ri ʃuraka:ʔu — alʔɑŧʕimatu ʕindaŧŧɒbba:xi filmɒŧ-baxi — ʃuba:bi:kulbaytilkabi:ri kaθi:ratun — ʔinna filmadi:nati mada:risa kaθi:ratan — hal mafa:ti:ħul-madi:nati ʕindalħa:risi — la: hiya ʕindalʔami:ri — aʃʃuyu:xu walʕaja:ʔizu ja:lisu:na [ja:lisatun] fi: ðillilʔa-ʃja:ri — alkila:bu kaθi:ratun ʕinda qɒbi:latin min qɒba:ʔilil-ʕarabi — ʔinna raða:ʔilalxa:s̶s̶ɒti fɑđɒ:ʔilulʕa:mmati —

ʔinnalʔarɣifata min daka:ki:nilxabba:zi:na — alʔaʃra:fu ʃuraka:ʔulʔumara:ʔi fi: ħafðilmuduni — daka:ki:nulbaqqɒ:li:na fi: su:qin xa:s̶s̶ɒtin.

10

the farmers and merchants are the pillars of the land — the boy's fingers are dirty — the slaves are servants (of God) — wheat is the food of the nobles and barley the food of the poor — the owners of fine clothing are in king's palaces — Syrian fruits are good — the children of the nobles are in special schools — the girl's nails are clean but (and) the boy's nails are dirty — dogs are the watchmen of the Arabs — the winds on the islands are cold — the hearts of men are between the fingers of God.

LESSON 6

PERSONAL PRONOUNS

The independent personal pronoun can be used only in the nominative case. When a pronoun is in an oblique case, it is expressed by a suffix added to a verb, noun, or particle. The same suffixes are used for both the accusative and genitive except in the first person singular.

	Singular.	Dual.	Plural.
third masc.	هُ *hu*		هُمْ *hum*
third fem.	هَا *ha:*	هُمَا *huma:*	هُنَّ *hunna*
second masc.	كَ *ka*		كُمْ *kum*
second fem.	كِ *ki*	كُمَا *kuma:*	كُنَّ *kunna*
first	يَ or ـِي *ya, i:*		نَا *na:*

As direct object appended to a verb the first person singular is *ni:*.

The suffixes are very like the independent pronoun but with *k* instead of *t* in the second person.

After *i* and *ay* the *u* of the third person becomes *i* by assimilation.

Before liaison *-hum* and *-kum* become *-humu:* and *-kumu:*.

For the first person singular *ya* is used after *i:*, *a:*, and *ay:* ; everywhere else *i:* is used.

With nouns the suffixes are added to the construct state ; that means that nunation is dropped and, of course, the *alif* of the masculine accusative. The *ni* of the dual and the *na* of the sound masculine plural are also dropped.

The *i:* of the first singular swallows up the case ending.

These suffixes make the noun definite so an adjective agreeing with it must be also definite. An adjective is defined by giving it the definite article.

قَدَمِي *qvdami:* my foot (all cases) كَلْبُهُ *kalbuhu* his dog (nom.).

جَارِهِ *ja:rihi* his neighbour (gen.) وَلَدَهُ *waladahu* his son (acc.).

عَيْنَايَ *ʕayna:ya* my two eyes (nom.) أُذُنَيَّ *ʔudunayya* my two ears (oblique).

خَادِمِيَّ *xa:dimiyya* my servants (all cases ; the *u:* of the nominative is assimilated to the *y* of the suffix).

مَدْرَسَةُ مَدِينَتِهِ ٱلْجَدِيدَةُ The new school of (in) his town.

يَدِهِ ٱلْقَوِيَّةِ his strong hand (gen.).

فَضَائِلَكُمُ ٱلشَّرِيفَةَ your noble virtues (acc.).

These suffixes are added to prepositions. Note the following :—

	me	thee	him	them
لِ	لِي	لَكَ	لَهُ	لَهُمْ
بِ	بِي	بِكَ	بِهِ	بِهِمْ
مِنْ	مِنِّي	مِنْكَ	مِنْهُ	مِنْهُمْ
عَنْ	عَنِّي	عَنْكَ	عَنْهُ	عَنْهُمْ
إِلَى	إِلَيَّ	إِلَيْكَ	إِلَيْهِ	إِلَيْهِمْ

Note that before all suffixes except the first singular لِ becomes لَ.

Sometimes the object suffix cannot be appended to a verb so, as it cannot stand alone, it is added to *ʔiyya:* which has no meaning but serves as a base for the suffix.

إِيَّاهُ — إِيَّاكَ — إِيَّايَ — إِيَّاهُنَّ

The suffixes are also added to إِنَّ and particles like it.

إِنَّا or إِنَّنَا — إِنِّي or إِنَّنِي — but إِنَّكُمْ — إِنَّهُ.

كَ as, like does not take suffixes ; the construct of the noun مِثْلٌ *miθlun* ‘ likeness ’ is used instead, or the compound كَمِثْلِ *kamiθli.*

لَهَا أَجْنِحَةٌ مِثْلُ ٱلْخُفَّاشِ. they have wings like the bat.

(The feminine pronoun in *laha:* refers to a broken plural.)

Arabic is fond of bringing a word or phrase to the front and referring to it by a pronoun in the actual sentence. 'Zaid's native land is Egypt' can be translated literally :—

وَطَنُ زَيْدٍ مِصْرُ.

It is quite as likely to be :—

زَيْدٌ وَطَنُهُ مِصْرُ

Zaid, his native land is Egypt.

مِصْرُ هِيَ وَطَنُ زَيْدٍ

Egypt, it is Zaid's native land.

وَطَنُ زَيْدٍ هُوَ مِصْرُ

Zaid's native land, it is Egypt.

The difference between these modes of expression is less than it is in English.

بَعْضٌ *baʕđun,* 'someone, some' (sing. or pl.). Usually with a following genitive.

بَعْضُ ٱلنَّاسِ فِي ٱلْبَيْتِ وَبَعْضُهُمْ فِي ٱلْبُسْتَانِ

Some of the folk are in the house and some (of them) in the garden.

شِعْرٌ لِبَعْضِ ٱلشُّعَرَاءِ

A poem by some poet.

Vocabulary 6

وَطَنٌ (a) native land.

شَاعِرٌ (شُعَرَاءُ) poet.

وَزْنٌ (a) weight.

سَرِيعٌ swift.

شَرَفٌ honour.

لَبَنٌ (a) milk.

ضَعِيفٌ weak.

جَمَلٌ (c) male camel.

نَاقَةٌ (نُوقٌ) female camel.

مَعْزٌ goats.

ثَوْرٌ (ثِيرَانٌ) bull.

زَيْتُونٌ olives, olive trees.

زَيْتٌ olive oil, oil.

شِعْرٌ (a) poetry, poem.

قَوِىٌّ strong.

قُوَّةٌ (قُوًى) strength.

عَقْلٌ (b) reason, intelligence.

هِمَّةٌ (هِمَمٌ) care, anxiety.

تَجْرِبَةٌ (تَجَارِبُ) experience.

كَثْرَةٌ multitude, abundance.

مَعْلُومٌ known.

شَاةٌ (شَاءٌ) a sheep.

بَقَرٌ cattle (sing. بَقَرَةٌ).

خَيْلٌ horses, horsemen.

جَامُوسٌ (جَوَامِيسُ) buffalo.

Exercise 11

يَدِى نَظِيفَةٌ ـ يَدَا كُمْ نَظِيفَتَانِ ـ أَفْرَاسُهُ ٱلْحَسَنَةُ سَرِيعَةٌ ـ
زَيْدٌ بِنْتُهُ حَسَنَةٌ ـ إِنَّ بَقَرَهُ لَهَا لَبَنٌ كَثِيرٌ ـ وَزْنِى عِنْدَهُ
كَوَزْنِ ٱلْكَلْبِ ـ قُوَّةُ ٱلإِنْسَانِ فِى عَقْلِهِ وَلِسَانِهِ ـ
شُعَرَاءُ ٱلْعَرَبِ وَفَوَارِسُهَا كَثِيرَةٌ ـ لَهُ وَلَدَانِ كَبِيرُهُمَا
قَصِيرٌ وَصَغِيرُهُمَا طَوِيلٌ ـ شَرَفُ ٱلرَّجُلِ أَوْلَادُهُ

وَهِمَّتُهُ دَارُهُ وَجَارُهُ ـ أَشْعَارُكُمُ ٱللَّطِيفَةُ مَعْلُومَةٌ بَيْنَ ٱلنَّاسِ كُلِّهِمْ ـ لِصَاحِبِي ٱلْفَقِيرِ حِمَارَانِ وَلِصَاحِبَتِكُنَّ أَفْرَاسٌ كَثِيرَةٌ ـ صُنْدُوقُكَ ٱلْكَبِيرُ خَفِيفٌ وَصُنْدُوقُهَا ٱلصَّغِيرُ ثَقِيلٌ.

12

my wheat and my barley are in my big chests — her two hands are indeed clean — our native land is dear to us — boys, have you your books ? — your gracious letters are in the keeping of my master — my two hands and my two feet — your sister and her maids are sitting beside my cook — their chiefs are masters of wisdom — the two hands and two eyes of the old woman are weak — the weight of a man is the weight of his intelligence — the wisdom of the chief is from the multitude of his experiences.

LESSON 7

VERB

The verb has no tenses. Apart from the imperative, there are two finite forms which denote respectively completed and incompleted action. It is convenient to call them the perfect and imperfect, some prefer perfective and imperfective, remembering that these terms do not mean what they mean in English. Normally the perfect indicates a finished and therefore past act while the imperfect denotes an unfinished and therefore present or future act. The simplest part of the verb is the third masculine singular of the perfect which is used as the name of the verb; we speak of the verb 'to write', Arabs speak of *kataba* 'he wrote'.

The verb is highly developed but on lines foreign to us. By additions to the root modifications of the original meaning are expressed. The plain root is called the simple or first and the enlarged stems are also called by numbers.

It is convenient to call the vowel, which follows the second radical whether in the perfect or imperfect, the characteristic.

In this book a strong verb is one which comes from a root having three different radicals, neither of them being *ʔ*, *w*, or *y*.

Perfect of the Strong Verb, Stem I

Before reading the following notes, study carefully the perfect in Table I.

The perfect is made by the addition of suffixes to the root. Those of the second person are the same as the endings of the personal pronoun, and closely resemble the pronominal suffixes.

In the third feminine singular and dual the *t* is the feminine *t*.

a: is the sign of the dual as in the nominative of the noun.

u: is masculine plural as in the external nominative plural of the noun. The *alif* following this *u:* has no meaning but is always written after a plural *u:* in the finite verb; in some weak verbs it is useful for distinguishing the plural from the singular. It is dropped before a pronominal suffix.

In Stem I there are three classes of perfect فَعَلَ — فَعِلَ — فَعُلَ; the inflections are the same for all. فَعِلَ فَعُلَ are usually intransitive. Many verbs have more than one form.

هَلِكَ — هَلَكَ he perished.

With verbs denoting a state, the perfect must be translated by the English present. شَبِعَ 'he is satisfied (with food)', i.e. he has eaten enough and now does not want to eat more.

The third person singular of the verb may contain its own subject. شَبِعَ 'he is satisfied', شَبِعَتْ 'she is satisfied' are complete sentences. You can also say, شَبِعَ زَيْدٌ 'Zayd is satisfied'; شَبِعَتْ زَيْنَبُ 'Zaynab is satisfied'. All other parts of the perfect or imperfect contain their subjects.

One grammar gives twenty-one rules for the agreement of subject and verb. You can write correctly if you remember this much :—

If the verb comes before the subject, it is third masculine singular unless the subject is a woman or women and follows the verb immediately when it is third feminine singular.

If the subject comes first, the verb agrees with it.

Other agreements are possible but not necessary.

دَخَلَ ٱلرَّجُلُ ٱلدَّارَ وَخَرَجَ مِنْهَا

The man went into the house and came out of it.

دَخَلَ ٱلرِّجَالُ ٱلْبَيْتَ وَخَرَجُوا مِنْهُ

The men went into the house and came out of it.

لَبِسَتِ ٱلْعَجُوزُ ثِيَابَهَا وَخَرَجَتْ مِنْ حُجْرَتِهَا

The old woman put on her clothes and came out of her room.

لَعِبَتِ ٱلْبَنَاتُ ثُمَّ رَجَعْنَ إِلَى بُيُوتِهِنَّ [بُيُوتِهَا]

The girls played, then returned to their houses (homes).

both right	كَتَبَ إِلَى أُخْتِهَا زَيْنَبُ كَتَبَتْ إِلَى أُخْتِهَا زَيْنَبُ	Zaynab wrote to her sister.

Arabic does not distinguish between being and becoming; thus لَبِسَ means both 'to wear clothes' and 'to put them on'.

The addition of pronominal suffixes makes no difference to the parts of the perfect except the second masculine plural and, sometimes, the second feminine singular.

The object suffix of the first person singular is *ni:*.

كَتَبَهُ he wrote it; بَعَثَتْنِي she sent me;

دَخَلْتُمُوهُ you (pl.) entered it; ضَرَبُوهُ they hit him;

لَبِسْتِهِ you (fem. sing.) put it on, or لَبِسْتِيهِ.

A nominal sentence begins with a noun.

A verbal sentence begins with a verb.

This distinction is important because some particles must be followed by a noun and others by a verb.

The verb comes first unless there is a reason for some other order. The direct object of a transitive verb is in the accusative.

Most verbs, which are transitive in English, are so in Arabic; many, which are intransitive in English, are transitive in Arabic.

Vocabulary 7

(The vowel after a verb is that of the imperfect; the noun is the infinitive.)

ضَرَبَ i. ضَرْبٌ hit, strike.

طَلَبَ u. طَلَبٌ seek, look for.

خَرَجَ u. خُرُوجٌ go, come out.

ذَهَبَ a. ذَهَابٌ go away.

كَسَرَ i. كَسْرٌ break.

بَعَثَ a. بَعْثٌ send.

سَمِعَ سَمْعٌ hear.

كَتَبَ u. كِتَابَةٌ write.

لَعِبَ لَعْبٌ play.

ذَكَرَ u. ذِكْرٌ remember, mention.

شَبِعَ شَبَعٌ be satisfied (with food).

كَلَامٌ speech, what is said.

جَبَلٌ (c) mountain.

فَهِمَ فَهْمٌ understand.

فَتَحَ a. فَتْحٌ open, conquer.

دَخَلَ u. دُخُولٌ enter.

رَجَعَ i. رُجُوعٌ return.

نَزَلَ i. نُزُولٌ come down, dismount, camp.

شَرِبَ شُرْبٌ drink.

قَطَعَ a. قَطْعٌ cut, cut off.

حَفِظَ حِفْظٌ keep, guard.

صَعِدَ صُعُودٌ go up.

صَرَخَ u. صُرَاخٌ cry for help.

صَوْتٌ (a) voice, noise.

لَبَنٌ (a) milk.

Exercise 13

ضَرَبَ ٱلشَّيْخُ رَأْسَ ٱلْوَلَدِ ـ فَهِمَتِ ٱلْعَجُوزُ كَلَامَ
ٱلْجَارِيَةِ ـ أَطَلَبْتُمْ طَعَامًا مِنَ ٱلْمَطْبَخِ ـ طَلَبْتُ
لَحْمًا مِنْ دُكَّانِ ٱلْجَزَّارِ ـ خَرَجَ ٱلْأَوْلَادُ مِنَ ٱلْمَسْجِدِ

وَدَخَلُوا فِى ٱلْمَدْرَسَةِ ـ ذَهَبَتِ ٱلْخَيَّاطَاتُ مِنْ مَدِينَتِنَا
وَرَجَعْنَ إِلَى وَطَنِهَا [وَطَنِهِنَّ] ـ يَا بَنَاتُ هَلْ
شَرِبْتُنَّ ٱلْمَاءَ ـ بَلْ شَرِبْنَا ٱللَّبَنَ ـ هَلْ سَمِعْتُمَا أَصْوَاتَ
ٱلطَّيْرِ عَلَى ٱلشَّجَرِ ـ قَطَعْتُ ٱللَّحْمَ قِطَعًا صَغِيرَةً ـ
بَعَثَتْنِى أُمِّى إِلَيْكَ ـ نَزَلَ ٱلرِّجَالُ مِنْ رَأْسِ
ٱلْجَبَلِ وَفَتَحُوا ٱلْمَدِينَةَ .

14

have you (sing. and plu.) written the letters? — the boy broke the dog's leg with a stone — they heard what the governor said and returned to their homes — the kings entered the land and conquered it — I opened the window and a dog came in — the guardians of the cattle have called for help; did you hear them? — the doctors amputated the man's hand and foot — did you go into the room? — girls, did you play with the big dog? — evil men cut off the ears of the cattle — you two girls, have you sent a present to your sister?

LESSON 8

IMPERFECT INDICATIVE

Read Table 1. The inflection of the imperfect is by prefixes and sometimes also by suffixes. The first radical has no vowel.

The prefixes denote the person except in the third

feminine singular and dual where the *t* is feminine. Elsewhere *ya* stands for the third person, *ta* for the second, *ʔa* for the first singular (cf. أَنَا) and *na* for the first plural (cf. نَحْنُ).

a: is again the sign of the dual; *u:* of the masculine plural (except in the first person); *-na* of the feminine plural (cf. أَنْتُنَّ هُنَّ and كَتَبْنَ).

The imperfect has three forms يَفْعَلُ — يَفْعِلُ — يَفْعُلُ but the inflections are the same for all of them.

فَعُلَ has the imperfect يَفْعُلُ (no exceptions) كَرُمَ يَكْرُمُ

فَعِلَ has the imperfect يَفْعَلُ (perhaps five exceptions) غَضِبَ يَغْضَبُ

فَعَلَ has any of the three forms but يَفْعَلُ usually occurs when one of the second or third radicals is a guttural consonant.

The word سَوْفَ or the particle سَ is prefixed to the imperfect when it is desired to show that it refers to the future.

It suffers no change when pronominal suffixes are added to it. It often denotes an act growing out of another. 'He came out and looked' may be translated خَرَجَ يَنْظُرُ or خَرَجَ وَيَنْظُرُ.

The imperfect suggests a close connection of the two acts; خَرَجَ وَنَظَرَ suggests two unconnected acts. Thus the imperfect often refers to past acts, as in the preceding example, when the whole sentence refers to the past.

An imperfect linked to the main sentence by 'and' or a pronoun or by both indicates an attendant circumstance:

دَخَلَ وَهُوَ يَضْحَكُ he came in and he was laughing.

he came in laughing—while laughing.

Interrogative Adverbs

أَيْنَ where, whither? أَيْنَ أَنْتَ where are you?

أَيْنَ تَذْهَبُونَ where are you going?

مِنْ أَيْنَ whence; مِنْ أَيْنَ خَرَجُوا (from) where did they get out?

كَيْفَ how? كَيْفَ حَالُكَ how is your condition? how are you?

كَيْفَ فَعَلَ رَبُّكَ how did your Lord act?

These words make no change in the form of the sentence.

كَمْ how much? how many?

When it asks a question, it is followed by a noun in the accusative singular:—

كَمْ حُجْرَةً فِى ٱلْبَيْتِ

how many rooms are in the house?

كَمْ إِنسَانًا فِى ٱلْجَمَاعَةِ

how many persons are in the company?

بِكَمْ دِينَارًا ٱلثَّوْبُ

for how many dinars is the costume?

When exclamatory, it is followed by the genitive of a singular or of a broken plural; if there is a verb, it is in the perfect.

كَمْ كَأْسٍ شَرِبْتُ—كَمْ كُؤُوسٍ

what a lot of cups I have drunk!

In both usages, كم may be followed by من with a genitive:—

كَمْ مِنْ حُجْرَةٍ فِى ٱلْبَيْتِ

how many rooms in the house?

Vocabulary 8

نظر u. نَظَرٌ look at, see.

غَضِبَ غَضَبٌ be angry.

فَعَلَ a. فِعْلٌ do, act.

جَمَعَ a. جَمْعٌ collect (trans.).

سَبَحَ a. سِبَاحَةٌ swim.

عَدُوٌّ (a) enemy.

شِتَاءٌ winter.

صَفٌّ (b) row, rank.

جَيْشٌ (b) army.

بَلَدٌ (c) town.

كَأْسٌ (b) (fem.) cup.

دِينَارٌ (دَنَانِيرُ) dinar, gold coin (Latin denarius).

ثَوْبٌ (c) piece of cloth, clothing.

كَرُمَ كَرَامَةٌ be noble, generous.

ضَحِكَ ضَحِكٌ laugh.

صَنَعَ a. صُنْعٌ make, do.	صَيْفٌ summer.
جَلَسَ i. جُلُوسٌ sit.	خَشَبٌ wood.
قَدِمَ قُدُومٌ advance, arrive.	بِلَادٌ (بُلْدَانٌ) country.
نَبَحَ a. نَبْحٌ bark.	جَمَاعَةٌ party, company.
طَبْلٌ (b) drum.	

Exercise 15

دَخَلَ ٱلْأَوْلَادُ ٱلْبَحْرَ يَسْبَحُونَ ـ بَعَثَ ٱلنَّجَّارُ إِلَى
يَطْلُبُ خَشَبًا ـ جَلَسْنَا عِنْدَ ٱلْعَيْنِ نَشْرَبُ وَنَضْحَكُ ـ
خَرَجَ أَمِيرُ ٱلْجَيْشِ يَصْعَدُ فِي ٱلْجَبَلِ وَيَنْظُرُ إِلَى
صُفُوفِ ٱلْعَدُوِّ ـ ذَهَبَ ٱلرُّفَقَاءُ مِنَ ٱلشَّامِ إِلَى ٱلْقُدْسِ
يَنْزِلُونَ كُلَّ لَيْلَةٍ فِي بَلَدٍ ـ إِنَّ ٱلنَّاسَ فِي ٱلصَّيْفِ
يَخْرُجُونَ مِنَ ٱلْبِلَادِ ٱلْحَارَّةِ وَيَنْزِلُونَ فِي بِلَادٍ
قَرِيبَةٍ مِنَ ٱلْبَحْرِ ـ قَدِمَ ٱلتَّاجِرُ مَدِينَةَ ٱلْمَلِكِ يَجْمَعُ
ٱلدَّنَانِيرَ مِنْ أَصْحَابِهِ ـ سَتَسْمَعُونَ صَوْتَ ٱلطُّبُولِ .

16

God will conquer the town by (on) the hand of his prophet — the dogs came out barking — men wear heavy clothes in winter — you sat down and listened to the words of the poet — do the girls make their clothes? — the king strikes good dinars — the children went out to play — the army advanced beating their drums — the carpenter made cups of wood for us to drink from — we heard the watchmen calling for help against the enemy — I looked at him and he was angry at what I had said.

LESSON 9

DEMONSTRATIVE PRONOUNS

The letters *ð, h, l, k* have demonstrative force, the pronouns are compounded from them. We have already met *l* in the definite article and the emphatic *la*.

This. The simplest pronoun is *ða:* but more common is the compound *ha:ða:* which is usually written هٰذَا or هَذَا.

	Singular.	Dual.	Plural.
masc.	هٰذَا	هٰذَانِ هٰذَيْنِ	هٰـؤُلَاءِ *ha:ʔula:ʔi*
fem.	هٰذِهِ . هٰذِي	هٰتَانِ هٰتَيْنِ	

The inflections of ذَا can be found by cutting off the prefix *ha:*.

That.

	Singular.	Dual.	Plural.
masc.	ذَاكَ	ذَانِكَ ذَيْنِكَ	أُولَائِكَ *ʔula:ʔika*
fem.	تَاكَ تِيكَ	تَانِكَ تَيْنِكَ	

More common in the singular are ذٰلِكَ (masc.) تِلْكَ (fem.).

A demonstrative pronoun precedes its noun and, as it is by nature definite, the noun must be definite also.

هٰذَا ٱلرَّسُولُ this messenger; هٰذِهِ ٱلدَّابَّةُ this riding beast.

But if the noun has a pronominal suffix, the demonstrative follows it.

قُوتُكَ هٰذَا this your food = this food of yours.

If the noun is indefinite you have a sentence :—

هٰذَا قَلَمٌ this is a (reed) pen; تِلْكَ أَمَةٌ that is a slave girl.

When the predicate of a sentence is definite, the pronoun of the third person is put between the demonstrative and the predicate.

ذَلِكَ هُوَ ٱلْحَكِيمُ

that is the doctor (literally, wise man).

هٰذِهِ هِيَ ٱلضَّيْعَةُ this is the village (estate).

أُولَائِكَ هُمْ أَصْحَابُ ٱلْحُكُومَةِ

those are the members of the government.

In sentences like these, the demonstrative is a nominative absolute and the real sentence is the personal pronoun plus the predicate. It is a mistake to say that the personal pronoun takes the place of the copula 'is', 'are'.

Interrogative pronouns.

مَنْ 'who?' مَا 'what?' These are indeclinable.

مَـا when combined with the preposition لِ is often abbreviated لِمَـا or لِمَ.

مَنِ ٱلْوَكِيلُ who is the agent?

مَنْ صَرَخَ who shouted for help?

مَنْ ذَكَرْتَ whom did you mention?

لِمَنِ ٱلْجَوْهَرُ whose is the jewel?

لِمَ نَـظَرْتَ إِلَيْهَـا for what (why) did you look at her?

مَنْ and مَـا are also used as indefinite pronouns and then they behave like conditional particles.

أَيٌّ أَيَّةٌ 'which of' is always followed by a genitive or a pronominal suffix.

أَيُّـكُمْ صَعِدَ فِي رَأْسِ ٱلْمَنَـارَةِ

which of you went up to the top of the minaret?

Vocabulary 9

مَشْهُورٌ well known, famous.	حُكُومَةٌ government.
فِرَاشٌ (d) bedding, furniture (i.e. cushions and rugs).	ضَيْعَةٌ (c) estate, village.
	قُوتٌ (a) food.
أَهْلٌ (أَهَالٍ) family.	أَمَةٌ (إِمَاءٌ) slave girl.

وَكِيلٌ (وُكَلَاءُ) agent, man of business.

جَهْلٌ ignorance.

مَدْخَلٌ (مَدَاخِلُ) entrance.

فِضَّةٌ silver.

صِرَاطٌ path.

حَدِيدٌ sharp.

عَسِيرٌ difficult.

قَبِيلَةٌ (قَبَائِلُ) tribe.

قَوْلٌ (a) speech, word, what is said.

مَنَارَةٌ (مَنَاوِرُ) lighthouse, minaret.

دَابَّةٌ (دَوَابُّ) riding animal.

قَلَمٌ (a) reed pen.

حَكِيمٌ (حُكَمَاءُ) wise man.

ذَهَبٌ gold.

مَالٌ (a) wealth, property, money.

مَخْرَجٌ (مَخَارِجُ) exit.

وَرَقٌ (a) leaf, paper.

سَيْفٌ (b) sword.

دَقِيقٌ fine, thin (lit. powdered).

يَسِيرٌ few, easy.

Exercise 17

هٰذَانِ ٱلرَّجُلَانِ هُمَا شَيْخَا ٱلْقَبِيلَةِ ـ هٰذِهِ هِيَ ٱلْأَمَةُ ٱلصَّادِقَةُ ـ ضَيْعَتِي هٰذِهِ مَشْهُورَةٌ فِي ٱلْبِلَادِ ـ تَلْعَبُ هٰذِهِ ٱلْبَنَاتُ فِي صَحْنِ ٱلْمَدْرَسَةِ ـ نَزَلَ أُولَائِكَ ٱلرِّجَالُ عِنْدَ مَدْخَلِ ٱلْبَلَدِ ـ سَمِعْتُ كَلْبَكَ ذٰلِكَ يَنْبَحُ ـ هٰذَا فِرَاشُكَ ـ لِمَنْ هٰذِهِ ٱلْجَوَاهِرُ ـ هِيَ لِوَكِيلِ صَاحِبِ ٱلضَّيْعَةِ هٰذِهِ ـ أُولَائِكَ إِمَاءٌ مِنْ أَهْلِ

اُلشَّيْخِ - مَنْ صَنَعَ كُؤُوسَكَ وَصُحُونَكَ تِلْكَ - مَنْ بَعَثْتَ إِلَىَّ - مِنْ قَوْلِ مَنْ هَذَا .

18

short poems are the well-known ones — I am angry at what you have done — that agent has much silver and gold — whose is that estate ? — the watchman went up the minaret of that mosque and raised the alarm (cried for help) — the children will write on that paper with these pens — that poor friend of yours has gone away to look for food — this agent of yours has collected much wealth — the leaves of these trees are food for sheep — escape (exit) from his ignorance is hard for the ignorant — my wealth is my sword and my books.

LESSON 10

ADJECTIVES

Some of the common adjectival forms have already been mentioned.

فَعِيلٌ is often passive in meaning : قَتِيلٌ killed.

فَاعِلٌ the active participle is often used as an adjective or noun : عَادِلٌ just ; شَاهِدٌ a witness, martyr.

مَفْعُولٌ the passive participle is used as an adjective: مَشْهُورٌ famous.

فَعُولٌ is intensive. جَاهِلٌ ignorant ; جَهُولٌ very ignorant ; كَاذِبٌ untruthful كَذُوبٌ a great liar ; كَسُولٌ very lazy.

فَعْلَانُ (without nunation) the feminine is فَعْلَى : غَضْبَانُ — غَضْبَى angry ; تَعْبَانُ — تَعْبَى tired ; كَسْلَانُ — كَسْلَى lazy.

أَفْعَلُ has two meanings.

1. It denotes colours and bodily defects :—

	Masculine.	Feminine.	Plural
black	أَسْوَدُ	سَوْدَاءُ	سُودٌ
white	أَبْيَضُ	بَيْضَاءُ	بِيضٌ
red	أَحْمَرُ	حَمْرَاءُ	حُمْرٌ

The dual of the feminine changes the final ʔ into *w* ; سَوْدَاوَانِ two black (women).

2. The elative, the 'adjective of superiority'. Arabic has only one form which does duty for both our comparative and superlative, it denotes intensity, the quality of the simple adjective raised to a higher power. The form is :—

Masculine.	Feminine.	Plural.
أَفْعَلُ	فُعْلَى	فُعَلٌ

Roughly, when this form is indefinite, it is comparative; when it is definite, it is superlative.

When indefinite or when defined by a following genitive or pronominal suffix, the masculine is used for both genders and all numbers. When defined by the article, it is inflected for both gender and number. Of course, it is always inflected for case.

'Than' is expressed by مِنْ.

big كَبِيرٌ أَكْبَرُ كُبْرَى كُبَرٌ

اَلرَّجُلُ أَكْبَرُ مِنْ وَلَدِهِ

the man is bigger than his son.

دَارِى أَكْبَرُ مِنْ دَارِهِ

my house (fem.) is bigger than his.

شَوَارِعُ ٱلْعَاصِمَةِ أَنْظَفُ مِنْ شَوَارِعِ ٱلْقَرْيَةِ

the streets of the capital are cleaner than those of the village.

هُوَ ٱلْأَطْوَلُ فِى أَهْلِهِ

he is the tallest in his family.

هُوَ أَطْوَلُ ٱلْجَمَاعَةِ

he is the tallest of the party.

هِىَ أَطْوَلُهُنَّ ذِرَاعًا

she is the longest of them as to arm
= she has the longest arm of any.

هِىَ ٱلطُّولَى ذِرَاعًا

she is the longest in arm.

When the second and third radicals are the same, the forms of the elative are :—

few	قَلِيلٌ	أَقَلُّ	قُلَّى	قُلُلٌ
strong	شَدِيدٌ	أَشَدُّ	شُدَّى	شُدُدٌ

To make the elative from adjectives denoting colours or bodily defects, an adjective meaning 'strong' in the elative is used with the noun denoting the colour. The noun is in the accusative.

هٰذَا أَشَدُّ بَيَاضًا مِنْ ذٰلِكَ

this is more white than that.

There are two irregular elatives.

خَيْرٌ as a noun means any sort of 'goodness' and, as an adjective, 'better,' 'best.'

شَرٌّ as a noun means any sort of 'badness' and, as an adjective, 'worse,' 'worst.'

Feminines of the form فَعْلَاءُ belong, of course, to the second declension with only two case endings and those of the form فُعْلَى are indeclinable (Lesson 5).

Vocabulary 10

لَوْنٌ (a) colour, course (at a meal).

زَهْرٌ (b) flower.

مُصِيبَةٌ (مَصَائِبُ) calamity.

صَلَاةٌ (صَلَوَاتٌ) prayer, the Muslim form of worship.

مَوْهِبَةٌ (مَوَاهِبُ) gift.

ذِرَاعٌ (e) forearm, arm, cubit.

تَمْرٌ dates, sing. تَمْرَةٌ.

خُضْرَةٌ greenness, being a dark colour.

صُفْرَةٌ yellowness.

سَوَادٌ blackness.

أَزْرَقُ blue.

أَصْفَرُ yellow, pale.

نَوْمٌ sleep.

أَسْمَرُ brown.

نَخْلٌ sing. نَخْلَةٌ palm tree.

حُمْرَةٌ redness.

زُرْقَةٌ blueness.

بَيَاضٌ whiteness.

أَخْضَرُ green, dark coloured.

أَطْرَشُ deaf.

أَخْرَسُ dumb.

أَحْدَبُ hunch-backed.

حُلْوٌ sweet.

أَعْوَرُ one-eyed.

أَعْرَجُ lame.

مُرٌّ bitter, sour.

Exercise 19

اَلْعَبْدُ أَسْوَدُ ـ هٰذَا ٱلْفَرَسُ أَبْيَضُ ـ ذٰلِكَ كَلْبُكَ
ٱلْأَسْوَدُ فِي ٱلْحُجْرَةِ ٱلْحَمْرَاءِ ـ هٰذِهِ ٱلشَّجَرَةُ خَضْرَاءُ
فِي ٱلصَّيْفِ ـ عَيْنَا ٱلْبِنْتِ زَرْقَاوَانِ ـ اَلصِّرَاطُ أَحَدُّ
مِنَ ٱلسَّيْفِ وَأَدَقُّ مِنَ ٱلشَّعَرِ ـ لَوْنُ هٰذَا ٱلزَّهْرِ مَا

هُوَ ـ لَهُ لَوْنَانِ أَزْرَقُ وَأَصْفَرُ ـ إِنَّ أَوْرَاقَ ٱلشَّجَرِ سَمْرَاءُ وَحَمْرَاءُ فِي ٱلْخَرِيفِ ـ اَلذَّهَبُ أَثْقَلُ مِنَ ٱلْفِضَّةِ ـ اَلصَّلَاةُ خَيْرٌ مِنَ ٱلنَّوْمِ ـ خَيْرُ ٱلْمَوَاهِبِ ٱلْعَقْلُ وَشَرُّ ٱلْمَصَائِبِ ٱلْجَهْلُ ـ اَلْأَمَةُ ٱلْخَرْسَاءُ هِيَ ٱلْحُسْنَى ـ بِنْتِي أَطْوَلُ مِنِّي.

20

he has some deaf black slave-girls — our army is smaller in number (fewer) than that of our enemies — the sheep in the land of the Arabs are black — the food most dear to the Arabs is the two blacks, meat and dates — the palm is taller than the olive — your estate is smaller than mine — this bird has a yellow breast and red wings — my friends sent me many presents but (and) your present is the best — God sent his prophet to all men, the black, the white, and the red — your youngest (smallest) sister is the kindest of them.

LESSON 11

IRREGULAR NOUNS

Three nouns are half way to having three radicals :—

أَبٌ (آبَاءٌ) 'father': أَخٌ (إِخْوَةٌ—إِخْوَانٌ)

'brother': حَمٌ (أَحْمَاءٌ) 'husband's father'.

There is nothing peculiar about them when they have one of the articles :—

: اَلْأَخَ – اَلْأَخِ – اَلْأَخُ – أَبًا – أَبٍ – أَبٌ

Of course these forms are rare.

In the construct state the final vowel is lengthened :

أَبَا – أَبِى – أَبُو

and the dual is أَبَوَانِ 'two parents' أَبَوَيْنِ .

The pronominal suffixes are added to the construct state :—

أَبُوكَ 'your father' (nom.) أَبَاهُ 'his father' (acc.)

أَبِيهِ 'his father' (gen.) but : أَبِى 'my father' (all cases)

أَبُو ٱلْمُلُوكِ 'the father of kings' : أَبُو زَيْدٍ 'Zayd's father'.

When a man has a son, he is known not by his own name but as the father of his son.

ذُو 'possessor of' occurs only in the construct state :—

	Sing. Masc.	Sing. Fem.	Dual. Masc.	Dual. Fem.	Plural. Masc.	Plural. Fem.
nom.	ذُو	ذَاتُ	ذَوَا	ذَوَاتَا	ذَوُو أُولُو	ذَوَاتُ
acc.	ذَا	ذَاتَ	ذَوَىْ	ذَوَاتَىْ	ذَوِى أُولِى	ذَوَاتِ
gen.	ذِى	ذَاتِ				

ذُو is never used with suffixes : it often takes the place of an adjective :—

ذُو عِلْمٍ 'learned', 'a learned man'.

ذُو عَقْلٍ 'intelligent' : ذَاتُ مَالٍ 'rich', 'a rich woman'.

سَنَةٌ 'year' has two plurals سَنَوَاتٌ and سِنُونَ ; the oblique case of the latter is سِنِينَ with assimilation.

فَمٌ 'mouth' is regular but in the construct فُو—فَا—فِى may also be used ; with suffixes : فُوهُ—فَاهُ—فِيهِ but فِىَّ 'my mouth' (all cases).

A few nouns begin with liaison :—

اِبْنٌ (أَبْنَاءٌ) 'son' : اِبْنَةٌ (بَنَاتٌ) 'daughter' : اِثْنَانِ (masc.) 'two' : اِثْنَتَانِ (fem.) 'two' : اِسْمٌ (أَسْمَاءٌ) 'name' : اِمْرَأَةٌ (نِسَاءٌ—نِسْوَةٌ) 'woman' : اِمْرُؤٌ 'man' اِمْرَأً (acc.) اِمْرِئٍ (gen.).

اِمْرُؤٌ and اِمْرَأَةٌ drop the liaison after the definite

article and become اَلْمَرْءُ and اَلْمَرْأَةُ ; the other nouns keep the liaison : اَلِابْنُ — اَلِابْنَةُ .

اِبْنٌ has a sound plural بَنُونَ — بَنِينَ which is used in the names of tribes : بَنُو بَكْرٍ 'the tribe Bakr'.

Note the following spellings :—

بِسْمِ اللّٰهِ 'in the name of God'.

زَيْدُ بْنُ مُحَمَّدٍ *Zaydubnu muḥammadin*
Zayd, the son of Muhammad.

زَيْدٌ اِبْنُ مُحَمَّدٍ *Zaydunibnu muḥammadin*
Zayd is the son of Muhammad.

In the last example the connecting vowel *i* is not indicated in writing even in vocalized texts.

كِلَا ; fem. كِلْتَا 'both' is used only in the construct state. With a suffix it is inflected for case like any dual, with a noun it is not.

Vocabulary 11

مَوْتٌ death.

جَمَالٌ beauty.

نَزَعَ i. نَزْعٌ take away.

عَرَفَ i. مَعْرِفَةٌ know.

جَدٌّ (a) grandfather.

عَمٌّ (a) paternal uncle.

عَمَّةٌ paternal aunt.

مَطَرٌ rain.

هَوَاءٌ air.

شِمَالٌ north.

شَرْقٌ — مَشْرِقٌ east.

شَهْرٌ (b — e) month.

نَهَارٌ day, daylight.

جِدَارٌ (d) wall.

قَلْبٌ (b) heart.

نَجَحَ a. نَجَاحٌ succeed.

تَبِعَ تَبَعٌ and VIII follow.

جَدَّةٌ grandmother.

خَالٌ (a) maternal uncle.

خَالَةٌ maternal uncle.

نَوْءٌ (a) storm.

نَسِيمٌ (c) breeze.

جَنُوبٌ south.

غَرْبٌ — مَغْرِبٌ west.

دَقِيقَةٌ (دَقَائِقُ) minute.

ظَهْرٌ (b) back.

ظُهْرٌ noon.

Exercise 21

سَمِعَ أَبِى وَأَخُوكَ أَصْوَاتَ ٱلدَّوَابِّ ـ طَلَبَتِ ٱلْابْنَةُ
أَبَاهَا فِى ٱلسُّوقِ ـ جَمَعَ ٱلشَّيْخُ أَبْنَاءَهُ عِنْدَ فِرَاشِهِ
قَبْلَ ٱلْمَوْتِ ـ نَزَعَتِ ٱبْنَةُ ٱلْبَقَّالِ ٱلْأَوْرَاقَ ٱلْبَيْضَاءَ
مِنْ يَدِ أَخِيهَا ـ دَخَلَتِ ٱلْمَرْأَةُ مَعَ أَبْنَائِهَا بَيْنَ يَدَيِ
ٱلْخَلِيفَةِ ـ يَا أَبْنَاءُ هَلْ تَعْرِفُونَ أَسْمَاءَ ٱلزُّهُورِ ـ نَعَمْ
نَعْرِفُ ٱسْمَ كُلِّ زَهْرٍ فِى ٱلْبُسْتَانِ ـ تَبِعْتُ أَخَاكَ
فِى ٱلطَّرِيقِ أَكْتُبُ ٱسْمَهُ عَلَى جِدَارِ كُلِّ بَيْتٍ ـ

إِنَّ أَبَوَيْكَ يَفْرَحَانِ عَلَى نَجَاحِكَ ـ اَلْمَرْءُ بِأَصْغَرَيْهِ قَلْبِهِ وَلِسَانِهِ ـ جَمَالُ ٱلْمَرْءِ فِى لِسَانِهِ وَجَمَالُ ٱلْمَرْأَةِ فِى عَقْلِهَا.

22

do you and your brother understand what I have said ? — my two brothers and two sisters play with your brothers and sisters — did your father send your brother to me ? — the woman sent her sons to seek wealth in distant lands — what is your name ? my name is well known, it is the best known of the names of the Arabs — woman, have you any children ? — yes I have a son and two daughters — this man has two fathers, the father of his body and the father of his intelligence — did you stop at the house of my friend's father ? — the possessors of knowledge and wealth are the fewest of men.

LESSON 12

IMPERATIVE. PARTICIPLES. INFINITIVE

The imperative (Table 1), being a command, is an incomplete action and so connected with the imperfect. It has no prefixes and the inflections are cut short. The loss of the prefix makes a helping vowel necessary; this is *u* when the characteristic is *u* and otherwise *i*.

أُكْتُبْ write ; إِسْمَعْ hear ; إِضْرِبْ hit.

The imperative is confined to the second person and is affirmative only; a negative command is expressed differently.

It can take the object suffixes.

The active participle is كَاتِبٌ ; فَعَلَةٌ and فُعَّالٌ are common forms for the plural.

When derived from a transitive verb, it can take an object and, being a noun, it takes its object in the genitive case :—

قَاتِلُ زَيْدٍ Zaid's murderer ;

طَالِبُو عِلْمٍ seekers after knowledge, scholars.

It is obvious that this participle easily passes into a noun or adjective.

The passive participle is مَكْتُوبٌ : the plural is مَفَاعِيلُ.

In themselves the participles contain no idea of time.

Infinitive.—There is no fixed form for the infinitive of the simple stem ; فَعْلٌ is common but the infinitive of each verb has to be learnt.

Many verbs of motion have the form فُعُولٌ :—

خُرُوجٌ — دُخُولٌ — نُزُولٌ but ذَهَابٌ.

فَعِلَ usually has فَعَلٌ :—

فَرِحَ rejoice فَرَحٌ — غَضِبَ be angry غَضَبٌ

As the infinitive is a noun, it can govern a genitive which may be either subject or object of the verbal idea.

قَتْلُ زَيْدٍ the killing of Zaid.
the killing by Zaid.

Therefore it is sometimes best translated as passive :—

إِنْ يُقْتَلُوا فَالْقَتْلُ أَكْرَمُ مِيتَةٍ

if they are killed, being killed is the noblest mode of death.

When both subject and object are mentioned, the subject is put in the genitive and the object in the accusative.

ضَرْبُ خَالِدٍ الْوَلِيدَ Khalid's hitting Waleed

بَعْثِي إِيَّاهُ my sending him.

The object can always be put in the accusative.

The object both of an infinitive or a participle is often introduced by لِ especially when the verbal noun is in the adverbial accusative.

قُمْتُ إِكْرَامًا لَهُ

I stood up to do him honour (Lesson 15).

The infinitive takes the place of the two English forms 'to write' and 'writing'.

It passes easily into an abstract noun and even into a concrete one.

وُجُودٌ existence (وَجَدَ 'find').

تَصْوِيرٌ picture (from a derived stem 'give shape to').

Vocabulary 12

طِفْلٌ (a) infant.

عَظِيمٌ glorious, great.

أَمْرٌ (b) thing, affair.

سَهْلٌ level, easy.

قَتَلَ u. قَتْلٌ kill.

خَدَمَ i.u. خِدْمَةٌ serve.

مَنْزِلٌ — مَنْزِلَةٌ (مَنَازِلُ) house, camp, stage (of a journey).

غُلَامٌ (غِلْمَانٌ) young man, servant, boy.

عذب II punish.

سَرَقَ i. سَرَقٌ steal.

شَفَةٌ lip.

أَنْفٌ (b) nose.

جُبْنٌ cheese.

سِرٌّ (a) secret.

أَمِينٌ faithful.

أَمْرٌ (أَوَامِرُ) command.

شَرَفٌ honour, nobility.

كَتَمَ u. كِتْمَانٌ hide (trans.).

ضَيْفٌ (a) guest.

عَذَابٌ punishment.

خَدٌّ (b) cheek.

جَبْهَةٌ (c) forehead.

جَفْنٌ (b) eyelid.

جَوْزٌ nut.

Exercise 23

يَا نِسَاءُ اسْمَعْنَ صَوْتَ أَطْفَالِكُنَّ ـ اَلدُّخُولُ فِى
هٰذَا ٱلْأَمْرِ أَسْهَلُ مِنَ ٱلْخُرُوجِ مِنْهُ ـ يَا خَادِمَةُ
اُذْهَبِى إِلَى ٱلسُّوقِ وَٱطْلُبِى مِنَ ٱلْخَيَّاطَةِ ثِيَابِى
ٱلْجَدِيدَةَ ـ إِنَّ كَاتِمَ ٱلسِّرِّ صَدِيقٌ أَمِينٌ ـ فَتْحُ نَفْسِكَ
هُوَ ٱلْفَتْحُ ٱلْعَظِيمُ ـ أَيُّهَا ٱلْأَمِيرُ ٱنْزِلْ مِنْ فَرَسِكَ

وَادْخُلْ مَنْزِلِي وَهٰذَا لِي شَرَفٌ عَظِيمٌ ـ اَلْمَطْلُوبُ
مِنْكَ اَلرُّجُوعُ مِنَ اَلْبِلَادِ اَلْبَعِيدَةِ إِلَى بَيْتِ
أَبَوَيْكَ ـ اَلْمَخْدُومُ عِنْدَكُمْ هُوَ خَادِمُ كُلِّكُمْ ـ إِنَّا
لِلّٰهِ وَإِنَّا إِلَيْهِ رَاجِعُونَ ـ خِدْمَةُ اَلرَّجُلِ أَخَاهُ شَرَفٌ.

24

my daughter, hear what I say — seek knowledge from all, from men and women — entering into wealth is difficult and the going out from it easy — knowledge of yourself is the greatest knowledge and the most difficult — the king rejoiced at the return of his army after its defeat of his enemies — cutting off the hand is the punishment of the thief — the generous man rejoices at the arrival of guests — your keeping your tongue from evil is the fear of God — the object of my sending this young man to you is his entry into your service.

LESSON 13

MOODS

The perfect has only one form which serves for indicative, conditional, and optative.

The imperfect has three besides the indicative (Table 1).

Subjunctive.—This is a suitable name for this mood usually follows a subordinating conjunction. The *u* of the indicative is changed to *a*; the *ni* and *na* of the two syllabled inflections are cut off; while the feminine plurals are not changed.

It is used after the conjunctions لِ and كَيْ ' in order

that ' and also after أَنْ when that follows a verb expressing any sort of wish or purpose.

طَلَبَ مِنِّى أَنْ أَذْهَبَ إِلَى ٱلْقُدْسِ

he sought from me that I should go to Jerusalem.

أَنْ with the subjunctive can always be replaced by an infinitive :—

طَلَبَ مِنِّى ٱلذَّهَابَ الى القدس

Jussive.—This is formed by dropping the inflection *u* of the indicative ; in other places it is the same as the subjunctive.

It gets its name because it provides the imperative for the first and third persons and the negative imperative for the second :—

أُكْتُبْ write ; لَا تَكْتُبْ do not write ;

لِيَكْتُبْ let him write ; لَا يَكْتُبْ let him not write.

As a positive imperative the jussive always takes the prefix لِ ; after وَ and فَ the لِ loses its vowel.

وَلْيَكْتُبْ and let him write.

The jussive has other uses which have nothing to do with the imperative.

Energetic.—Roughly speaking, it is formed by adding *anna* to the indicative ; but the individual forms must be learnt.

With the emphatic لَ it is used in solemn statements, especially after oaths. It is also used to express commands and wishes.

قَدْ حَلَفَ لَيَقْتُلَنَّ he had sworn, he will kill.

Note.—Arabic has no strict rules for indirect speech as have English and Latin.

Conditional sentences.—The conjunction is إِنْ 'if'; either the perfect or the jussive may be used in both parts of the sentence.

إِنْ فَعَلْتَ هٰذَا هَلَكْتَ
إِنْ تَفْعَلْ هذا تَهْلِكْ } if you do this, you will perish.

إِنْ لَا 'if not' is often contracted to إِلَّا.

مَنْ and مَا, when indefinite pronouns, are often treated as conditional particles:—

من سَكَتَ سَلِمَ he who keeps silent is safe.

Vocabulary 13

حَلَفَ i. حَلْفٌ swear.

مَسَحَ a. مَسْحٌ measure.

شَهِدَ شُهُودٌ be present at.

نَدِمَ نَدَمٌ repent.

كَشَفَ i. كَشْفٌ uncover, disclose.

مَزْرَعَةٌ (مَزَارِعُ) field.

مَرَضٌ (a) illness.

حَيَاةٌ life.

سَكَتَ u. سُكُوتٌ be quiet.

شُجَاعٌ bold.

سُمٌّ (b) poison.

سَقَطَ u. سُقُوطٌ fall.

بَدْوٌ bedouins, nomads.

هَلَكَ i. هَلْكٌ perish.

هَلِكَ perish.

عَجِلَ عَجَلٌ hurry.

صَبَرَ i. صَبْرٌ be patient, endure.

كَرِهَ كُرْهٌ be unwilling, not like.

عَيْبٌ (b) fault, defect.

مَرِيضٌ (مَرْضَى) ill, sick.

فَرِيسَةٌ prey.

سَلِمَ سَلَامٌ be safe.

شَجَاعَةٌ bravery.

حَطَبٌ firewood.

ظَهَرَ a. ظُهُورٌ be manifest, conquer.

بَدَوِيٌّ a nomad.

Exercise 25

مَنْ يَعْجَلْ يَنْدَمْ ـ بَعَثَ ٱلْحُكُومَةُ غِلْمَانَهَا لِيَمْسَحُوا
ٱلْمَزَارِعَ ـ طَلَبَ مِنِّي ٱلطَّبِيبُ أَنْ أَشْرَبَ لَبَنًا
كَثِيرًا ـ إِنْ شَهِدْتَ ٱلْحَرْبَ عَرَفْتَ أَيُّ ٱلْجَيْشَيْنِ
أَشْجَعُ ـ لِيَنْزِعْ مِنْ فَمِ ٱلْأَسَدِ فَرِيسَتَهُ لِنَعْرِفَ قُوَّتَهُ
وَشَجَاعَتَهُ ـ أَكْرَهُ أَنْ تَنْظُرَ إِلَى عُيُوبِ جِيرَانِكَ ـ
كَتَبَ ٱلْخَلِيفَةُ إِلَى أَمِيرِ جَيْشِهِ لَا تَقْتُلِ ٱلشُّيُوخَ
وَٱلْأَطْفَالَ وَلَا تَقْطَعِ ٱلْأَشْجَارَ ـ إِنْ تَخْرُجْ مِنَ

هَذَا ٱلْأَمْرِ تَفْرَحُ كُلَّ حَيَاتِكَ ـ مِنَ ٱلشَّجَاعَةِ
أَنْ تَصْبِرَ عَلَى ٱلْمَصَائِبِ وَٱلْمَكْرُوهِ ـ طَلَبَ
ٱلْأَبُ حَكِيمَيْنِ لِيَكْشِفَا عَنْ مَرَضِ ٱبْنِهِ.

26

do not play with that sharp sword — I shall certainly discover his secret — let the youth be silent before one who is older than he — let me go into your house that I may look at your carpets — they broke the cup that the posion in it might fall to the ground — send the servant to gather the dates fallen on the ground — the women of the tribe go out every day to collect firewood — be not angry with a friend — it is part of nobility to disapprove of defects in oneself.

LESSON 14

NEGATIVES

There are several negatives, each with its special uses. The negative stands at the beginning of the sentence, except when it denies a single word.

إِنَّكَ عِنْدِي كَلَا شَيْءٍ

in my opinion you were as nothing.

لَا is ' no ' and also ' not '.

A nominal sentence may be denied by مَا :—

مَا قَوْمٌ كَقَوْمِي

a tribe is not like my tribe—no tribe is like my tribe.

مَا هُوَ مِنَ ٱلْكِتَابِ

it is not from the Book (Koran).

A general negation may be expressed by لَا 'which denies the class'; the noun loses nunation and is in the accusative :—

لَا رَجُلَ فِي ٱلدَّارِ no man is in the house.

If there are two clauses, the nominative may be used in both :—

لَا خَوْفٌ عَلَيْهِمْ وَلَا فَزَعٌ

no fear is on them and no terror.

The defective verb لَيْسَ 'it is not' has no imperfect.

لَيْسَ — لَيْسَتْ — لَسْتَ — لَيْسَا — لَسْتُمَا — لَيْسُوا

— لَسْنَ, etc., is followed by a noun in the accusative or by

ب with the genitive :—

لَسْتُ عَالِمًا — لَسْتُ بِعَالِمٍ I am not learned.

Sometimes it is reduced in meaning to 'not' :—

لَسْتُ أَقْصِدُ ٱلْحَرْبَ I do not intend war.

Verbal sentences.—The past is denied by مَا with the perfect or by لَمْ with the jussive :—

لَمْ يَكْتُبْ — مَا كَتَبَ he did not write.

The future is denied by لَنْ with the subjunctive ; here the subjunctive stands in a main sentence.

لَنْ يَكْتُبَ he will not write — he will never write.

مَا with the imperfect denies the present :—

مَا يَكْتُبُ he is not writing (at the present moment).

لَا with the imperfect is a general negation and may refer to any time.

لَا يَكْتُبُ he does not write.

After another negative لَا may be used to continue a series of denials ; the time is that of the first.

لَمْ يَدْخُلِ ٱلدَّارَ وَلَا نَظَرَ إِلَى شَيْءٍ فِيهَا

he did not enter the house and did not look at anything in it.

لَا with the perfect denies a wish :—

لَا رَحِمَهُ ٱللّٰهُ may God not have mercy on him.

لَا after an oath denies the future :—

وَٱللهِ لَا فَتَحْتُ هٰذَا ٱلْبَابَ

by God I will not open this door.

لَا with the jussive is a negative command as was ṣaid in the previous lesson.

لَمَّا with the jussive means 'not yet' :—

لَمَّا يَكْتُبْ he has not yet written (but still has time).

بَلْ introduces a correction :—

اِضْرِبْ زَيْدًا بَلْ زَيْنَبَ beat Zaid ; no, Zainab.

لَا تَضْرِبْ زَيْدًا بَلْ زَيْنَبَ do not beat Zaid but (beat) Zainab.

غَيْرٌ is a noun meaning 'change'; in the construct state it means first 'other' and then 'not' :—

اَلْمُلُوكُ وَغَيْرُهُمْ the kings and others.

غَيْرُ ٱلْعَرَبِ non-Arabs.

وَجْهُهُ إِلَى غَيْرِ مِصرَ his face was not towards Egypt.

Vocabulary 14

شَيْءٌ (أَشْيَاءُ no nunation) thing.

قَوْمٌ (a) people, tribe, some.

فَزِعَ (فَزَعٌ) be afraid, seek refuge.

قَصَدَ i. قَصْدٌ aim at, purpose.

هَرَبَ u. هَرَبٌ run away.

شُغْلٌ (a) work, labour.

حَدِيثٌ (أَحَادِيثُ) story, report.

عَلِمَ عِلْمٌ know.

فَقْرٌ poverty.

حِرْصٌ greed.

أَسَدٌ (b) lion.

حُسْنٌ goodness, beauty.

سَمَاءٌ (سَمَوَاتٌ) sky, heaven.

أَحَدٌ fem. إِحْدَى one.

وَقْتٌ (a) time.

كَفٌّ restraint.

وَرَعٌ piety.

حَزِنَ حَزَنٌ be sorry.

رَحِمَ رَحْمَةٌ have mercy on.

خَوْفٌ fear.

خَبَرٌ (a) story, news.

قَنِعَ قَنَاعَةٌ be content, satisfied.

بَلَاءٌ trial, misfortune.

شَرَهٌ greed.

حَرٌّ heat.

تَدْبِيرٌ management.

خُلْقٌ (a) nature, character.

Exercise 27

لَا تَضْرِبُوا أَوْلَادَكُمْ ـ لَمْ يَبْعَثْنِي أَبِي لِأَطْلُبَ كِتَابًا
لَكَ ـ لَنْ يُكْرَمَ مَنْ لَا يَكْتُمُ ٱلْأَسْرَارَ ـ لَمْ نَسْمَعْ
مِثْلَ هٰذَا ٱلْحَدِيثِ ـ اَللّٰهُ أَحَدٌ لَيْسَ كَمِثْلِهِ شَيْءٌ ـ
لَا نَرْجِعُ مِنْ شُغْلِنَا فِي ٱلْمَزَارِعِ وَٱلشَّمْسُ

فِي ٱلسَّمَاءِ ـ لَمْ نَفْرَحْ فِي هٰذَا ٱلْخَبَرِ وَلَا حَزِنَّا ـ
لَا فَقْرَ وَلَا بَلَاءَ كَٱلْحِرْصِ وَٱلشَّرَهِ وَلَا مَالَ
كَٱلْقَنَاعَةِ ـ لَا عَقْلَ كَٱلتَّدْبِيرِ وَلَا وَرَعَ كَٱلْكَفِّ
وَلَا حُسْنَ كَحُسْنِ ٱلْخُلْقِ ـ ٱلْهَرَبُ فِي وَقْتِهِ خَيْرٌ مِنَ
ٱلصَّبْرِ فِي غَيْرِ وَقْتِهِ ـ اِثْنَانِ لَا يَشْبَعَانِ طَالِبُ عِلْمٍ
وَطَالِبُ مَالٍ.

28

our enemies, may God not have mercy on them, are many — do not be afraid of work — the prophet never ate his fill of meat in his life — be not satisfied with a little knowledge — the days which have gone will never return — I do not seek gifts from the government to-day — do not take refuge with (إِلَى) another than God — do not laugh, my daughter, at the misfortune of the poor and be not angry at the success of the rich — he is the possessor of wealth, estates, and houses but (and) he is not yet content — you are not the possessor of wisdom.

LESSON 15

MORE ABOUT CASES

Accusative.—This is the adverbial case, for true adverbs are few.

Cognate accusative.—The infinitive, usually qualified in some way, carries on the idea of the verb :—

ذَهَبَ ذَهَابًا سَرِيعًا

he went off a quick going (quickly).

أَخَذْنَاهُمْ أَخْذَ عَزِيزٍ

we laid hold on them the laying hold of a strong one = we took a good grip of them.

The infinitive may be left out :—

اُذْكُرُوا اللّٰهَ كَثِيرًا remember God much (often).

Extensions of this construction are :—

ضَرَبْتُهُ مَرَّتَيْنِ I hit him twice.

ضَرَبْتُهُ سَوْطًا I hit him with a whip.

Accusative of reason or cause.—It is the infinitive of a verb of sensation or thought referring to the same time as the main verb :—

لَا تَقْتُلُوا أَوْلَادَكُمْ خَشْيَةَ إِمْلَاقٍ

do not kill your children from fear of poverty.

Accusative of extent in time or place.—All nouns of time may be used in this way :—

ذَهَبَ لَيْلًا he went away by night.

سَكَنَ فِي مَكَّةَ سِنِينَ [أَيَّامًا]

he dwelt some years (days) in Mecca.

For place only names of direction, measure, and general words can be used :—

ذَهَبَ مِيلًا he went away a mile.

نَظَرَ يَمِينًا وَيَسَارًا [شِمَالًا] he looked right and left.

جَلَسْتُ مَجْلِسَ زَيْدٍ ـ جَلَسْتُ مَكَانَ زَيْدٍ

I sat in Zaid's place.

but جَلَسْتُ فِي الْمَسْجِدِ I sat in the mosque.

Accusative of nearer definition.—This is used with weights, measures, verbs of filling and such like ; it is always indefinite :—

هِيَ أَطْوَلُهُنَّ ذِرَاعًا she was the longest of them in arm.

رِطْلٌ عَسَلًا a *roll* of honey.

مَلَأَ الْكِيسَ ذَهَبًا he filled the purse with gold.

Accusative of accompanying circumstance.—It is indefinite and English would use the nominative :—

قَدِمَ الرَّجُلُ رَاكِبًا the man advanced riding.

أُدْخُلُوا رَجُلًا رَجُلًا come in, one by one.

The accusative may refer to any part of the sentence :—

نَظَرْتُ إِلَى زَيْدٍ جَالِسًا

I looked at Zaid as he was sitting.

دَخَلْتُ ٱلْبُسْتَانَ زَاهِرًا

I went into the garden when it was in bloom.

ضَرَبْتُ زَيْدًا رَاكِبَيْنِ

I hit Zaid when we were both mounted.

Genitive.—This is used more freely than in English ; possession is only one of the ideas expressed by it. Examples will make the usage clear.

رِطْلُ عَسَلٍ a *roll* of honey.

كُرْسِيُّ خَشَبٍ a chair of wood.

سَمُّ سَاعَةٍ poison of a moment (instantaneous).

'My knowledge' means 'what I know'.

عِلْمِي means 'what I know' and 'what others know about me'.

In technical terms the English genitive is subjective, the Arabic may be subjective or objective.

فَخَرْتَ بِأَيَّامٍ لِغَيْرِكَ فَخْرُهَا

you boasted of days (battles) the boasting in which belonged to others.

We have just seen the genitive describing a noun ; it can also describe an adjective :—

قَلِيلُ ٱلْعَقْلِ little of understanding, foolish.

In this construction the adjective, unlike the noun, can take the definite article :—

اَلاِبْنَةُ ٱلْحَسَنَةُ ٱلْوَجْهِ the girl, the pretty of face.
the girl with the pretty face.

اَلرَّجُلُ ٱلْكَثِيرُ ٱلْمَالِ the man the much of property.
the rich man.

Vocabulary 15

مَرَّةٌ (c) time (repetition).

يَوْمٌ (أَيَّامٌ) day (24 hours).

لَيْلَةٌ one night.

مَكَانٌ (أَمْكِنَةٌ) place.

كِيسٌ (a) bag, purse.

سَاعَةٌ (سَاعَاتٌ) hour, moment.

سَكَنَ u. سُكُونٌ be quiet, dwell.

سَجَدَ u. سُجُودٌ bow down.

فَخَرَ u. فَخْرٌ boast.

مَكَثَ u. مَكْثٌ stay, remain.

غَرَسَ i. غَرْسٌ plant.

حَرِيرٌ silk.

جُبْنٌ cowardice.

سَوْطٌ (a) whip.

لَيْلٌ (لَيَالٍ) night.

خَشْيَةٌ fear.

كُرْسِيٌّ (كَرَاسِيُّ) chair.

ٱلْبَارِحُ yesterday.

رَكِبَ رُكُوبٌ ride.

زَهَرَ a. زُهُورٌ bloom, shine.

قَعَدَ u. قُعُودٌ sit, stay at home.

غَرَبَ u. غُرُوبٌ be, go far off set (star).

صُوفٌ wool.

Exercise 29

هُوَ أَصْفَرُ ٱللَّوْنِ ـ زَيْدٌ قَلِيلُ ٱلْعَقْلِ وَعَمْرٌو أَقَلُّ ٱلْعَقْلِ مِنْهُ ـ ٱلرِّيحُ ٱلْيَوْمَ أَشَدُّ مِنْهَا ٱلْبَارِحَ ـ هَرَبَ مِنَ ٱلْبِلَادِ خَوْفًا مِنْ غَضَبِ ٱلسُّلْطَانِ ـ ذَهَبَ يَمِينًا وَيَسَارًا يَطْلُبُ طَعَامًا ـ مَكَثُوا غَيْرَ طَوِيلٍ ـ قَعَدْتُ عَنِ ٱلْحَرْبِ جُبْنًا ـ غَرَسَ ٱلْفَلَّاحُونَ مَزَارِعَهُمْ شَعِيرًا ـ أَنَا أَشَدُّ مِنْهُ خَوْفًا مِنْهُ مِنِّي ـ قَصَدْتُ خِدْمَةَ كَبِيرٍ مِنَ ٱلْكِبَارِ طَلَبًا لِلْمَالِ ـ فَرِحْتُ وَأَكْتُمُ مَا بِي حَزَنًا عَلَى ٱلْمَرِيضِ ـ سَجَدْتُ لِلّٰهِ فَرَحًا فِي بَعْثِهِ ٱلنَّبِيَّ.

30

she was much afraid — no one ran away as I did — I lived in that town for many years — he has little money but (and) is quite content in his poverty — the heat to-day is greater than it was yesterday — he is as brave as a lion — he is braver than a lion — he was silent for a long time — I do not go to hot countries for fear of illness — he wore garments of silk in his joy at having gathered much wealth — he is strong in the arm and weak in the leg.

LESSON 16

WEAK—HOLLOW—VERBS

In these verbs (Tables 4—5) the middle radical is *w* or *y*. In the perfect the first radical has *a:* in an open syllable and *u* or *i* in a shut syllable according as the middle radical is *w* or *y*. Thus the perfect has only two syllables in place of the three of the strong verb.

In the imperfect the vowel after the first radical is long in an open and short in a shut syllable and is *u* or *i* as the middle radical is *w* or *y*.

In the jussive the forms with no final vowel have a shut syllable after the first radical, so the vowel in it is short.

The imperative is made as usual by cutting off the prefix of the jussive and what is left needs no helping vowel.

The active participle always has a glottal stop; قَائِلٌ may come from the root *qwl* or *qyl*.

The passive participle is مَقُولٌ from *qwl* and مَقِيلٌ from *qyl*.

The infinitive is often فَعْلٌ, i.e. قَوْلٌ and قَيْلٌ, but there are many exceptions.

There is also a special intransitive form corresponding to فَعِلَ.

In this the long vowel of the perfect is *a:* and the short vowel always *i*. The vowel of the imperfect and its derivatives is *a*, long or short, as the syllable is open or closed.

The verb كَانَ يَكُونُ 'become' takes the place of the missing 'be' when it is necessary to indicate past or future time :—

اَلرَّجُلُ فِي اَلدَّارِ the man is in the house.

كَانَ اَلرَّجُلُ فى الدار the man was in the house.

يَكُونُ اَلرَّجُلُ فى الدار the man will be in the house.

(A future particle is not needed, for the verb would not be used for the present.)

كَانَ is also an auxiliary verb; the perfect of it is used with another perfect to express the pluperfect; قَدْ is sometimes added.

مَاتَ اَلرَّشِيدُ بِطُوسَ وَكَانَ خَرَجَ إِلَى خُرَاسَانَ

Rasheed died in Tus and (after) he had gone to Khurasan.

The perfect is also used with an imperfect to denote an act repeated in the past :—

كَانَ يَرْكَبُ فِي كُلِّ يَوْمٍ عِدَّةَ مِرَارٍ

he used to ride (rode) every day a number of times.

The imperfect with the perfect of another verb expresses the future perfect :—

يَكُونُ زَيْدٌ كَتَبَ Zaid will have written.

When it is an independent verb, the subject is in the nominative and the complement in the accusative :—

يَكُونُ اَلرَّسُولُ عَلَيْكُمْ شَهِيدًا

the apostle will be a witness against you.

كُونُوا حِجَارَةً أَوْ حَدِيدًا be stone or iron.

Peculiar is the construction—

مَا كَانَ لِ he is not the one to.

لَمْ يَكُنْ زَيْدٌ لِيَشْرَبَ خَمْرًا

Zaid was not the man to drink wine.

يَصِيرُ ــ صَارَ 'become' and other verbs also take the complement in the accusative.

قَدْ with the perfect shows that it has the sense of the English perfect or pluperfect :—

إِنَّ ٱبْنَتَكَ قَدْ مَاتَتْ

your daughter has died (is dead).

قَدْ أَمَرَتْ بِالْبُخْلِ أُمُّ مُحَمَّدٍ

Umm Muhammad (name of a woman) had given an order about stinginess ; had told me to be stingy.

قَدْ with the imperfect means 'sometimes' :—

قَدْ يَعْلَقُ ٱلْقَلْبُ حُبًّا ثُمَّ يَتْرُكُهُ

the heart sometimes attaches itself to love, then leaves it.

The verb يَمُوتُ ــ مَاتَ 'die' is irregular ; in the perfect both مُتُّ and مِتُّ are possible.

Vocabulary 16

قَصُرَ قِصَرٌ be short.

قَالَ u. قَوْلٌ say.

قَالَ i. قَيْلٌ take a siesta.

عَلِقَ عُلُوقٌ be attached to.

صَارَ i. صَيْرٌ become.

قَامَ u. قِيَامٌ stand, stand up.

عَادَ u. عَوْدٌ return.

بَاعَ i. بَيْعٌ sell.

عِدَّةٌ number.

حَدِيدٌ iron.

حُبٌّ love.

حُجَّةٌ (حُجَجٌ) argument.

قَافِلَةٌ (قَوَافِلُ) caravan.

وَحْدٌ (always with a suffix) alone.

طَالَ u. طُولٌ be long.

كَانَ u. كَوْنٌ become, be.

تَرَكَ u. تَرْكٌ leave.

مَاتَ u. مَوْتٌ die.

سَارَ i. سَيْرٌ go, travel.

خَافَ a. خَوْفٌ fear.

مَالَ i. مَيْلٌ incline.

غَلَبَ i. غَلْبٌ overcome.

بُخْلٌ avarice.

حَجَرٌ (a) stone.

لُصٌّ (b) thief, brigand.

حَبْلٌ (e) rope.

Exercise 31

مَن قَصُرَتْ حُجَّتُهُ طَالَ لِسَانُهُ ـ قُمْ يَا وَلَدِي وَسِرْ
إِلَى جَدِّكَ ـ كَانَ ٱلْأَوْلَادُ تَلْعَبُ فِي ٱلشَّارِعِ ـ
خَافَتِ ٱلْجَارِيَةُ مِنْ شِدَّةِ ٱلرِّيحِ ـ عَادَتِ ٱلْقَافِلَةُ
خَوْفًا مِنَ ٱللُّصُوصِ ـ لَا تَخَافِي يَا بِنْتِي لَا
تَسِيرِينَ عَلَى وَحْدِكِ ـ لِيَقُلْ مَا فِي قَلْبِهِ ـ كُنْتُ

ٱبْنَ أَبِى ثُمَّ صِرْتُ أَبَا ٱبْنِى - إِنَّ لَوْنَ ٱلْحَيَّةِ خُضْرَةٌ
تَمِيلُ إِلَى ٱلسَّوَادِ - كَانَ ٱلْبَدْوُ يَبِيعُونَ جُلُودَ ٱلْغَنَمِ
وَٱلْمَعْزِ مِنَ ٱلْفَلَّاحِينَ - يَكُونُ ٱلْجَيْشُ قَدْ غَلَبَ
عَلَى أَعْدَائِهِ قَبْلَ غُرُوبِ ٱلشَّمْسِ.

32

he rose from his bed and the sun had inclined to its setting — if a chief of our people dies, a chief arises — the caravan will have travelled for many days — the whole company had heard what I was saying — everybody takes a siesta in the hot days of summer — many say other than what they think — do not fear the unpleasantnesses of the road — the woman had been making clothes for her children — the guests will not have risen from their beds before your departure — my grandmother, are you going with the other women to Jerusalem ?

LESSON 17

STRONG VERB—DERIVED STEMS

The derived are formed from the simple stem (consult Table 2) by additions of various sorts and express some modification of the original verbal idea. It is the custom in European grammars to number them, the simple stem being I. They have each only one variety, unlike I, and are made from فَعِلَ فَعَلَ and فَعُلَ .

The inflections are the same as for the simple stem.

The derived stems fall into four groups determined by the vowel sequence in the imperfect.

1.

II is formed by doubling the second radical: كَتَّبَ impf. يُكَتِّبُ.

III by lengthening the first vowel: كَاتَبَ impf. يُكَاتِبُ.

IV by prefixing ʔa and dropping the vowel of the first radical: أَكْتَبَ impf. يُكْتِبُ.

The prefix of the imperfect has *u* and the characteristic is *i*. Note that in the imperfect of IV the ʔ is dropped though it reappears in the imperative, أَكْتِبْ.

2.

V is made by prefixing *ta* to stem II: تَكَتَّبَ impf. يَتَكَتَّبُ.

VI by prefixing *ta* to III: تَكَاتَبَ impf. يَتَكَاتَبُ.

The imperfect has the vowel *a* throughout, except of course in the final inflection.

3.

VII is made by prefixing *n* with liaison: اِنْكَتَبَ impf. يَنْكَتِبُ.

VIII by inserting *t* after the first radical; the form begins with liaison : اِكْتَتَبَ impf. يَكْتَتِبُ.

X by prefixing *sta* with liaison. This is really a form like VIII made from *saktaba* which does not occur in Arabic though it is found in other Semitic languages.

اِسْتَكْتَبَ impf. يَسْتَكْتِبُ

In this group the prefix of the imperfect has *a*, and the characteristic is *i*.

4.

IX and XI cannot be made from anything, which we should call a verb; they denote colours, and are best treated with the doubled verb.

Summary.—The perfects have *a* throughout, except of course in liaison.

If the imperfect has five syllables, the fourth has *a*.

Few verbs have all the nine stems.

In good Arabic VII is not made from roots beginning with *ʔ, w, y, r, l,* and *n*.

In VIII partial or total assimilation occurs when the root begins with *t, θ, d, ð, z, s, đ ŧ, ǧ*.

دَرَكَ	اِدَّرَكَ			overtake
ذخر	اِدَّخَرَ	or	اِذَّخَرَ	store up
زحم	اِزْدَحَمَ			crowd together
صنع	اِصْطَنَعَ			take into one's employment
ضرب	اِضْطَرَبَ			be confused

ضجع اِضْطَجَعَ or اِضَّجَعَ lie down

طلع اِطَّلَعَ know (survey from above)

ظلم اِظَّلَمَ or اِطَّلَمَ suffer wrong

Each stem has its own meaning or meanings.

II is

intensive : كَسَرَ break كَسَّرَ smash

causative (this is an encroachment on IV) :

عَلِمَ know عَلَّمَ teach

declarative : صَدَقَ speak truth صَدَّقَ say that one speaks truth, believe

denominative : كَبَّرَ say, ' God is very great ' (اَللّٰهُ أَكْبَرُ)

III is

conative : قَتَلَ kill قَاتَلَ try to kill, fight

نَزَعَ take away نَازَعَ try to take away, quarrel

It takes as direct object the indirect object of I :—

كَتَبَ write كَاتَبَ correspond with

رَكِبَ ride رَاكَبَ ride with (a person)

It is always transitive.

IV is

causative : جَلَسَ sit down أَجْلَسَ set down

V is the reflexive of II and then passive :

فَرَقَ divide (trans.) تَفَرَّقَ scatter (intrans.)

VI is

reciprocal : ضَرَبَ hit تَضَارَبَ hit one another, have a free fight

pretence : نَعَسَ sleep تَنَاعَسَ pretend to sleep

VII is reflexive, then passive : إِنْكَسَرَ be broken

هَزَمَ defeat إِنْهَزَمَ let oneself be defeated

VIII is
reflexive (sometimes passive) :

جَمَعَ collect (trans.) إِجْتَمَعَ collect (intrans.)

X is to ask or think that the simple verbal idea should be done.

حَسُنَ be good اِسْتَحْسَنَ think good, approve

غَفَرَ pardon اِسْتَغْفَرَ ask pardon from (trans.)

It is almost causative :

خَرَجَ go out اِسْتَخْرَجَ extract from a mine, make productive, till.

It takes considerable ingenuity to fit many verbs into this scheme; thus كَلَّمَ speak to (trans.) تَكَلَّمَ speak (intrans.). Here are two sample roots :—

	خَلَفَ u. خَلُفَ	سَلاَمٌ سَلِمَ
I.	remain behind	be safe, well
II.	خَلَّفَ leave behind	سَلَّمَ greet (denominative) make safe, protect, surrender (trans.)
III.	خَالَفَ oppose	سَالَمَ make peace with, treat peaceably
IV.	أَخْلَفَ break (promise) (make your word lag behind)	أَسْلَمَ submit turn Muslim
V.	تَخَلَّفَ hold back from	تَسَلَّمَ receive the surrender, turn Muslim
VI.	تَخَالَفَ disagree with	تَسَالَمَ make peace together
VIII.	اِخْتَلَفَ differ, be different	اِسْتَلَمَ kiss (the Black Stone)
X.	اِسْتَخْلَفَ appoint a successor, take in exchange	اِسْتَسْلَمَ submit keep to the middle of the road

فَ 'and' denotes a closer connection than وَ and may often be rendered 'so', 'then'. In a conditional sentence it cannot be translated. Sometimes it denotes a change of subject.

Vocabulary 17

فَرَقَ u. i. فَرْقٌ separate.	هَزَمَ i. هَزْمٌ defeat.
غَفَرَ i. غُفْرَانٌ cover, pardon.	بَلَغَ u. بُلُوغٌ arrive at.
صَرَفَ i. صَرْفٌ turn (trans.).	VII turn away, go away.
نظر IV cause to wait.	VIII expect, wait for.
قَبِلَ قَبُولٌ receive.	IV go forward.
قبل III compare.	نزع III try to take away, quarrel.
ضرب VIII be confused, in commotion.	حصر III besiege.
زَحَمَ a. زَحْمٌ push.	VIII crowd.
ذَخَرَ a. ذُخْرٌ select.	VIII store up.
دَرَسَ u. دَرْسٌ study.	II teach.
ثَلْجٌ (b) snow.	حَاجَةٌ need, business, thing.
عِيدٌ (a) festival.	حِصْنٌ (b) fortress.
علم II teach.	IV tell, make known.
V learn.	غَابَ i. غُيُوبٌ be absent.

Exercise 33

كَلَّمْتُهُ وَلَمْ أَتَكَلَّمْ مَعَ غَيْرِهِ - أَطْعَمَ ٱلْغَنِيُّ فُقَرَاءَ
كَثِيرَةً فَٱنْصَرَفُوا شَاكِرِينَ - لَا تُخَالِفُوا آبَاءَكُمْ يَا
أَيُّهَا ٱلْأَوْلَادُ - كُنَّا نَتَّبِعُ ٱلْفَلَّاحَ وَٱنْفَرَدْنَا عَنْ
أَصْحَابِنَا - اِنْتَظِرْنِي فِي ٱلسُّوقِ وَلَا تَنْصَرِفْ - كَانَ

سُكَّانُ ٱلْبَلَدِ يَضْطَرِبُونَ عِنْدَ بُلُوغِ خَبَرِ ٱنْهِزَامِ ٱلْجَيْشِ ـ كُلُّ شَيْءٍ تَسْتَحْسِنُهُ فِي ٱلْكَلْبِ فَٱطْلُبْهُ فِي ٱلْفَرَسِ ـ كَانَتِ ٱلنِّسَاءُ يَزْدَحِمْنَ عِنْدَ بَابِ ٱلْقَصْرِ لِيَقْبَلْنَ تُحَفَ ٱلْمَلِكَةِ ـ غَلَبَ ٱللُّصُوصُ عَلَى ٱلْمَدِينَةِ وَأَهْلَكُوا كُلَّ مَا فِيهَا ـ طَلَبْتُ مِنْ فَلَّاحِيَّ أَنْ يَدَّخِرُوا ٱلثَّلْجَ فِي حُجَرٍ تَحْتَ ٱلْأَرْضِ ـ كَرِهْتُ أَنْ تُقَابِلَ فَخْرِي بِفِعْلِي ـ سَلَّمَ ٱلرَّئِيسُ ٱلْحِصْنَ إِلَى ٱلْمُحَاصِرِينَ.

34

I asked pardon of God and he pardoned me — let me wait till the arrival of the guests that I may hear their news — I shall expect you after sunset — brothers sometimes quarrel with their sisters — I shall punish thieves and all doers of evil — he tried to overcome me and I overcame him — no child thinks its mother ugly — the company differed about (فِي) what they should do — the governor appointed his son deputy during his absence — everyone dresses his children in new clothes on the two great festivals — does your father sometimes bring a poor man into the house and give him food ?

LESSON 18

PASSIVE

The passive (Tables 3, etc.) is made by a change of vowels inside the verb. The inflections are the same as for the active except the vowel of the prefix of the imperfect. In stem I the perfect is *kutiba* and the imperfect *yuktabu*. The same scheme holds good for the derived stems; if there are more than three syllables, the extra one has *u* in the perfect and *a* in the imperfect.

a: in the perfect of III and VI becomes *u:* in the passive.

The passive imperfect of IV is the same as that of I.

Hollow verb, stem I.—Some typical forms are put side by side to make the differences apparent.

w. active.	قَالَ	قُلْتُ	يَقُولُ	يَقُلْنَ	يَقُلْ
passive.	قِيلَ	قِلْتُ	يُقَالُ	يُقَلْنَ	يُقَلْ
y. active.	بَانَ	بِنْتُ	يَبِينُ	يَبِنَّ	يَبِنْ
passive.	بِينَ	بِنْتُ	يُبَانُ	يُبَنَّ	يُبَنْ

The passive can only be used when the agent is not mentioned.

'Zaid was killed' قُتِلَ زَيْدٌ

'Zaid was killed by Muhammad' cannot be translated into Arabic, which can only say: قَتَلَ مُحَمَّدٌ زَيْدًا 'Muhammad killed Zaid'.

If an active verb has two objects, the first becomes the subject of the passive and the second stays in the accusative.

وَعَدَنَا ٱللهُ ٱلْحَيَاةَ ٱلأَبَدِيَّةَ God promised us eternal life.

وُعِدْنَا ٱلْحَيَاةَ ٱلأَبَدِيَّةَ we were promised eternal life.

A verb may take two pronominal suffixes provided that they do not both refer to the same person or thing. When both are third person they cannot be of the same number and gender; indeed, it is better to make one of them independent by using *ʔiyya:*.

أَنْكَحَنِيهَا he gave her to me in marriage.

نُلْزِمُكُمُوهَا (we make you stick to it). we compel you to take it.

أَسْكَنَهُمُوهُ he made them dwell in it.

Vocabulary 18

فَتَلَ i. فَتْلٌ twist.

حَمَلَ i. حَمْلٌ carry.

طَعَنَ u. طَعْنٌ thrust, pierce, criticise.

حَرَمَ i. حَرِيمٌ forbid.

نَشَدَ u. نَشْدٌ seek, adjure.

صَامَ u. صَوْمٌ fast.

ٱلإِسْتَانَةُ Stamboul.

مِيتَةٌ mode of death.

عِنَايَةٌ care.

فَرْسَخٌ parasang (about three miles).

مَشْكُوكٌ doubted.

زُبْدٌ butter.

خبر IV tell, report.

II put a burden on, load.

حَرُمَ حَرَامٌ be unlawful, tabu.

نشد IV recite (poetry).

لَامَ u. لَوْمٌ blame.

ضَاقَ i. ضِيقٌ be narrow.

رِفْقٌ kindness.

هَنْدَسَةٌ engineering.

سِكَّةٌ (سِكَكٌ) coin, road.

نَسَبٌ (a) pedigree, family honour.

تَمْرٌ dates (coll.) تَمْرَةٌ a date.

رَمَضَانُ ninth month of Muslim year.

Exercise 35

ضُرِبَتْ تِلْكَ ٱلسِّكَّةُ فِى ٱلْإِسْتَانَةِ ـ إِنَّ ٱلْإِنْسَانَ
يُعْرَفُ بِرُفَقَائِهِ ـ سِيرَ مِيلَانِ ـ إِنْ تُقْتَلُوا فَٱلْقَتْلُ
أَكْرَمُ مِيتَةٍ ـ حُمِّلْتُ عِنَايَةَ إِخْوَانِى ٱلصَّغِيرَةِ
بَعْدَ مَوْتِ أَبِينَا ـ كَانَ مَشْكُوكًا فِى نَسَبِهِ
مَطْعُونًا عَلَيْهِ ـ مَنْ حُرِمَ ٱلرِّفْقَ حُرِمَ ٱلْخَيْرَ كُلَّهُ ـ
هٰذَا أَمْرٌ ٱخْتُلِفَ فِيهِ ـ صِيمَ رَمَضَانُ ـ مَاتَ
ٱلْخَلِيفَةُ وَٱسْتُخْلِفَ ٱبْنُ عَمِّهِ ٱلْأَصْغَرُ ـ اَلدُّخُولُ
مَمْنُوعٌ ـ حُمِلَ عَلَى أَفْرَاسِ ٱلْحُكُومَةِ إِلَى
مِصْرَ ـ هَلْ تَعَلَّمْتُمْ عِلْمَ ٱلْهَنْدَسَةِ نَعَمْ عَلَّمَنَاهُ
ٱلْمُعَلِّمُ ـ زُرِعَ ٱلْمَزَارِعُ زُهُورًا.

36

his poetry is recited before the great ones of the land — the fields were sown with wheat, barley, and millet — entry to the mosques is forbidden — the leader was killed and the army defeated — the earth was made a bed for you — his face was turned from his goal — his boasting is suspect — his father was killed, a man from Egypt killed him — he goes forward like a laden camel — he was blamed for his much fasting — his secret will be disclosed.

LESSON 19

THAT—CONJUNCTION

In the sentences :—

1. He said that he had done it.
2. That you are pleased pleases me.
3. The rain has been so heavy that the crops are good.
4. I sent him to school that he might not be spoiled at home.

In 1 'that' introduces indirect speech ; in 2 it introduces a sentence which takes the place of a noun and may be subject or object in a bigger sentence ; in 3 it denotes a consequence ; in 4 a purpose. Arabic does not distinguish sharply the first three types and only sometimes the fourth.

إِنَّ

We have seen that it is used to introduce an independent nominal sentence and it cannot be translated. After قال 'he said' it is a conjunction.

قَالَ إِنَّ زَيْدًا مُسَافِرٌ he said that Zaid was travelling.

أَنَّ

This is used after all other verbs or substitutes for verbs to introduce a nominal sentence.

أُخْبِرْتُ أَنَّ مَلِكًا مِنْ مُلُوكِ ٱلْهِنْدِ كَانَ لَهُ زَوْجَةٌ

I was told that a king of India had a wife.

(Note how the impossibility of putting an indefinite noun before a definite genitive is evaded.)

وَفِى ٱلْحَدِيثِ أَنَّ رَجُلًا قَالَ

and it is in the tradition that a man said.

زَعَمُوا أَنَّهَا أَخْبَرَتْ they claim that she related.

(This can also be expressed زَعَمُوهَا أخبرت).

A verbal sentence can only follow أَنَّ if it is separated from it by a pronoun of the third person which cannot be translated.

أَنَّهُ كَانَ فِي بَغْدَادَ تَاجِرٌ وَهُوَ ذُو مَالٍ وَافِرٍ

that there was in Baghdad a merchant possessed of abundant wealth.

It is also used after prepositions :—

شَهِدْتُ بِأَنَّ ٱللّٰهَ حَقٌّ لِقَاءُهُ

I testify that God the meeting him is truth — that meeting God is a fact.

اَلدَّلَائِلُ عَلَى أَنَّهُ لَا يَعِيشُ إِلَّا ٱلْأَنْسَبُ كَثِيرَةٌ

the proofs are many that only a man of the best family will live.

Or when a noun governs a sentence :—

مَا دَلِيلُ أَنَّكَ صَادِقٌ

what proof is there that you are truthful ?

(دليل loses nunation because it is in the construct state before a sentence.)

Note.—The pronoun, which cannot be translated, is also used after إِنَّ :

يَا مُوسَى إِنَّهُ أَنَا ٱللّٰهُ ٱلْعَزِيزُ ٱلْحَكِيمُ

O Moses, I am the mighty wise God.

أَنْ

It introduces direct speech :—

بَلَغَنِى أَنْ زَيْدٌ مُسَافِرٌ غَدًا

it has reached me (I have heard) that Zaid is travelling to-morrow.

سَمِعْتُ أَنْ زَيْدٌ عَالِمٌ I have heard that Zaid is learned.

When the main verb does not contain any wish or purpose, أَنْ may govern the perfect or the imperfect indicative :—

أَعْجَبَنِى أَنْ قُمْتَ it pleased me that you stood up.

أَعْلَمُ أَنْ يَنَامُ I know that he is asleep.

But these two sentences would be more often put :—

أَعْجَبَنِى أَنَّكَ قُمْتَ ـ أَعْلَمُ أَنَّهُ يَنَامُ

It is used with the subjunctive when the main verb contains any sort of wish or intention :—

أَمْ حَسِبْتُمْ أَنْ تَدْخُلُوا الْجَنَّةَ

do you reckon that you will enter the garden (paradise) ?

أَمَرَ أَنْ لَا يُولَدَ مَوْلُودٌ ذَكَرٌ إِلَّا ذَبَحَهُ

he gave orders that no male child should be born except one killed it.

أَبْلِغْ رَبِيعَةَ أَنْ يَغْضَبُوا

convey to Rabiʻa that they should be angry.

The negative is أَنْ لَا or أَلَّا by assimilation.

إِنْ خِفْتُمْ أَلَّا يُقِيمَا حُدُودَ ٱللّٰهِ

if you fear that those two will not cause the limitations of God to stand (observe God's laws).

لَيْسَ عَلَيْكُمْ جُنَاحٌ أَلَّا تَكْتُبُوهَا

it is no sin for you that you do not write it.

حَتَّى

With the subjunctive it means 'so that', 'until' if any wish or purpose is intended.

لِكَيْ – كَيْ – لِأَنْ – لِ

These may mean 'in order that', but لِ and لِأَنْ may express consequence or even a substantival idea; they govern the subjunctive :—

قَدْ أَمَرَتْ لِأُقْتَلَ

she had given orders that I should be killed.

تُبْ لِيَغْفِرَ لَكَ ٱللّٰهُ

repent in order that God may pardon you.

تَعَلَّمُوا لِكَيْ تُعَلِّمُوا

learn in order that you may teach.

أُمِرْتُ لِأَنْ أَكُونَ أَوَّلَ ٱلْمُسْلِمِينَ

I was commanded that I should become the first of those who submit (the Muslims).

لِئَلَّ — لِأَنْ لَا is used as the negative of لِ ; كَيْلَا and لِكَيْلَا are usually written as one word.

Vocabulary 19

صَفَحَ u. صَفْحٌ pardon.

عَقَدَ i. عَقْدٌ tie, knot.

كَبُرَ كِبَرٌ be big.

خَطَبَ u. خُطْبَةٌ preach, خِطَابٌ ask a woman in marriage.

طَلَقَ u. طَلَاقٌ be divorced.

عَتَبَ u. i. عَتْبٌ blame.

كَفَرَ u. كُفْرٌ be an unbeliever ; كُفْرَانٌ be ungrateful.

دَمٌ (دِمَاءٌ) blood.

زَوْجٌ (a) pair, husband.

حَقٌّ (b) truth, duty, right.

رَسُولٌ (d) messenger, apostle.

شغل VIII work, be busy.

حَمَّ u. حَمٌّ be hot.

حُمَّى fever.

فَاقَ u. فَوْقٌ be superior to.

عقد VIII believe.

كبر V be proud, act proudly.

IV divorce.

III blame, speak contemptuously to.

رَبٌّ (a) lord.

زَوْجَةٌ wife.

إِنَّمَا only (adv.).

خَلَطَ i. خَلْطٌ mix.

حُمَّ (passive), suffer from fever.

حَمَّامٌ bath (Turkish).

Exercise 37

هَلْ لَكَ أَنْ تَذْهَبَ — لَا يَكْرَهُ كَاتِبٌ أَنْ يَكْتُبَ —

اِنْزِلْ مِنَ الْجَنَّةِ فَمَا يَكُونُ لَكَ أَنْ تَتَكَبَّرَ

فِيهَا ـ لَمْ نَشْتَغِلْ بِذِكْرِ ذَلِكَ كَيْلَا يَطُولَ ٱلْكِتَابُ ـ
مَا أَعْتَقِدُ أَنْ يَفُوقَ أَحَدٌ زَيْدًا فِى عِلْمٍ أَوْ أَدَبٍ ـ
إِنَّ ٱلصَّفْحَ ٱلْجَمِيلَ أَنَّكَ لَا تُعَاتِبُ مَنْ صَفَحْتَ
عَنْهُ ـ إِنَّ دِمَاءَكُمْ عَلَيْكُمْ حَرَامٌ إِلَى أَنْ تَقُومُوا
بَيْنَ يَدَىْ رَبِّكُمْ ـ خَطَبَ أَحَدٌ ٱمْرَأَةً فَقَالَتْ لَا
حَتَّى تُطَلِّقَ زَوْجَتَكَ ـ لَسْتُ أَخَافُ عَلَيْكَ أَنْ
تَخَافَ وَإِنَّمَا أَخَافُ عَلَيْكَ أَنْ لَا تَخَافَ ـ ٱلطِّفْلُ
ثَقِيلٌ حَتَّى لَا تَحْمِلَهُ أُمُّهُ ـ سَمِعَ أَعْرَابِىٌّ رَجُلًا
يَقُولُ أَشْهَدُ أَنَّ مُحَمَّدًا رَسُولَ ٱللّٰهِ فَقَالَ يَفْعَلُ
مَا ذَا.

38

his sermon was so long that the hearers went to sleep — we believe that God is one and that he pardons the penitent — the husband did not wish to divorce his elderly wife out of pity for her — I listened attentively for fear that anything of his speech should escape me (fall from me) — what prevented you from prostrating yourself? (two versions) — he sends his servants to bring down snow from the mountains to preserve his food in the hot days — we fear that the two parties will quarrel, one with the other — tell him that I made this melody (voice) for him.

LESSON 20

ADVERBS

There are a few adverbs, mostly by-forms of prepositions; they are indeclinable.

بَعْدُ yet (in negative sentences); مِنْ بَعْدُ after, afterwards; قَبْلُ ـ مِنْ قَبْلُ before (time); تَحْتُ ـ مِنْ تَحْتُ below; فَوْقُ ـ مِنْ فَوْقُ above; حَيْثُ where; مِنْ حَيْثُ whence.

لَمْ يَمُتْ بَعْدُ he is not yet dead.

لِلّٰهِ ٱلْأَمْرُ مِنْ قَبْلُ وَمِنْ بَعْدُ

God's is the command, before and after = the business is in God's hands.

The infinitive takes the place of an adverb (Lesson 15). Some English adverbs are replaced by verbs while the English verb takes a subordinate place as imperfect or participle.

Always.

زَالَ ـ يَزَالُ or بَرِحَ ـ يَبْرَحُ 'cease' with a negative:—

مَا زَالَ يَقُولُ ـ لَمْ يَزَلْ يَقُولُ

he did not cease talking = was always talking.

لَا يَزَالُ يَرْكَبُ he is always riding.

لَا تَزَلْ ذَاكِرَ ٱلْمَوْتِ always remember death.

Almost.

يَكَادُ ـ كَادَ be on the point of doing (never used alone).

كَادَ يَقْتُلُهُ he almost killed him; كِدْتُ أَفْهَمُ I almost understood.

Scarcely.

يكاد ـ كاد with a negative :—

لَا يَكَادُ يَتَحَرَّكُ he scarcely moves.

وَجَدَ قَوْماً لَا يَكَادُونَ يَفْقَهُونَ قَوْلاً

he found a people who scarcely understood speech.

ذَبَحُوهَا وَمَا كَادُوا يَفْعَلُونَ

they sacrificed it but were nearly not doing so.

Again.

يَعُودُ ـ عَادَ 'return'; يَزِيدُ ـ زَادَ 'increase' :—

عَادَ يَضْرِبُهُ he hit him again.

زَادَ يَشْتِمُهُ he abused him again.

At once, immediately.

لَبِثَ 'remain'; نَشِبَ ـ يَنْشَبُ 'stick to' with a negative :—

لَمْ يَلْبَثْ أَنْ قَالَ لَهَا at once he said to her.

لَمْ يَنْشَبُوا أَنْ بَلَغَهُمُ ٱلْخَبَرُ بِذٰلِكَ

they did not stick that: immediately the news about this came to them.

Soon, quickly.

أَوْشَكَ, IV of a verb first 'w', more usually the imperfect يُوشِكُ with أَنْ and the subjunctive; rarely the imperfect indicative. Three constructions are possible :—

يُوشِكُ أَنْ يَدْخُلَ زَيْدٌ ـ يُوشِكُ زَيْدٌ أَنْ يَدْخُلَ ـ

يُوشِكُ زَيْدٌ يَدْخُلُ

Zaid will soon come in.

The subordinate sentence ان يدخل زيد is the subject of the verb.

Perhaps.

The defective verb عَسَى of which only the perfect exists. Commonly the third masculine singular alone is used.

عَسَى أَنْ تَكْرَهُوا شَيْئًا

perhaps you do not like something.

Less common is the construction :—

عَسَى ٱلْأَيَّامُ أَنْ يُرْجِعْنَ قَوْمًا

perhaps the days will bring a tribe back.

There is also the particle لَعَلَّ which is construed like أَنَّ .

لَعَلَّ ٱللّٰهَ غَافِرٌ perhaps God is a pardoner.

لَعَلَّهُ يُسَافِرُ perhaps he will go on a journey.

In the morning.

أَصْبَحَ IV do, be in the morning, become morning.

أَصْبَحَ زَيْدٌ مَرِيضًا in the morning Zaid was ill.

أَصْبَحْتُ أَحْزَنُ عَلَى مُعَاكَسَةِ ٱلْأَيَّامِ بِى

in the morning I was grieved by the contrariness of the days (fate) to me.

The verb may be followed by a noun or by a sentence with the imperfect ; often it loses all sense of time and means no more than كان or صار ' become '.

أَمْسَى (IV of a verb third weak) ' do, be in the evening ' behaves just like اصبح .

In many other places the English adverb or adverbial expression becomes a verb in Arabic.

أَسْرَعَ ٱلذَّهَابَ

he made quick the going = he departed hurriedly.

أَبْعَدَ ٱلنَّظَرَ

he made distant the look = he looked into the distance.

A verbal sentence follows such phrases as :—

قَلِيلًا مَا ـ قَلَّ أَنْ ـ قَلَّ مَا seldom.

كَثِيرًا مَا ـ رُبَّمَا often.

طَالَ مَا it has lasted long.

قَلَّمَا رَأَيْتُ seldom have I seen.

قَلَّ مَا يَدُومُ وِصَالٌ seldom do (lovers') meetings last.

Vocabulary 20

حرك II move (trans.).

عاد u. عَوْدٌ return, do again.

شَتَمَ u. i. شَتْمٌ abuse.

نَشِبَ نُشُبٌ be attached to.

سَرُعَ سُرْعَةٌ be quick.

بَعُدَ بُعْدٌ be far, distant.

ذَبَحَ a. ذَبْحٌ cut the throat, sacrifice.

فَقِهَ فِقْهٌ understand.

عَكَسَ i. عَكْسٌ turn upside down.

حَسُنَ حُسْنٌ be good.

صُبْح (a) morning.
صبح II attack in the morning.
مَسَاءٌ evening.
حَصَلَ u. حُصُولٌ come to, befall (not of motion).
— II obtain.
رَزَقَ u. رَزْقٌ provide.
سَفَرٌ (a) journey.
نَصِيحَةٌ advice, help.
حرك V move (intrans.).
هٰهُنَا — هُنَا here.
ثَمَّ there.
زاد i. زِيَادَةٌ increase (trans and intrans.).
لَبِثَ لَبْثٌ remain, stay.
سفر III journey, travel.
سرع IV make quick, go fast.
بعد II, IV make distant.
علج III treat (illness, etc.).
عكس III oppose.
حسن IV make good, do well.
صَبَاحٌ morning.
صبح VIII drink in the morning.
غَدٌ next day.
غَدًا to-morrow.
رِزْقٌ (a) daily food, rations.
أُسْوَةٌ (إِسًا) model.
هُنَالِكَ — هُنَاكَ there.
حِينَئِذٍ then.

Exercise 39

لَا يَلْبَثُ أَنْ يَرْجِعَ مِنْ سَفَرِهِ ـ لَا يَكَادُ ٱلْمَرِيضُ
يَتَحَرَّكُ عَلَى فِرَاشِهِ ـ لَمْ تَزَلْ تَنْفَعُنِي بِنَصِيحَتِكَ
وَأُسْوَتِكَ ـ إِنْ حَدَّثَنَا أَحْسَنَ ٱلْحَدِيثَ وَإِنْ حَدَّثْنَاهُ
أَحْسَنَ ٱلِاسْتِمَاعَ ـ أَمِثْلُ هٰذَا يَقُولُ ٱلشِّعْرَ أَو

يُحْسِنُ شِعْرًا ـ حَصَلَنَا عِدَّةُ لَيَالٍ لَا نَنَامُ مِنَ
ٱلْبَرْدِ وَكِدْنَا نَهْلِكُ ـ أَصْبَحَ ٱلتَّاجِرُ وَٱلنَّاسُ
يَزْدَحِمُونَ قُدَّامَ دُكَّانِهِ ـ تَعَلَّمُوا ٱلْعِلْمَ فَإِنْ تَكُونُوا
صِغَارَ قَوْمٍ فَعَسَى أَنْ تَكُونُوا كِبَارَ قَوْمٍ آخَرَ ـ
إِنْ أَنْكَحَكَهَا فَعَسَى أَنْ تُرْزَقَ وَلَدًا مِثْلِي ـ
أَكَادُ أَخَافُ مِنْ صَوْتِ ٱلرِّيحِ.

40

I almost believed what he was saying — they fled quickly (two versions) — he went in without delay — perhaps they will come back to-morrow (two versions) — she scarcely blamed her son for swimming in the great river though (and) he did not swim well — the proud will soon repent of their pride — that young man almost turned the world upside down — they defeated us once and will not do so again — two men of great strength moved the stone but it scarcely moved — don't do this again.

LESSON 21

VERBS FIRST 'W' AND 'Y'

First 'w' (Table 7).

Deviations from the strong verb occur in the imperfect of I and in VIII.

If the characteristic vowel of the imperfect of I is or ought to be 'i', the 'w' is omitted.

وَلَدَ produce young; يَلِدُ imperfect; لِدْ imperative.

In some verbs a final guttural has turned this 'i' into 'a' but the 'w' is still omitted.

وَضَعَ	place	يَضَعُ	ضَعْ	وَضْعٌ
وَقَعَ	fall	يَقَعُ	قَعْ	وُقُوعٌ
وَدَعَ	leave	يَدَعُ	دَعْ	وَدْعٌ
وَزَعَ	restrain	يَزَعُ	زَعْ	وَزْعٌ

A few have 'i' in the perfect and in the imperfect contrary to rule.

وَرِثَ inherit يَرِثُ وَفِقَ find suitable يَفِقُ

وَثِقَ trust يَثِقُ وَرِمَ be swollen يَرِمُ

وَلِيَ be near يَلِي (this is also third 'y')

In the imperfect of IV the 'w' combines with the preceding 'u' to form a long vowel. From وَجَدَ find IV means 'cause to be findable' and then 'create': أَوْجَدَ — يُوجِدُ — أَوْجِدْ — إِيجَادٌ.

There is no VII.

In VIII the 'w' is assimilated to the 't':—

وهم اِتَّهَمَ suspect; وفق اِتَّفَقَ agree.

Verbs of the forms فَعُلَ فَعِلَ are regular in the imperfect of I:—

وَجِلَ be afraid; يَوْجَلُ impf. اِيجَلْ impv. but وَوْجَلْ

وَبُلَ be unhealthy يَوْبُلُ اُوبُلْ فَوْبُلْ

Some nouns from these roots lose the first radical:—

جِهَةٌ direction ثِقَةٌ reliability.

سَعَةٌ (width) wealth, ability.

Though only two radicals are visible, there is no doubt about the root. Feminine nouns from hollow roots have a long vowel in the middle: قَامَةٌ 'stature'; those from a third weak root have a long vowel after the second radical: زَكَاةٌ 'act of sacrificing'. A few nouns from third weak roots are without the long vowel but they all have 'u' in the first syllable: لُغَةٌ 'language'.

Verbs first 'y'.

There are only a few of these and the variations from the strong verb are few.

Two verbs have two imperfects in I :—

يَبِسَ be dry يَيْبَسُ and يَيْبِسُ

يَئِسَ despair يَيْأَسُ يَيْئِسُ

Note the imperative I : يَسَرَ — يَيْسِرُ — إِيسِرْ be easy.

The imperfect and participle IV : يُوسِرُ مُوسِرٌ become rich.

In VIII assimilation occurs : اتَّأَسَ despair.

Plurals, which can be deduced from the singular, are no longer put in the vocabulary.

Vocabulary 21

وجه II (turn the face) send.

وَجَدَ وُجُودٌ find.

وَقَفَ وُقُوفٌ stand.

وَسِعَ a. سَعَةٌ be wide, include, be able.

وَجَبَ وُجُوبٌ be necessary.

وَرِثَ i. وِرْثٌ inherit.

وَدَعَ a. وَدْعٌ leave.

وَكَلَ وَكْلٌ entrust.

وهم VIII suspect.

صِفَةٌ (صِفَاتٌ) description, quality.

عَدْلٌ justice.

فَيْلَسُوفٌ (فَلَاسِفَةٌ) philosopher.

مَقْدَرَةٌ strength.

سُوءٌ evil, badness.

وجه V (send oneself) go.

وَصَلَ وُصُولٌ reach, arrive at, give.

وَصَفَ وَصْفٌ describe.

وسع VIII be wide.

وَرَدَ وُرُودٌ go down.

وَضَعَ وَضْعٌ put, put down.

ودع II say good-bye.	فِكْرٌ (a) thought, idea.
وكل II appoint as agent.	مَعْذِرَةٌ excuse.
— VIII rely on.	مَفْجَرَةٌ sin (of any sort).
وفق VIII agree.	سَيِّءٌ bad.
حَالٌ f. (a) condition.	

Exercise 41

اَللّٰهُ أَحَدٌ لَمْ يَلِدْ وَلَمْ يُولَدْ ـ هُوَ رَجُلٌ لَا يُوصَفُ صِفَتُهُ ـ لَمْ يَدَعِ ابْنَهُ ٱلصَّغِيرَ يَرِثُ مَعَ ٱلْكَبِيرِ ـ دَعُوا ٱلْمَعَاذِرَ فَإِنَّ أَكْثَرَهَا مَفَاجِرُ ـ إِنَّ ٱللّٰهَ يَسَعُ عِلْمُهُ أَفْعَالَ عِبَادِهِ وَأَفْكَارَهُمْ ـ اَلْعَدْلُ أَنْ تَضَعَ ٱلْأَشْيَاءَ فِي أَمْكِنَتِهَا ـ مَنْ أَسْوَءُ ٱلنَّاسِ حَالًا قَالَ مَنِ ٱتَّسَعَتْ مَعْرِفَتُهُ وَضَاقَتْ مَقْدِرَتُهُ وَبَعُدَتْ هِمَّتُهُ ـ اِتَّهَمُوهُ بِٱلْكُفْرِ لِدَرْسِهِ كُتُبَ ٱلْفَلَاسِفَةِ ـ يَجِبُ عَلَى ٱلْمُتَعَلِّمِ أَنْ يَطْلُبَ ٱلْحَقَّ ـ اِنْتَظَرْتُ وُصُولَ ٱلْأَخْبَارِ وَلَمْ تَصِلْ بَعْدُ ـ يُوشِكُ ٱلطَّبِيبَانِ أَنْ يَتَّفِقَا عَلَى عِلَاجِ ٱلْمَرِيضِ.

42

describe the conditions of your disease (symptoms) — fresh news was arriving every hour — the earth became narrow on him and it had been wide (his condition changed for the worse) — I sent him to you but he did not go — we heard you describing what you had done — we shall find them standing in the street — there is not found ingratitude like that of an ungrateful child — I heard his friends saying good-bye to him — was it necessary for you to entrust this business to someone else? — put your hand on the book of God and swear.

LESSON 22

RELATIVE CLAUSES

There is no relative pronoun in Arabic.

When the antecedent is indefinite, the relative clause is added without any connecting link.

أَطْلُبُ رَجُلًا يَقُومُ عَلَى بُسْتَانِى

I am looking for a man who will stand over (look after) my garden.

When the antecedent is definite, اَلَّذِى is used as a link between the antecedent and the relative clause. It is inflected as follows:—

	sing.	dual, nom.	oblique	plural
masc.	اَلَّذِى	اَللَّذَانِ	اَللَّذَيْنِ	اَلَّذِينَ
fem.	اَلَّتِى	اَللَّتَانِ	اَللَّتَيْنِ	اَللَّوَاتِى

The link agrees in case with the antecedent; this is visible only in the dual.

When the English relative is in an oblique case, the link has to be supplemented by a personal pronoun in the relative clause. This pronoun is often omitted when it should be in the accusative.

اَلرَّجُلُ ٱلَّذِى قَتَلَ أَبِى

the man who killed my father.

اَلرَّجُلُ ٱلَّذِى قَتَلَهُ أَبِى

the man whom my father killed.

اَلْمَرْأَةُ ٱلَّتِى كَانَ عِنْدَهَا ٱبْنِى

the woman with whom my son was.

أَبْعَثُ إِلَيْكَ ٱلْمَرْأَتَيْنِ ٱلَّتَيْنِ تَطْلُبُ مِنْهُمَا خَبَرَ ٱبْنَتِكَ

I am sending to you the two women from whom you can ask news of your daughter.

If the antecedent is first or second person, the pronoun in the relative clause may agree with it or be in the third person to agree with the link.

أَأَنْتِ ٱلَّتِى ٱسْتَوْدَعْتُكِ ٱلسِّرَّ

are you she to whom I entrusted the secret?

كُنْ أَنْتَ ٱلَّذِى تُكَلِّمُهَا

be you he who speaks to her.

نَحْنُ ٱلَّذِينَ بَايَعُوا مُحَمَّدًا

we are those who did homage to Muhammad.

'He who' is rendered by الذى or مَنْ ; 'that which' by الذى or مَا .

من may take the verb in the singular or plural ; ما always has a singular verb.

مَنْ أَشْعَرُ ٱلْعَرَبِ قَالَ ٱلَّذِى يَقُولُ....

who is the most poetical of the Arabs ? he said, he who says . . . .

يَا مَنْ لَا يَمُوتُ أَرْحَمْ

O, he who dies not, have mercy = you who die not have mercy.

عَرَفْتُ مَا عَرَفْتَهُ

I know what you know.

أَىُّ 'which of' is always followed by a genitive, either a noun or a pronominal suffix. It may be singular or plural and may belong to the main sentence or the relative clause.

سَلِّمْ عَلَى أَيُّهُمْ أَفْضَلُ

or

سَلِّمْ عَلَى أَيِّهِمْ أَفْضَلُ

greet those (him) of them who are most worthy.

Vocabulary 22

جازَ u. جَوَازٌ be allowable.

طَرَحَ a. طَرْحٌ throw down.

رسل III write letters to.

زَعَمَ a. زَعْمٌ think, claim.

رَغِبَ . رَغْبٌ فِي like, be pleased with ; عَنْ dislike.

زَرَعَ a. زَرْعٌ sow.

دَاءٌ (a) disease.

عِلْمٌ (b) knowledge, science.

سَرِيرٌ (أَسِرَّةٌ) anything on which one can sit or lie.

خاتَمٌ (خَوَاتِمُ) seal.

بَدَنٌ (a) body.

ذِهْنٌ mind, intellect.

جوز III pass beyond.

قَسَمَ i. قَسْمٌ divide.

رسل IV send.

وَجِعَ i. وَجَعٌ feel pain.

حَصَدَ u. حَصَادٌ reap.

دَوَاءٌ (أَدْوِيَةٌ) medicine, remedy.

أَدَبٌ (a) manners, arts.

صِحَّةٌ health.

ذَكَاءٌ sharpness (metaphorical).

صَحِيحٌ healthy, true.

Exercise 43

كَانَ لَهُ بَنُو عَمٍّ وَرِثُوهُ ـ مَا أَنْتُمُ ٱلَّذِينَ يَهْرُبُونَ مِنَ ٱلْحَقِّ ـ ٱلَّذِى يَزْرَعُهُ ٱلْإِنْسَانُ ٱلْيَوْمَ يَحْصُدُهُ غَدًا ـ نَزَلْتُ عَنِ ٱلسَّرِيرِ ٱلَّذِى كُنْتُ مَطْرُوحًا عَلَيْهِ ـ كَانَ ذَلِكَ خَاتَمُ أَعْمَالِهِ ٱلْحَسَنَةِ ٱلَّتِى تُجَاوِزُ ٱلْوَصْفَ ـ كَيْفَ لَا تَرْغَبُ فِى تَدْبِيرٍ يَجْمَعُ

لَكَ صِحَّةُ ٱلْبَدَنِ وَذَكَاءُ ٱلذِّهْنِ وَكَثْرَةُ ٱلْمَالِ ـ
اَلْجَارِيَتَانِ ٱلَّتَانِ وَجَّهْتُهُمَا إِلَى مَدْرَسَةِ ٱلْبَنَاتِ
قَدْ صَارَتَا ذَوَاتَيْ عِلْمٍ وَأَدَبٍ ـ كُنْ لَهُمْ كَٱلطَّبِيبِ
ٱلَّذِي لَا يَعْجَلُ بِٱلدَّوَاءِ قَبْلَ مَعْرِفَةِ ٱلدَّاءِ ـ هَلْ بِعْتِ
ٱلْعَبْدَيْنِ ٱلَّذَيْنِ تَرْغَبِينَ عَنْهُمَا ـ صِفِي لِي مَنْ
كَلَّمَكِ.

44

I appointed as my agent one in whom I trust — he asserts that what came down on him had never come down on another — he who does not know the disease does not know the remedy — they do not wish to sell the two books which they inherited from their uncle — we sowed the fields which we had found unsown — these are the two men who found the wounded man and carried him to my house — I came out by the same door as in I went — the duties, which were incumbent on me, were beyond my strength — I said good-bye to the work in which I took pleasure and turned to work in which I took no pleasure.

LESSON 23

DOUBLED VERBS

In these verbs (consult Tables 8 and 9) the second radical is the same as the third.

The variations from the strong verb can be summarized in three rules :—

1. When the third radical has a vowel, the second loses its vowel and the two consonants are written once with *shadda.*
2. When the third radical has no vowel, the second keeps its vowel and the two consonants are written separately.
3. In the imperfect, when Rule 1 applies, the vowel of the second radical is thrown back to the first.

Rule 2 applies, in the perfect, to the first and second persons and to the third feminine plural; in the imperfect to the feminine plurals only.

(The word, contraction, is avoided for there is no reason to think that these verbs were originally strong.)

The jussive has two forms; one is regular according to Rule 2, the other is short like the imperfect indicative. A final double consonant cannot be pronounced so a short vowel, usually 'a', is added; the result is that the jussive cannot be distinguished by form alone from the subjunctive. Both forms existed side by side.

The imperative may be formed from the short form of the jussive and then needs no liaison.

A long vowel between the second and third radicals prevents them from coalescing; examples are the infinitives of stems II, VII, VIII, and X and the passive participle of I.

Stems IX and XI of the strong verb are only special forms of doubled verb and present no difficulties (Table 9).

The derived stems follow the same rules; II is no exception, for the second radical is already doubled and no consonant can be tripled.

V is sometimes irregular, the third radical being changed into 'y' and resembling a verb third weak.

تَظَنَّنْتَ becomes تَظَنَّيْتَ you think.

Peculiar is the change from قَصَصْتَ to قَصَّيْتَ you cut.

Other forms behave like hollow verbs : ظَلْتَ or ظِلْتَ from ظَلَّ remain أَحَسْتُ for أَحْسَسْتُ I feel.

Nouns from these roots also follow the same rules. مَحَلٌّ (مَحَالٌّ) 'place' come from theoretical *mahlalun* and *maha:lilu* ; حَلَالٌ (loosed) not taboo, lawful, permissible.

The connection of ideas is this :—

حَلَّ u. حَلٌّ loose, untie.

When the bedouin unties his baggage, he camps dwells so :—

حَلَّ u. حُلُولٌ dwell.

The antithesis of loosing and binding is familiar from the Gospels :—

صَاحِبُ ٱلْحَلِّ وَٱلْعَقْدِ

the master of loosing and binding—holder of supreme power.

So حَلَّ i. حِلٌّ be not taboo, be lawful, allowable.

The opposite of this is حَرُمَ حَرَامٌ be taboo, sacred, unlawful. حَرَمَ i. or حَرِمَ a. حَرِيمٌ forbid, prevent.

The two senses appear in one sentence :—

سَفَكُوا دَمَ ٱلْحَرَامِ فِي شَهْرِ ٱلْحَرَامِ فِي بِلَادِ ٱلْحَرَامِ

they shed forbidden blood in the sacred month, in the holy place.

These verbs go back to a time before morality had been associated with religion.

In the last example a noun in the genitive case acts as an adjective :—

رِجَالُ ٱلسَّوْءِ evil men.

Vocabulary 23

سَرَّ u. سُرُورٌ please, delight.

حسّ IV to perceive, know.

عَدَّ u. عَدٌّ count.

مرّ u. مُرُورٌ pass by.

مَدَّ u. مَدٌّ stretch.

رَدَّ u. رَدٌّ come back, send back.

خفّ i. خِفَّةٌ be light (weight).

عَفّ i. عِفَّةٌ be chaste, temperate.

قصّ u. قَصٌّ tell a story, cut.

قَرَّ i. قَرَارٌ be firm, fixed.

دَلَّ u. دَلٌّ guide.

لِقَاءٌ (inf. of لَقِيَ) meeting.

حَيَّةٌ (حَيَّاتٌ) snake.

مُصْعَبٌ a man's name.

ظَنّ u. ظَنٌّ have an opinion.

فَرّ i. فِرَارٌ run away.

عدّ IV prepare (trans.).

عدّ X prepare oneself.

مرّ X continue.

مدّ IV help, reinforce.

مدّ X ask for help.

خفّ X despise.

حبّ IV love, like.

مَلّ a. مَلَلٌ be disgusted with.

قَرَّ u. قَرٌّ be cold.

— IV acknowledge, confirm.

ضَلَّ i. ضَلَالٌ go astray.

فِتْنَةٌ (فِتَنٌ) temptation, civil war.

حَيَاءٌ shame, modesty.

اَلْبَصْرَةُ Basra.

Exercise 45

أُحِبُّهَا وَتُحِبُّنِي وَيُحِبُّ جَمَلِي نَاقَتَهَا ـ ظَنَنْتُ أَنَّهُ يَسْتَعِدُّ لِلصُّعُودِ فِي ٱلْجِبَالِ ـ لَا تَظُنَّنِي أُخَالِفُكَ ـ مَنْ عَفَّ خَفَّ عَلَى ٱلصَّدِيقِ لِقَاؤُهُ وَأَخُو ٱلْحَوَائِجِ وَجْهُهُ مَمْلُولٌ ـ ذُكِرَ فِي أَمْرِ مُصْعَبٍ وَعَزْلِ أَخِيهِ إِيَّاهُ عَنِ ٱلْبَصْرَةِ وَرَدِّهِ إِيَّاهُ إِلَيْهَا غَيْرُ هٰذِهِ ٱلْقِصَّةِ ـ أَسْرَعُ ٱلنَّاسِ إِلَى ٱلْفِتْنَةِ أَقَلُّهُمْ حَيَاءً مِنَ ٱلْفِرَارِ ـ إِنِّي أَحْسَسْتُ بِصَوْتِ مُرُورِ حَيَّةٍ أَلَمْ تُحِسَّ بِهِ ـ مُدَّ يَدَكَ إِلَى حَبْلِ ٱللهِ وَيُمِدُّكَ ـ عُدُّوا ٱلْمَرْضَى وَأَعِدُّوا ٱلْأَدْوِيَةَ لِعِلَاجِهِمْ ـ مَرَّ بِٱلْأَوْلَادِ يَقُصُّ عَلَيْهِمْ قِصَصَ ٱلنَّبِيِّ.

46

guide me to what will delight me — I thought that you were guiding me aright and you have led me astray — the boy used to ask the teacher for help and he helped him — you want to become chief of the tribe ; then despise what folks may say — we thought that the women were fleeing in fear while (and) they were hurrying to meet their husbands — we do not know what to think — unbelievers are misled and mislead others — I saluted the company and they returned my salute — do you think they will acknowledge my rights ? — there is none to turn back what God does.

LESSON 24

HOLLOW VERBS—*Continued* (Table 6)

Stems II, III, V, and VI are like the strong verbs ; ' w ' verbs differ from ' y ' roots :—

زَوَّجَ give in marriage ; تَزَوَّجَ marry ;

بَيَّنَ distinguish, make plain ; تَبَيَّنَ make plain to oneself, be plain ;

بَايَعَ do, receive homage ; جَاوَبَ answer.

In the other stems there is no distinction between the two classes. A long vowel appears in place of the middle radical just as in I ; in the perfects that vowel is *a:* which is shortened where necessary to *a.*

In the imperfect of IV and X the vowel is *i:*, shortened where necessary to *i.*

In VII and VIII the imperfect unexpectedly has ' a '

long or short as is required. اِنْقَادَ obey (let himself be led) ; اِخْتَارَ choose.

Indicative.	Jussive.	Imperative.	Infinitive.
يَنْقَادُ	يَنْقَدْ	اِنْقَدْ	اِنْقِيَادٌ
يَخْتَارُ	يَخْتَرْ	اِخْتَرْ	اِخْتِيَارٌ

Note the infinitive of IV and X; the middle radical is lost and the feminine ending ' at ' is added as compensation.

إِقَامَةٌ IV اِسْتِقَامَةٌ X.

Some verbs have both strong and weak forms :—

أَرْوَحَ — أَرَاحَ give rest ; اِسْتَرْوَحَ ، اِسْتَرَاحَ rest.

A few of the type فَعِلَ have strong forms only:

سَوِدَ be black ; أَسْوَدَ blacken ;

but اِسْوَدَّ XI be black and سَوَّدَ II blacken are more common.

Vocabulary 24

سوف II make future, postpone. جوب III, IV answer.

صَادَ i. صَيْدٌ hunt, fish. قَادَ i. lead.

رود IV wish, will. خير II give a choice to.

قوم IV stay, set up.

وَعَدَ i. وَعْدٌ promise.

طوع IV obey.

طَوْعاً willingly.

عون IV help.

يَهُودُ Jews. يَهُودِىٌّ (sing.).

خُفَّاشٌ (خَفَافِيشُ) bat (animal).

بَالٌ mind.

صوب II think right.

حول VIII employ devices, tricks.

عَوْنٌ help.

بيع VIII buy.

صيد VIII take by hunting.

حوج VIII need, be in want (always with إِلى).

نَقَدَ u. نَقْدٌ pay cash.

قيد VII obey.

خير VIII choose.

قوم X be straight.

وعد IV threaten.

طوع X be able.

وَعِيدٌ threat.

عون X ask the help of.

نَصْرَانِىٌّ (نَصَارَى) Christian.

سَتَرَ u. سَتْرٌ hide.

مَا بَالُ what about, what is the matter with ?

صوب IV come upon, hit.

حِيلَةٌ (حِيَلٌ) trick, stratagem, device.

لَئِيمٌ (c) base, ignoble.

Exercise 47

وَعْدُ الْكَرِيمِ نَقْدٌ وَوَعْدُ اللَّئِيمِ تَسْوِيفٌ — صِدْنَا وَنَصْطَادُ — لَمْ تُرِدْ أُخْتِي أَنْ تُطِيعَ أَوَامِرَ مُعَلِّمَتِهَا — لِمَا لَا تُرِيدِينَ أَنْ تَتْرُكِي شُغْلَكِ —

اَلْخَفَافِيشُ تَسْتَتِرُ بِالنَّهَارِ خَوْفَ أَنْ تُصْطَادَ
لِحُسْنِهَا ـ أَرَادَ أَبِي أَنْ يَبْتَاعَ مَا يَحْتَاجُ إِلَيْهِ
أَهْلُهُ ـ سَمِعَ أَحَدٌ رَجُلًا يَسْتَعِينُ ٱللّٰهَ فِي أَمْرِ
أُمِّهِ فَقَالَ لَهُ مَا بَالُ أَبِيكَ قَالَ هُوَ رَجُلٌ
يَحْتَالُ لِنَفْسِهِ ـ أَخَيَّرَكَ أَبُوكَ فِي تَزَوُّجِكَ ـ لَا
اُخْتَارَتْ أُمِّي زَوْجَةً لِي ـ سَمِعْنَا يَهُودِيًّا يُوعِدُ
غُلَامَهُ ـ يَجِبُ عَلَيْكُمْ أَنْ تُجِيبُوا طَلَبَ
اَلْحُكُومَةِ ـ قَادَ ٱلشَّرَهُ تِلْكَ ٱلنِّسَاءَ أَنْ يَمِلْنَ
عَنْ طَرِيقِ ٱلرِّفْقِ وَٱنْقَدْنَ .

48

he kept quiet and was quiet for a long time — avarice makes men incline from the Straight Path — we asked for his help and he helped us — he set up a great stone as a reminder of the evil which had befallen the people — the brigands frightened the inhabitants of out-of-the-way (distant) houses — care for my family and property is killing me — that Jew does what he likes and the Jews and Christians think him right — the wise man learns from the misfortunes of others — she needed help but found no helper — I used every device to get out of the fortress in which I was a captive but did not find a way out — my wife bought clothes of silk and wool.

LESSON 25

VERBS WITH THE GLOTTAL STOP

Verbs with the glottal stop (consult Tables 10–12) are regular in pronunciation, apart from a few freaks. There remains the difficulty of writing; the rule of thumb given in the chapter on the alphabet and the following notes will help to remove this.

First Hamza

When two hamzas should occur in one syllable, the second drops and the vowel is lengthened. Thus *ʔaʔ* becomes *ʔa:*, *ʔuʔ* becomes *ʔu:*, and *ʔiʔ* becomes *ʔi:*. *ʔa:* is written with madda.

			Imperfect First Singular Active.	Imperfect First Singular Passive.
أَمَلَ	hope	يَأْمُلُ	آمُلُ	أُومَلُ

		Imperative.		
أمل	hope	أُومُلْ	but	فَأْمُلْ
أَسَرَ	take captive	يَأْسِرُ	اِيسِرْ	فَأْسِرْ

Two drop the hamza always in the imperative :—

أَخَذَ take يَأْخُذُ ـ خُذْ ; eat أَكَلَ ـ يَأْكُلُ ـ كُلْ

أَمَرَ drops hamza when the imperative stands alone but retains it after و and ف : مُرْ command but وَأْمُرْ.

Stem III

آكَلَ eat with يُوَٰاكِلُ impf. آكِلْ impv. أُوكِلَ perf. pass.

Stem IV

آكَلَ feed. يُؤْكِلُ impf. أُوكِلُ 1 per. آكِلْ impv. إِيكَالٌ infin.

There is no VII.

Stem VIII

اِيتَزَرَ wear a loin cloth but فَأْتَزَرَ.

يَأْتَزِرُ impf. اِيتَزِرْ impv. but فَأْتَزِرْ.

Passive

أُوتُمِنَ was given authority; اَلَّذِى أُؤْتُمِنَ he who was given authority.

أخذ assimilates ʔ to *t*: اِتَّخَذَ.

MIDDLE HAMZA

The spelling is often not rigid: يَسْئَلُ — يَسْأَلُ.

The passive perfect I is سُئِلَ; this spelling seems to be derived from a dialect which used the form *si:la*.

سَأَلَ has also an irregular imperative سَلْ, jussive يَسَلْ.

The active participle I is like that of the hollow verb so

سَئِرَ	be left over	سَائِرٌ
سَارَ ـ يَسِيرُ	go	
سَارَ ـ يَسُورُ	jump	

THIRD HAMZA

Some of the spellings are not rigid :—

3 masc. dual perfect قَرَآ ـ قَرَأَا

2 fem. sing. impf. تَقْرَئِينَ ـ تَقْرَأِينَ

3 masc. plu. impf. يَقْرَؤُونَ ـ يَقْرَاوُنَ

Vocabulary 25

ادب II educate.

أَمِنَ أَمَانٌ be safe from.

أَجَرَ u.i. أَجْرٌ hire out.

اثر II make a mark on, influence.

اثر IV prefer.

سَأَلَ a. سُؤَالٌ ask, beg.

نبأ IV tell.

كفأ III reward.

أَنِسَ أُنْسٌ be friendly.

قَرَأَ a. قِرَاءَةٌ read, repeat.

أَسِيرٌ (أَسْرَى) prisoner.

دِينٌ (a) religion.

حَسَدَ u.i. حَسَدٌ envy.

أَذِنَ إِذْنٌ permit.

بَدَأَ a. بَدْءٌ and VIII begin.

امن IV believe.

اجر X hire, rent.

اثر V receive a mark, be influenced.

لجأ VIII take refuge.

الف II compose (a book), unite (men), win over.

هنأ II congratulate.

انس III treat kindly.

اخر II make late.

— V be late.

مَلَاكٌ ـ مَلَكٌ (مَلَائِكَةٌ) angel.

جِسْمٌ (a) body.

آخِرٌ last.

نَصِيبٌ share.

Exercise 49

مَنْ أَدَّبَ وَلَدَهُ صَغِيرًا سُرَّ بِهِ كَبِيرًا ـ آمَنْتُ بِاللّٰهِ

وَبِمَلَائِكَتِهِ وَبِرُسُلِهِ وَبِكُتُبِهِ وَبِالْيَوْمِ الْآخِرِ ـ

هَلْ يَأْذَنُ لِي الْقَائِدُ بِسُؤَالِ الْأَسْرَى ـ كُنْتُ

أَسْتَأْجِرُ مَنْزِلِي مِنْ تَاجِرٍ وَأَدْفَعُ أَجْرَهُ لَهُ كُلَّ

شَهْرٍ ـ اِبْتَدَأْنَ الْعِيدَ بِقِرَاءَةِ الْقُرْآنِ الْكَرِيمِ ثُمَّ

خَاطَبَتِ امْرَأَةٌ مِنَ النِّسَاءِ تَنَبِّئُ نَبَأَ الرَّسُولِ ـ

كَانَ الشَّيْخُ يُؤَانِسُ السَّائِلِينَ وَالْمُلْتَجِئِينَ ـ

اِكْتَسَبَ مُكَافَأَةً عَظِيمَةً بِتَأْلِيفِهِ كِتَابًا يُدَافِعُ
عَنْ دِينِ ٱلنَّصَارَى ـ كَانَ ٱلنَّاسُ يُهَنِّئُونَهُ بِرُجُوعِهِ
سَالِمًا عَنِ ٱلْحَرْبِ ـ اِقْرَأُوا عَلَيْهِ ٱلسَّلَامَ وَأَنْبِئُوهُ
بِوُصُولِي إِلَيْهِ غَدًا ـ مَا كُنْتُ لِأُوثِرَ بِنَصِيبِي مِنْكَ
أَحَدًا ـ أَأَمِنَ أَحَدٌ ٱلْمُصِيبَةَ.

50

give this beggar food and tell him to go away — he was not safe from the devices of the envious — have you hired men to harvest your fields ? — I treated these people with friendliness and they rewarded me richly — your friends will eat and drink with me — I shall feed it on bread and dates — then the poets will ask the governor's permission to begin the recitation of their poems — the sun left its mark on the face of the peasant but the strength of his body was not affected — the caravan is late ; rain has delayed it.

LESSON 26

VERBS—THIRD WEAK (Tables 13–16)

These verbs have 'w' or 'y' as third radical.

فَعَلَ. The third masculine singular of the perfect and the short forms of the imperfect have only two syllables instead of the three of the strong verb. In the simple stem of verbs third 'w' the third masculine singular of the perfect is written with *alif*, in those third 'y' and in all the derived stems of both classes it is written with 'y'. This probably points to an original difference in pronunciation but this has long been ignored. When the inflections of the perfect begin with a consonant, the forms are like those of the strong verb except that the weak radical forms a diphthong with the characteristic vowel. Elsewhere there is contraction for which no rules can be given. The third masculine dual cannot be contracted for the inflection is already long.

Most verbs with 'w' have 'u' in the imperfect and most with 'y' have 'i'. The radical combines with the characteristic to form a long vowel. When a back vowel is followed by a front vowel, the weak consonant reappears to separate them, as in the dual. When two back vowels come together, one is lost; the survivor is the vowel of the inflection for, if that were lost, the significant form would be destroyed. Thus تَدْعِينَ (root *dʕw*) second feminine singular; if the 'u' had survived, the resulting word would be تَدْعُونَ which is second masculine plural.

Again, يَرْمُونَ (root *rmy*) third masculine plural; if the 'i' had been kept, the result would be يَرْمِينَ which is third feminine plural.

The subjunctive explains itself.

The short forms of the jussive lose the letter of prolongation and with it all trace of the third radical.

The emphatic can only be learnt.

The imperative, of course, has liaison.

فَعِلَ. In verbs third 'w' there is partial assimilation of 'w' to 'y' so there is only one form for both classes.

Perfect. The characteristic 'i' is separated from 'a'

of the inflection by the third radical and is lost before *u:*. When the inflection begins with a consonant, 'y' coalesces with the characteristic to form *i:*.

Imperfect. As in the transitive the short forms have only two syllables, the vowel of the second being *a:*. Before a back vowel, this is shortened and forms a diphthong. Before a consonant, it is resolved into the diphthong *ay*. Before *a:* (in the dual) it is resolved into 'a' and 'y' which begins the next syllable.

Passive. What has been said about the intransitive applies to the passive also.

Derived stems. Both classes become third 'y'.

Active participle. Contraction takes place in the nominative and genitive; the third radical and the case ending drop and nunation is given to the second radical :—

رَامٍ 'a shooter' (nom. and gen.) but رَامِيًا (acc.)

اَلرَّامِى 'the shooter' (nom. and gen.) but اَلرَّامِىَ (acc.)

This applies to all active participles of the derived stems and to all nouns from these roots with 'i' before the weak radical.

Something similar happens in some plurals :—

فَاعِلَةٌ has for plural فَوَاعِلُ.

So جَارِيَةٌ should have جَوَارِىُ but *iyu* is contracted to 'i' and nunation is added to indicate the contraction.

جَوَارٍ (nom. and gen.) جَوَارِىَ (acc.)

اَلْجَوَارِى (nom. and gen.) اَلْجَوَارِىَ (acc.)

Passive participle. In stem I verbs final 'w' have forms

like مَدْعُوٌّ and final 'y' like مَرْمِيٌّ with assimilation because the resulting word cannot be confused with any other part of the verb.

When a noun from these roots has 'a' after the second radical, contraction occurs; the case ending is dropped and nunation put over the second radical. *Alif* is written in the 'w' roots and 'y' in those with 'y'.

فَتًى (فِتْيَانٌ) a man in the prime of life اَلْفَتَى

عَصًا (عِصِيٌّ) stick اَلْعَصَا

These nouns are indeclinable. All passive participles of the derived stems are of this form. مُلْقًى ـ مُصْطَفًى ـ مُسْتَلْقًى.

Infinitive. Stem II shortens the *i:* and adds *at* for compensation. تَسْلِيَةٌ.

Stem III. In the form مُفَاعَلَةٌ contraction occurs مُلَاقَاةٌ; the dotted 'h' shows that it cannot be a feminine plural.

Stems V and VI. The 'u' is assimilated to the 'y' and contraction occurs.

V تَلَقٍّ VI تَرَاضٍ

When the second radical has *a:*, the final radical becomes ʔ :—

رِدَاءٌ (أَرْدِيَةٌ) cloak (final ' y ').

كِسَاءٌ (أَكْسِيَةٌ) covering, dress (final ' w ').

Stems III, IV, VII, VIII, and X form their infinitives in this way.

اِسْتِلْقَاءٌ ـ اِبْتِلَاءٌ ـ إِلْقَاءٌ ـ لِقَاءٌ

أَفْعَلُ. The elative, like the imperfect, has only two syllables :—

أَعْلَى عُلْيَا عُلًى higher, etc.

In the feminine the radical ' w ' is usually changed to ' y ', so the *a:* is indicated by *alif* to avoid the repetition of ' y '.

Similarly أَعْمَى blind عَمْيَاءُ ـ عُمْيٌ .

فَعِيلٌ becomes قَوِيٌّ ـ غَنِيٌّ.

فُعُولٌ by assimilation becomes مُضِيٌّ infinitive of يَمْضِي مَضَى.

Further assimilation occurs occasionally :—

عِصِيٌّ plural of عَصًا is the form فُعُولٌ as is قِسِيٌّ the irregular plural of قَوْسٌ bow (weapon).

مَفْعَلٌ. Place nouns always have 'a' in the second syllable :—

مَنْجًى place of safety, refuge. Plural مَنَاجٍ ـ اَلْمَنَاجِي

Note.—The elative أَعْلَى has probably been influenced by the IV stem. The passive participles are inflected for number as follows :—

dual	مُصْطَفَيَانِ	مُصْطَفَيَيْنِ
plural	مُصْطَفَوْنَ	مُصْطَفَيْنَ

Vocabulary 26

أخذ u. أَخْذٌ take.

نسى نِسْيَانٌ forget.

جنى i. جَنْىٌ gather, جِنَايَةٌ commit a crime.

هجا u. هِجَاءٌ lampoon.

غنى IV make rich, self-sufficient.

لها u. لَهْوٌ play.

غزا u. غَزْوٌ raid, go to war.

بكى i. بُكَاءٌ weep.

نهى a. نَهْىٌ forbid.

ولى i. وَلْيٌ be near.

— IV do a kindness.

حوط IV surround.

فقر IV make poor.

بغض IV hate, dislike.

حق X deserve.

قل i. قِلٌّ be little.

—X think little, be independent.

سَيِّدٌ (سَادَاتٌ سَادَةٌ) prince, chief.

اخذ VIII make, choose.

عِمَامَةٌ (عَمَائِمُ) turban.

قِلَادَةٌ (قَلَائِدُ) necklace.

عصب i. عَصْبٌ fold, tie.

حصى IV count.

غنى X be self-sufficient.

لهو IV distract attention.

كفى i. كِفَايَةٌ be sufficient for.

شرى VIII buy.

بقى بَقَاءٌ remain.

نهى VIII let oneself be forbidden, desist.

ولى II make one governor.

فقر VIII be poor, in need.

جاء i. جَيْءٌ come.

ركض u. رَكْضٌ run.

مَعْرُوفٌ known, kind act.

قلّ IV make little, support.

مُعَمَّمٌ wearing a turban.

Exercise 51

إِذَا اُتَّخَذْتُمْ عِنْدَ رَجُلٍ يَدًا فَانْسَوْهَا ـ لَا خَيْرَ فِي
الْمَعْرُوفِ إِذَا أُحْصِيَ ـ سَتَرَ رَجُلٌ مَا أَوْلَى وَنَشَرَ
مَا أُولِيَ ـ اَلْعَرَبُ تَقُولُ سَيِّدٌ مُعَمَّمٌ يُرِيدُونَ أَنَّ
كُلَّ جِنَايَةٍ يَجْنِيهَا أَحَدٌ مِنْ قَوْمِهِ مَعْصُوبَةٌ بِرَأْسِهِ ـ
لِمَا لَا تُطِيلُ اُلْهِجَاءَ قَالَ يَكْفِيكَ مِنَ اُلْقِلَادَةِ
مَا أَحَاطَ بِالْعُنُقِ ـ اَلَّذِي أَرْضَاهُ لَا يَجِيئُنِي
وَاُلَّذِي يَجِيئُنِي لَا أَرْضَاهُ ـ أَغْنِنِي بِالْاِفْتِقَارِ إِلَيْكَ
وَلَا تُفْقِرْنِي بِالْاِسْتِغْنَاءِ عَنْكَ ـ إِنَّ مَا قَلَّ وَكَفَى
خَيْرٌ مِمَّا كَثُرَ وَأَلْهَى ـ مَا لَكَ لَا تَغْزُو فَقَالَ

لأُبْغِضُ ٱلْمَوْتَ عَلَى فِرَاشِى فَكَيْفَ أَمُرُّ إِلَيْهِ
رَكْضًا ـ اِشْتَرِ ٱلتَّمْرَ مِنَ ٱلْمَوْصِلِ وَٱحْمِلْهُ إِلَى
ٱلْبَصْرَةِ فَإِنَّكَ تُهْلِكُ مَالَكَ .

52

I will square (be sufficient for) him for you — whatever I forget, I shall not forget your friendliness — did you buy what you needed? — daughter, take what I give you and buy what you like — the women wept for the slain — those who weep now shall laugh — I think they will remain in (on) their present condition — let no play distract you from your studies — I forbade her and she stopped (let herself be forbidden) — their (masc. and fem.) attention was diverted from what they were making — the caliph, may God preserve him, does not forget to reward those who deserve it.

LESSON 27

VERBS DOUBLY WEAK

These verbs are regular according to both the classes to which they belong, except for occasional aberrations. The pronunciation is easy though the writing may cause difficulty. Here follow a few typical verbs.

Hollow and Hamza

Root اول 'return'

أُلْ يَؤُلْ يَؤُولُ أُلْتَ آلَ

Root جيء 'come'

جِئْ يَجِئْ يَجِيءُ جِئْتَ جَاءَ

The active participle is جَاءٍ اَلْجَائِي

Hamza and third 'y'

أَتَى 'come': the perfect is regular.

Imperfect يَأْتِي jussive يَأْتِ imperative اِيتِ and فَأْتِ.

رَأَى 'see': the perfect is regular.

In the imperfect the hamza is dropped :—

يَرَيْنَ يَرَوْنَ يَرَيَانِ تَرَيْنَ يَرَى

As in رَضِيَ the second feminine singular has the same form as the second feminine plural.

In IV the hamza is also dropped :—

perfect أَرَى أَرَتْ أَرَيْتَ

imperfect يُرِي تُرِينَ يُرُونَ

jussive يُرِ imperative أَرِ

The active participle I رَاءٍ and IV مُرٍ

Infinitive I رُؤْيَةٌ or رَأْىٌ ; IV إِرَاءَةٌ.

In verbs third weak with 'w' or 'y' as second radical the second is usually treated as a strong consonant.

حَيِيَ 'live' is irregular in places.

I may be treated as a doubled verb حَىَّ.

II. The infinitive is like that of a doubled verb with the feminine ending as compensation تَحِيَّةٌ.

X, when it means 'be ashamed', may be shortened :—

perfect إِسْتَحَيْتَ – إِسْتَحَى

imperfect يَسْتَحُونَ – يَسْتَحِى

First 'w' and third 'y'

وَفَى 'accomplish, fulfil'; the perfect is regular :—

imperfect يَفِينَ يَفُونَ يَفِيَانِ تَفِينَ يَفِى

imperative فِينَ فُوا فِى فِ

active participle اَلْوَافِى – وَافٍ infinitive وَفَاءٌ

A weak form can only be identified by grammar and common sense.

يدعو must be singular and must come from دعا.

يدعوا is plural and may be يَدْعُوا from دعا or يَدَعُوا from ودع.

يجد may come from وجد and be any form of the imperfect; it may be يَجُدْ or يُجِدْ jussive I or IV from جَادَ يَجُودُ; and it may be يَجْدُ or يَجْدِ jussive of جدا or جدى.

فِيهِ may mean 'in it', 'of his mouth' or 'accomplish it', imperative singular feminine of وفى.

Vocabulary 27

وصى IV make a will, give a dying charge.

شاء a. مَشِيئَةٌ wish, will.

عَيِيَ a. عَيٌّ be weary.

وَقَى i. وِقَايَةٌ guard.

عَفَا u. عَفْوٌ pardon, refrain; be abundant.

نَجَزَ u. نَجْزٌ finish off, fulfil.

وَدَعَ a. وَدْعٌ leave.

حيى II greet.

كرم IV honour.

حِلْمٌ statecraft, clemency, kindness.

قَدْرٌ amount, measure.

وَصِيَّةٌ (وَصَايَا) will, testament.

تُهْمَةٌ suspicion.

وعى i. وَعَى contain, understand.

عيى IV fatigue, distress.

وقى VIII be on one's guard, fear, be pious.

ودع II say good-bye.

ودع IV deposit.

نفع a. نَفَعَ be useful to.

وهم VIII suspect.

حَلْيٌ (حُلِيٌّ) jewels.

أَبَدًا (with a negative) never.

سَهْمٌ (c) arrow, share.

سَمَكٌ (sing. سَمَكَةٌ) fish.

Exercise 53

قَالَ دَعْنِي أُوصِي فَقَالَ أَوْصِ ـ رَأَوْا أَرْآءَ
الْفَلَاسِفَةِ ـ أَمَا تَسْتَحِي أَنْ يَكُونَ هٰذَا قَدْرَ حِلْمِكَ
عَنِ ٱبْنِكَ ـ إِذَا لَمْ تَسْتَحِ فَاصْنَعْ مَا شِئْتَ ـ مَا
لَكُمْ تَسْمَعُونَ وَلَا تَعُونَ ـ أَغْنُوهُ وَكَانَ قَلِيلَ الْوَفَاءِ
لَئِمْ ـ أَرَاكَ ٱللّٰهُ فِي بَنِيكَ مَا أَرَى أَبَاكَ فِيكَ
وَأَرَى ٱللّٰهُ بَنِيكَ فِيكَ مَا أَرَاكَ فِي أَبِيكَ ـ كَانَ
إِذَا وَعَدَ الْخَيْرَ وَفَى وَإِذَا أَوْعَدَ أَخْلَفَ وَعَفَا ـ آثِرْ
مَا تَلْقَاهُ غَدًا عَلَى مَا لَا تَرَاهُ أَبَدًا ـ كُنْتُ أَجِدُ
مَنْ يَعِدُ وَيَنْجِزُ فَقَدْ أَعْيَانِي مَنْ يَعِدُ وَلَا يَنْجِزُ ـ

اِسْتَحْيَيْتُ مِنْهُ وَبَعَثْتُ إِلَيْهِ بِالْحُلِيِّ ـ حَاجَتُكَ
عِنْدَنَا فَأْتِ مَنْزِلَكَ فَإِنَّهَا سَتَأْتِيكَ ـ لِيَقِ أَحَدُكُمْ
وَجْهَهُ ٱلنَّارَ ـ يُوَلِّي ٱلْخَلِيفَةُ مَنْ يَشَاءُ.

54

he told them to bring their books — what do you think of Egypt ? — these women, will they perform what they have promised ? — be on your guard against suspicion — they greeted us politely — show me how that will benefit me — ask the keeper to show you what the boxes contain — fear God and honour the king — I prefer that men should fear me than that they should fear God — bring me my share of the food and I will eat it by the river — did you not all see what your aunt wrote ? — much study wearies the young.

LESSON 28

CONDITIONAL AND EXCEPTIVE SENTENCES

The two main types of conditional sentences have been mentioned in Lesson 13. There are, however, many irregularities. Besides إِنْ the following words follow the same rules :—

مَنْ he who ; مَا that which ; أَيٌّ which of ; أَيْنَ ـ حَيْثُ where ; مَتَى when ; كَيْفَ how ; كُلَّمَا whenever ; إِذَا when.

مَا أَنْسَ لَا أَنْسَ

whatever I forget, I shall not forget . . .

كَيفَ قَضَيْتَ فَعِنْدَهُ أَخطَأْتَ

however you decide, in his opinion you will be wrong.

The apodosis must be introduced by فَ when it is :—

1. A nominal sentence.

إِنْ قُلتَ هٰذَا فَأَنْتَ مِنَ ٱلْكَافِرِينَ

if you say this you are of the infidels.

2. A sentence beginning with an incomplete verb, such as لَيسَ or عَسَى, one of the particles قَدْ ـ سَوْفَ ـ سَ or one of the negatives لَنْ ـ مَا .

إِنْ تَستَغْفِرْ لَهُمْ فَلَنْ يَغْفِرَ ٱللّٰهُ لَهُمْ

if you ask pardon for them, God will never pardon them

3. A verbal sentence expressing a wish or command.

أَيَّهُمَا شِئْتُمْ فَبَايِعُوا

do homage to which of the two you will.

4. When a perfect in the apodosis has to keep its meaning as a past tense.

إِنْ كَانَ قَمِيصُهُ قُدَّ مِنْ قُبُلٍ فَصَدَقَتْ

if his shirt is torn in front she has told the truth.

A condition may also be expressed by an imperative and a jussive :—

قِفِى أُخْبِرْكِ

stand, let me tell you = if you wait I will tell you.

قُمْ عَنْهُ يَقُلْ بِحَاجَتِهِ

stand away from him, he will speak of his need = if you stand back he will say what he wants.

إِمَّا follows the same rules as إِنْ but is often followed by the energetic.

وَإِنْ often means ‘ even if ’.

If the condition is improbable, لَوْ is used in place of إِنْ ; the same rules apply for tenses but the use of the simple imperfect is more common.

سَيَذْكُرُونَنِى لَوْ قَدْ جَرَّبُوا الْعُمَّالَ بَعْدِى

they will remember me should they have experience of governors after me.

لَوْ is also used to express an impossible wish :—

لَوْ كَانَ يَنْفَعُ الْإِنْظَارُ

if only postponement were of some use.

إِلَّا ‘ if not ’ is often used elliptically ; an example is the best explanation :—

إِنْ قَبِلْتَ رَأْيِى وَإِلَّا خَبُتْتَ

if you accept my opinion (all will go right), but if (you do) not, you will be disappointed.

لَوْلَا is also used elliptically:

لَوْلَا ٱلشَّمْسُ بَرَدَتِ ٱلْأَرْضُ

but for the sun the earth would grow cold.

A sentence following لولا is usually introduced by أَنَّ or أَنْ.

Exceptions.

The most common word for these is إِلَّا. When the main sentence is affirmative, the noun after إِلَّا is accusative unless, of course, it is governed by a preposition.

جَاءَ ٱلْقَوْمُ إِلَّا زَيْدًا the tribe came except Zaid.

فَرَضَ لِأَبْنَاءِ ٱلْبَدْرِيِّينَ أَلْفَيْنِ أَلْفَيْنِ إِلَّا حَسَنًا وَحُسَيْنًا

he allotted to the sons of those who fought at Badr (Lesson 31) two thousand apiece except Hasan and Husain.

When the exception comes before the main noun the accusative is used.

لَمْ يَكُنْ إِلَّا غَالِبًا مَيِّتٌ يَقْرِى

no dead man except Ghalib gave hospitality.

When the sentence is negative, actually or virtually, the exception is in the same case as the main noun.

مَا مَرَرْتُ بِأَحَدٍ إِلَّا زَيْدٍ

I passed by no one except Zaid.

When the sentence is negative and the main noun left out, the exception is in the case the main noun should have.

مَا جَاءَ إِلَّا امْرَأَتُهُ only his wife came.

ما مررت الا بِزَيْدٍ I passed only Zaid.

مَا يَخْدَعُونَ إِلَّا أَنْفُسَهُمْ

they deceive only themselves.

مَا كَانَ إِبْرَاهِيمُ إِلَّا يَهُودِيًّا

Ibrahim (Abraham) was only a Jew.

When the exception is of a different sort from the main noun, the accusative is used. One feels sometimes that this is a desperate attempt to bring the facts of language under rule.

مَا لَهُمْ بِهِ مِنْ عِلْمٍ إِلَّا اتِّبَاعَ الظَّنِّ

they have no knowledge of it but the following of fancy.

إِلَّا is often used loosely.

قَدْ أَدْرَكَنِي ٱلْمَوْتُ إِلَّا قَلِيلًا

death almost overtook me.

لَا يَبْقَى حَيٌّ إِلَّا مَاتَ

no living one remains without dying.

مَا شَعَرْتُ بِهِ إِلَّا وَقَدِ ٱحْتَمَلَنِي

I did not perceive him except he had picked me up = the next thing I knew was that he had carried me.

'Only.' As we have just seen, this is often expressed by إِلَّا with a negative. It can also be expressed by إِنَّمَا; the word excepted is put at the end of the sentence.

إِنَّمَا عَلِيٌّ شُجَاعٌ

Ali is only brave (has no other good qualities).

إِنَّمَا شُجَاعٌ عَلِيٌّ the only brave man is Ali.

Note.—The addition of مَا to أَنَّ makes no difference to its meaning.

Vocabulary 28

بقى X preserve, keep alive.	شبه III resemble.
تَابَ u. تَوْبَة repent.	X ask to repent.
سَلَكَ u. سُلُوك go.	جلس III sit with.
فوض III be partners, discuss.	نَكَحَ i.a. نِكَاح marry.
صَلَحَ u. صَلَاح be good, serviceable.	III make peace with.
— IV repair, restore.	عَبَأَ a. عَبْأ (with negative) ignore.
كَدَّ u. كَدّ work hard, persevere.	عَمَّ u. be general, concern many.
يَسَرَ i. يُسْر be easy, easy-going.	بِرّ goodness, filial piety.
— IV become rich.	II make easy.
قَمِيص (قُمْصَان) shirt.	فَضْل excellence, superiority.
حَرِيص eager, greedy	بَيْت (a) verse of poetry.
خِطْء خَطِيء sin.	بطؤ IV make slow, do slowly.
	IV make a mistake.
يقظ IV wake up (trans.).	X wake up (intrans.).

Exercise 55

إِنْ لَمْ تَقْتُلْهُ لَأَتَزَوَّجَنَّهُ فَيَكُونُ قَدْ قَتَلَ أَبَاكَ وَنَكَحَ
أُمَّكَ فَقَتَلَهُ ـ لَوْ كَانَ ٱلْبُخْلُ قَمِيصًا مَا لَبِسْتُهُ وَلَوْ
كَانَ طَرِيقًا مَا سَلَكْتُهُ ـ إِنْ كَانَ رِزْقِي فِي ٱلسَّمَاءِ
فَأَنْزِلْهُ وَإِنْ كَانَ فِي ٱلْأَرْضِ فَأَخْرِجْهُ وَإِنْ كَانَ

بَعِيدًا فَقَرِّبْهُ وَإِنْ كَانَ قَرِيبًا فَيَسِّرْهُ ـ إِذَا جَالَسْتَ
ٱلْعُلَمَاءَ فَكُنْ عَلَى أَنْ تَسْمَعَ أَحْرَصَ مِنْكَ عَلَى
أَنْ تَقُولَ ـ لَوْلَا أَنَّ أَفْعَالَهُ لَا تُوجِبُ ٱلْعَفْوَ عَنْهُ
لَكَانَ حَقِيقًا بِٱلِاسْتِبْقَاءِ لِهٰذَا ٱلْفَضْلِ ـ مَا ٱلْعِزُّ
إِلَّا تَحْتَ ثَوْبِ ٱلْكَدِّ ـ لِمَ لَا تُطِيلُ ٱلْهِجَاءَ قَالَ
لَمْ أَجِدِ ٱلشِّعْرَ ٱلسَّائِرَ إِلَّا بَيْتًا وَاحِدًا ـ أَوْدَعَ
ذٰلِكَ ٱلْمَالَ رِجَالًا فَذَهَبُوا بِهِ إِلَّا يَهُودِيًّا ـ مَا
جِئْتُ إِلَّا فِى أَمْرٍ يَخُصُّ ٱلْوَزِيرَ وَيَخُصُّنِى لَمْ تَصْلُحْ
مُفَاوَضَتُهُ فِيهِ إِلَّا عَلَى خَلْوَةٍ شَدِيدَةٍ ـ لِكُلِّ دَاءٍ
دَوَاءٌ إِلَّا ٱلْمَوْتَ ـ مَا أَنْتَ بِشَيْءٍ إِلَّا شَيْءٌ لَا يُعْبَأُ
بِهِ ـ هُمْ كُفَّارٌ يُسْتَتَابُونَ فَإِنْ تَابُوا وَإِلَّا ضُرِبَتْ
أَعْنَاقُهُمْ.

56

he who has never made a mistake has never made anything — all the inhabitants came except your father — if you think that he is right, follow his example — if you find that

I have come on business which concerns myself alone and does not concern the whole people, send me away — it was only the sun's heat on my back which awakened me — wherever you live you will meet friends — none of the children resemble their father except Muhammad — if you believe in what he says, you ought to act according to it — he did not leave any act of filial piety without doing it — if you eat slowly, you will prolong your life — if he dies, his heirs will fight over the inheritance — but for him the army had perished.

LESSON 29

TEMPORAL CONJUNCTIONS

لَمَّا with the perfect denotes a definite event in the past and means 'when' or 'after'.

لَمَّا أَنْبَأَهُمْ بِأَسْمَائِهِمْ قَالَ

when he had told them their names he said . . .

لَمَّا with the jussive means 'not yet' (Lesson 14).

مَتَى 'when' is first an interrogative adverb.

مَتَى تُسَافِرُ when will you travel ?

As a conjunction it is treated as a conditional particle.

إِذْ 'when' may be followed by the perfect or imperfect and usually refers to the past but often passes into 'because'.

لَوْ شَهِدْتُكَ إِذْ تَدْعُو تَمِيمًا

would that I had been with you when you summoned Tamim (a tribe).

قَدْ ظَلَمْتُمْ إِذْ حَبَسْتُمُوهُمْ

you did wrong when (because) you put them in prison.

It may be followed by a nominal sentence.

إِذَا 'when' refers to the future though the perfect is used with it; it is often treated as a conditional particle.

إِذَا رَأَيْتَهُمْ تُعْجِبُكَ أَجْسَامُهُمْ

when you see them their bodies will please you.

Both إِذْ and إِذَا are used to introduce a fact which is not the direct consequence of what has gone before; hence they often suggest the sudden or unexpected. إِذْ takes a verbal sentence after it and إِذَا (usually وَإِذَا or فَإِذَا) takes a nominal sentence:—

بَيْنَمَا ٱلْعُسْرُ إِذْ دَارَتِ ٱلْمَيَاسِيرُ

while distress (is present suddenly) easy times come round.

نَظَرْتُ إِلَى ٱلْمَقْتُولِ فَإِذَا هُوَ زَيْدٌ

I looked at the murdered man; lo and behold, it was Zaid.

إذا may be construed with بِ; two forms are possible :—

شَقَقْتُ ٱلْعَصَا وَإِذَا بِدَنَانِيرِى

شققت العصا وَإِذَا أَنَا بِدَنَانِيرِى

I split the stick and there were my dinars (and there was I with).

There is no real difference in meaning.

حَتَّى 'until' when temporal is used with the perfect or the imperfect indicative :—

زُرْتُكِ حَتَّى قِيلَ لَيْسَ لَهُ صَبْرٌ

I visited you until it was said, 'he has no patience' (self-control).

For حَتّى 'so that' see Lesson 19.

It is also used to co-ordinate two statements and means 'then, later on'; an example is the best explanation :—

زَرَعْتُهُ حَتَّى اشْتَرَيْتُ مِنْهُ بَقَرًا

I sowed it and then bought from it cattle.

I sowed and reaped the field and did this till I had gathered enough money to buy cattle.

بَيْنَمَا ـ بَيْنَا ' while ' take either a verbal or a nominal sentence :—

بَيْنَا نحنُ نَرْقُبُهُ أَتَانَا

بينا نرقبه أتانا

while we were on the look out for him he came.

Often combined with إِذْ.

بَيْنَا أَنَا فِى ٱلْحَدِيثِ إِذْ قَدِمَ زَيْدٌ

while I was in talk, Zaid came.

مَا is used with the perfect but refers to the present with the sense ' as long as ' :—

لَسْتَ ضَائِرَهَا مَا أَطَّتِ ٱلْإِبِلُ

you cannot hurt it as long as camels grunt.

مَا دَامَ حَيّاً as long as he continues alive.

كَمَا ' as ' ; اِفْعَلْ كَمَا يَفْعَلُ ٱلنَّاسُ do as others do ; it passes easily to a sense of time :—

سَلِّمْ كَمَا تَدْخُلُ salute as (soon as) you enter.

Note. كَمَا أَنْتَ stop where you are.

Many prepositions can be turned into conjunctions by combining them with أَنْ or مَا ; أن governs the subjunctive. إِلَى أن until; بَعْدَ أن after; قَبْلَ مَا before, etc.

Vocabulary 29

ثَارَ u. ثَوْرٌ be stirred up.

IV stir up.

شرك IV associate with (trans.).

VIII be associated with.

لَزِمَ لُزُومٌ and VIII be attached to, be necessary.

أَلِمَ أَلَمٌ suffer pain.

قلد II put a necklace on, invest with.

دَفَنَ i. دَفْنٌ bury.

دَعَا دُعَاءٌ and X call, summon.

سر III whisper to.

دَنَا دُنُوٌّ be near.

وفى III arrive.

مَضَى مُضِيٌّ go, be past.

IV execute (order, etc.).

عَدَا عَدْوٌ go, go against.

طَرَدَ u. طَرْدٌ drive, drive away, round up.

عَقَبَ u. عَقْبٌ come after.

رَهَنَ a. رَهْنٌ give a pledge to.

III wager.

رَبِحَ رِبْحٌ make a profit, be profitable.

عَاقِبَةٌ consequence.

نَوْعٌ (a) kind, sort.

عَادَةٌ (عَادَاتٌ) custom.

جَنَازَةٌ — جِنَازَةٌ (جَنَائِزُ) funeral.

وَزِيرٌ (وُزَرَاءُ) minister of state.

وِزَارَةٌ ministry.

Exercise 57

عَلِمَ أَنَّهُ مَتَى رَدَّهُمْ ثَارَتْ فِتْنَةٌ لَا يَأْمَنُ عَوَاقِبَهَا
وَأَنَّ ٱلرَّأْىَ يُوجِبُ ٱلرِّفْقَ بِهِمْ ـ بَيْنَا نَحْنُ نَدْفِنُهُ إِذْ
حُمِلَتْ جَنَازَةٌ أُخْرَى ـ أَلِمْتُ أَلَمًا شَدِيدًا فَلَمَّا كَانَ
فِى ٱللَّيْلِ سَكَنَ ٱلْأَلَمُ وَنِمْتُ ـ لَمَّا أَخْطَأَ آبَاءَكَ
لَمْ يُصِبْ إِلَّا أَنْتَ ـ لَمَّا ٱشْتَدَّ ٱلْمَرَضُ عَلَيْهِ لَزِمَ
فِرَاشَهُ ـ مَا مَضَى عَلَى هٰذَا إِلَّا دُونَ شَهْرٍ حَتَّى
ٱسْتَدْعَى ٱلْخَلِيفَةُ ٱبْنَ أَخِيهِ وَقَلَّدَهُ ٱلْوِزَارَةَ ـ إِنِّى
أُكَلِّمُهُ فَإِذَا بِفِتْيَانٍ فَٱسْتَدْنَى ٱلْأَكْبَرَ مِنْهُمْ فَسَارَّهُ
بِشَيْءٍ دُونِى وَدُونَ أَصْحَابِهِ ـ عَدَا مَعَهُ حَتَّى وَافَيَا
ٱلْبَيْتَ كَفَرَسَىِ ٱلرِّهَانِ ـ لَمْ يَشْعُرْ صَاحِبَاهُ وَقَدْ
سَاءَ ظَنُّهُمْ وَتَخَوَّفَا عَلَيْهِ حَتَّى إِذَا هُمَا بِهِ يَطْرُدُ
ٱلْإِبِلَ فَطَرَدَاهَا مَعَهُ ـ بَقِىَ فِى ٱلْمَدِينَةِ حَتَّى إِذَا
أَعْيَاهُ حَرَارَةُ ٱلصَّيْفِ خَرَجَ إِلَى ضَيْعَتِهِ.

58

after they had shared in the work they shared in the profit — I have not yet received my share of the pay — when did you see anyone resembling him in face ? — he associated me with himself in his request to the government — when you go to a foreign country, adopt its customs — I asked the shopkeeper for fish and he had several kinds — when they gave me my share, I was not satisfied with it — poverty befell him and then his friends stood by him — when she saw that forbidding was useless, she wept — he was busy writing till, when he had written many pages, the whiteness of the paper tired his eyes — a promise, when fulfilment which makes it true does not accompany it, is like words with no meaning.

LESSON 30

NUMERALS

The numerals are the nightmare of a bankrupt financier.

1 أَحَدٌ fem. إِحْدَى is a pronoun.

وَاحِدٌ fem. وَاحِدَةٌ is an adjective.

Both these agree in gender with the noun to which they refer.

2 إِثْنَانِ construct إِثْنَا fem. إِثْنَتَانِ const. إِثْنَتَا

oblique إِثْنَيْنِ construct إِثْنَيْ fem. إِثْنَتَيْنِ const. إِثْنَتَيْ

This is a noun which agrees in gender with the noun

numbered. Usually the dual takes its place but it is used in apposition for emphasis.

لَا تَتَّخِذُوا إِلٰهَيْنِ اثْنَيْنِ do not choose two gods.

3–10. Used with the masculine: with the feminine:

3	ثَلَاثَةٌ	ثَلَاثٌ
4	أَرْبَعَةٌ	أَرْبَعٌ
5	خَمْسَةٌ	خَمْسٌ
6	سِتَّةٌ	سِتٌّ
7	سَبْعَةٌ	سَبْعٌ
8	ثَمَانِيَةٌ	ثَمَانٍ acc. ثَمَانِيًا
9	تِسْعَةٌ	تِسْعٌ
10	عَشَرَةٌ	عَشْرٌ

These numerals are fully declined nouns, disagree in gender with the singular of the noun numbered, and put that noun in the genitive plural, if possible, a plural of paucity. (See below.)

ثَلَاثُ نِسَاءٍ three women; ثَلَاثَةُ رِجَالٍ three men.

When the thing numbered is definite, two constructions are possible :—

تَلَاثَةُ ٱلرِّجَالِ or ٱلرِّجَالُ ٱلثَّلَاثَةُ the three men.

Note.—The construct state of ثَمَانٍ is ثَمَانِى nom. and gen. ثَمَانِىَ acc.

Note.—ثَمَانِيهِنَّ the eight of them = the eight women.

11–12.	Masc.	Fem.
11	أَحَدَ عَشَرَ	إِحْدَى عَشْرَةَ
12	اِثْنَا عَشَرَ	اِثْنَتَا عَشْرَةَ (ثِنْتَا)
oblique	اِثْنَىْ عَشَرَ	اِثْنَتَىْ عَشْرَةَ

These numerals are not declined—except the part اِثْنَا and its variants. The noun is in the accusative singular. Both parts of the numeral agree in gender with the noun which is in the accusative singular.

Note the variations in the words for ' ten '.

13–19.	With masculine :	With feminine :
13	ثَلَاثَةَ عَشَرَ	ثَلَاثَ عَشْرَةَ
14	أَرْبَعَةَ عَشَرَ	أَرْبَعَ عَشْرَةَ

15	خَمْسَةَ عَشَرَ	خَمْسَ عَشْرَةَ
16	سِتَّةَ عَشَرَ	سِتَّ عَشْرَةَ
17	سَبْعَةَ عَشَرَ	سَبْعَ عَشْرَةَ
18	ثَمَانِيَةَ عَشَرَ	ثَمَانِيَ عَشْرَةَ
19	تِسْعَةَ عَشَرَ	تِسْعَ عَشْرَةَ

These are indeclinable and govern the noun in the accusative singular. The unit disagrees in gender with its noun and with the ten.

20–30.

20	عِشْرُونَ	50	خَمْسُونَ	80	ثَمَانُونَ
30	ثَلَاثُونَ	60	سِتُّونَ	90	تِسْعُونَ
40	أَرْبَعُونَ	70	سَبْعُونَ		

These are ordinary external plurals and have the two cases; they take the thing numbered in the accusative singular.

In compound numbers between 21 and 99 the unit comes first.

100 مِائَةٌ (anomalous spelling) *miʔatun.* 200 is مِائَتَانِ ; 300 ثَلَاثُ مِائَةٍ (sometimes written ثلاثمائة) with the hundred in the singular. مائة puts its noun in the genitive singular.

1000 أَلْفٌ . Note أَرْبَعَةُ آلَافٍ . The noun numbered is in the genitive singular.

Order of the numerals :—

3822. ثَلَاثَةُ آلَافٍ وَثَمَانِي مِائَةٍ وَاثْنَانِ وَعِشْرُونَ

Ordinal Numbers.

	M.	F.		M.	F.
first	أَوَّلُ	أُولَى	sixth	سَادِسٌ	سَادِسَةٌ
second	ثَانٍ	ثَانِيَةٌ	seventh	سَابِعٌ	سَابِعَةٌ
third	ثَالِثٌ	ثَالِثَةٌ	eighth	ثَامِنٌ	ثَامِنَةٌ
fourth	رَابِعٌ	رَابِعَةٌ	ninth	تَاسِعٌ	تَاسِعَةٌ
fifth	خَامِسٌ	خَامِسَةٌ	tenth	عَاشِرٌ	عَاشِرَةٌ

These are ordinary adjectives and offer no peculiarities.

11–19. These are indeclinable.

	M.	F.
11th	حَادِيَ عَشَرَ	حَادِيَةَ عَشْرَةَ
12th	ثَانِيَ عَشَرَ	ثَانِيَةَ عَشْرَةَ
13th	ثَالِثَ عَشَرَ	ثَالِثَةَ عَشْرَةَ

etc.

For higher numbers the cardinal forms are used.

Note the compounds with ' first ':—

nom. حَادٍ وَعِشْرُونَ   اَلْحَادِى وَٱلْعِشْرُونَ

gen. حَادٍ وَعِشْرِينَ   اَلْحَادِى وَٱلْعِشْرِينَ

acc. حَادِيًا وَعِشْرِينَ   الحادِىَ والعشرين

حَادِيَةٌ وَعِشْرُونَ   etc.

etc.

Four of the broken plural forms أَفْعَالٌ ـ أَفْعُلٌ ـ فِعْلَةٌ ـ أَفْعِلَةٌ are sometimes plurals of paucity, i.e. indicate a number less than ten. If a noun has two or more plurals and one of them is one of these four forms, it is used for numbers below ten.

بَقِىَ فِى ٱلسِّجْنِ شُهُورًا

he stayed in prison many months.

بقى فى السجن أَشْهُرًا

he stayed in prison a few months.

An undefined number between 3 and 10 is expressed by the noun بِضْعٌ (part): بِضْعُ رِجَالٍ a few men; بِضْعُ نِسَاءٍ a few women.

With larger numbers نَيِّفٌ is used: نَيِّفٌ وَعِشْرُونَ twenty odd.

Fractions.

$\frac{1}{2}$. نِصْفٌ.

$\frac{1}{3}$ to $\frac{1}{10}$ are expressed by فُعْلٌ (أَفْعَالٌ), e.g. ثُلْثٌ $\frac{1}{3}$.

Some fractions can be expressed by combinations of these words: ثُمْنُ رُبْعٍ $\frac{1}{32}$.

Others can only be expressed in words :—

سَهْمٌ مِنْ تِسْعَةٍ وَعِشْرِينَ سَهْمًا
قِطْعَةٌ مِنْ تِسْعٍ وَعِشْرِينَ قِطْعَةً } $\frac{1}{29}$

Distributives.

These may be expressed by repeating the numeral :—

فَرَضَ عَلَيْهِمْ أَلْفَيْنِ أَلْفَيْنِ he allotted them 2,000 apiece.

Time.

The day begins at sunset so the Arabs often count by nights: صُمْتُ عَشْرًا I fasted 10 nights (days).

عَشْرًا as لَيْلَةٌ is feminine.

Note.—عُمْرُهُ أَرْبَعُ سِنِينَ or هُوَ ابْنُ أَرْبَعٍ he is four years old.

Vocabulary 30

عجل II hasten, do quickly.

تَمَّ i. تَمٌّ be complete, perfect.

حَدَثَ u. حُدُوثٌ be new, happen.

— IV make new, produce.

شَمَلَ u. شَمْلاً and شَمِلَ be common to, concern; VIII surround, consist of (عَلَى).

عَمَدَ i. عَمْدٌ support, direct oneself towards.

شِرْكٌ polytheism.

دِيكٌ (b) cock.

عُمْرٌ (a) life, age.

خَفِيَ خَفَاءٌ be hidden.

فتى IV give counsel's opinion.

فَتَاةٌ (فَتَيَاتٌ) young woman.

II, IV complete.

شَكَّ u. شَكٌّ doubt.

صغر II make little.

حدث II tell.

حدث V, VI talk, converse.

زَلْزَلَةٌ earthquake.

دَجَاجٌ (دَجَاجَاتٌ) fowls, hens.

بِضَاعَةٌ (بَضَائِعُ) goods, merchandise.

عَنَى عَنَايَةٌ mean.

فَتْوَى counsel's opinion.

مَعْنًى meaning, idea.

شَكَا شَكْوَى complain.

Exercise 59

بَقِيتُ فِي بِلَادِ الشِّرْكِ أَرْبَعَةَ أَشْهُرٍ وَأَحَدَ عَشَرَ
يَوْمًا ـ اِشْتَرَتْ دِيكًا وَاحِدًا وَخَمْسَ دَجَاجَاتٍ ـ
اِشْتَمَلَ قَافِلَتُهُ عَلَى مِائَةِ إِبِلٍ وَخَمْسَةٍ وَعِشْرِينَ
حِمَارًا ـ وُلِدَ فِي سَنَةِ أَلْفٍ وَتِسْعِمِائَةٍ وَاثْنَتَيْنِ

وَثَلاَثِينَ ـ دَامَتِ ٱلْحَرْبُ سَنَتَيْنِ وَنِصْفَ سَنَةٍ ـ يَأْخُذُ ٱلْحُكُومَةُ ٱلْعُشْرَ مِنْ كُلِّ بَضَائِعِ ٱلتُّجَّارِ ٱلَّذِينَ يَدْخُلُونَ بِلاَدَهَا مِنَ ٱلْخَارِجِ ـ مَا أَكَلْتُ مُنْذُ ثَلاَثٍ شَيْئًا فَأُرِيدُ أَنْ تُقِيمَ عِنْدِي لِنَأْكُلَ وَنَتَحَدَّثَ ـ كَانَ مَوْتُهُ قَبْلَ ٱلزَّلْزَلَةِ ٱلْكَبِيرَةِ بِسَنَتَيْنِ ـ هُوَ ٱبْنُ خَمْسٍ وَسِتِّينَ سَنَةً ـ لاَ يَتِمُّ ٱلْمَعْرُوفُ إِلاَّ بِثَلاَثٍ تَعْجِيلِهِ وَتَصْغِيرِهِ وَسَتْرِهِ .

60

there are 72 kinds of dates — she is 17 years old — that chief was the father of his tribe, he had 16 sons and 12 daughters — she cut the meat into 12 shares — the guests went away by twos — he travelled for 19 days, crossing 3 rivers and climbing 7 mountains — forgive him 70 times — my messenger arrived three hours after me — his daughter inherited one-sixteenth of his property — he is the seventh son of a seventh son.

LESSON 31

NOUN FORMS

Every word form has its special meaning, sometimes more than one.

فَعِيلٌ is commonly an adjective but it is also an infinitive and a broken plural.

فَعْلَةٌ as an infinitive denotes the doing of the action once, whatever form the ordinary infinitive may have :—

نَصَرَهُ ٱللّٰهُ نَصْرَةً God helped him (gave him victory) once

infinitive نَصْرٌ

فَرَّ فَرَّةً he ran away once infinitive فِرَارٌ

فِعْلَةٌ as an infinitive denotes the doing of the act in a certain manner :—

هُوَ حَسَنُ ٱلْكِتْبَةِ he is good in (his style of) writing

infinitive كِتَابَةٌ

قُتِلَ قِتْلَةَ سَوْءٍ he was killed horribly infinitive قَتْلٌ

مَشَى مِشْيَةَ ٱلْمَرِيضِ he walked like a sick man

infinitive مَشْيٌ

فَعَّالٌ denotes one who follows a trade or does something habitually. Examples have been given in Lesson 4. It is also used as an emphatic :—

كَذَّابٌ a great liar.

Noun of place or time.

مَفْعُلٌ ـ مَفْعَلٌ When the characteristic of the imperfect is 'u' or 'a' the noun is مَفْعَلٌ. مَطْبَخٌ kitchen; مَخْرَجٌ exit.

There are a few exceptions; the commonest are—

مَسْكِنٌ dwelling house; مَسْجِدٌ mosque.

مَفْعِلٌ is used when the characteristic of the imperfect is 'i':—

مَقْصِدٌ goal; مَنْزِلٌ house, stage (of a journey);

مَوْضِعٌ place.

Note.—The 'a' in the imperfect is due solely to the guttural.

Roots middle 'w' have forms like مَقَامٌ place.

Those middle 'y' have forms like مَقِيلٌ place of the siesta.

Roots first 'w' have also a variant: مِيلَادٌ ـ مَوْلِدٌ birthday; مِيقَاتٌ ـ مِيعَادٌ appointed time..

Roots third weak have always 'a' in the second syllable (Lesson 26).

In the derived stems of all verbs the passive participle is used as the noun of place : مُسْتَشْفًى hospital.

مَفْعَلٌ may also be used as a noun of action (practically an infinitive) and as a concrete noun :—

مَقْدَمٌ arrival ; مَطْلَبٌ object, thing looked for ;

مَرْكَبٌ carriage, ship, riding beast.

Noun of instrument.

مِفْعَلَةٌ ـ مِفْعَالٌ ـ مِفْعَلٌ may express this :—

مِبْرَدٌ file (tool) ; مِفْتَاحٌ key مِكْنَسَةٌ broom ;

مِيزَانٌ scales ; مِقَصٌّ ـ مِقْرَاضٌ scissors.

Diminutive.

كُلَيْبٌ ـ فُعَيْلٌ a little dog, puppy. It is often used as a form of endearment ; very common is بُنَيَّ my little son.

Relative adjectives.

Adjectives can be made from most nouns by adding *iyyun* feminine *iyyatun* to the noun. If the noun has the feminine ending *at* it is dropped and a long second syllable is shortened. There are many irregularities.

بَلَدٌ town, village , رَجُلٌ بَلَدِيٌّ a country bumpkin

مِصْرُ Egypt ; مِصْرِيٌّ an Egyptian

مَدِينَةٌ town اَلْمَدِينَةُ al-Medina ; مَدَنِيٌّ a townsman, a man from al-Medina

مَكَّةُ Mecca ; مَكِّيٌّ a man from Mecca

قُرَيْشٌ Quraish (Muhammad's tribe) ; قُرَشِيٌّ a man of the tribe.

These adjectives are very common in modern Arabic.

أَصْلٌ (أُصُولٌ) root, principle. فَرْعٌ (فُرُوعٌ) branch.

مَسْأَلَةٌ أَصْلِيَّةٌ a problem involving first principles.

مَسأَلة فَرْعِيَّةٌ a question of detail.

The feminine is used as an abstract noun :—

كَيْفَ how ? كَيْفِيَّةٌ quality : كَمْ how much ? كَمِّيَّةٌ quantity.

Broken plurals.

فُعَّلٌ ـ فُعَّالٌ ـ فَعَلَةٌ are common as plurals of the active participle of Stem I.

فُعَلَةٌ is plural of the active participle of Stem I of verbs third weak : قَاضٍ judge قُضَاةٌ .

فَعَالٍ is plural of فَعْلَاءُ ـ فَعْلَى and فِعْلَى (p. 147).

عَذْرَاءُ virgin عَذَارٍ : فَتْوَى a legal opinion فَتَاوٍ .

فَعَالَى is plural of the same three forms and of فَعْلَانُ :—

حَيْرَانُ : كَسَالَى ـ كَسْلَانُ perplexed حَيَارَى ;

and of فَعِيلَةٌ from verbs third weak :—

هَدِيَّةٌ gift هَدَايَا : مَنِيَّةٌ fate مَنَايَا : مَطِيَّةٌ riding animal مَطَايَا .

Other plurals are فِعْلَانٌ ـ فِعَلَةٌ ـ فَعَلَةٌ ـ فُعُلٌ ـ فُعْلَانٌ ـ فَعْلَى .

مَفَاعِيلُ sometimes becomes مَفَاعِلَةٌ .

Second declension.

The grammarians give many rules for finding whether a noun belongs to this declension or not; it is simpler to trust to memory. To it belong :—

Some forms of the broken plural ;

All proper names which are feminine in form or belong to women (few exceptions) ;

Most foreign names of men, إِبْرَاهِيمُ Abraham ;

Some native names, especially those which resemble verbs, يَزِيدُ Yazid ;

All proper names with a suffixed *a:n*, نُعْمَانُ *Nuʕma:n* ;

The adjectives أَفْعَلُ and فَعْلَانُ ;

All nouns ending in *a:u*, صَحْرَاءُ desert.

Secondary roots.

These commonly have the radical ' t '.

تُهْمَةٌ ' suspicion ' from وهم through اِتَّهَمَ

تَقْوَى ' piety ' from وقى through اِتَّقَى

تَلِيدٌ ' born in the house, ancestral ' from ولد

Vocabulary 31

خَرَقَ u. خَرْقٌ tear rend.

جرب II test.

بَرَدَ u. بَرْدٌ file.

عَبَرَ u. عُبُورٌ pass over, cross.

تَعَبٌ تَعِبَ be tired.

تَعْبَانُ tired.

مِعْبَرٌ ferry.

مَخَاضٌ ford.

مَسْمَعٌ place from which is heard, ear.

مَأْمَنَةٌ place of safety.

مَبْعَثٌ time of sending, mission.

مَشْرِقٌ east, sunrise.

قَطُّ (with negative) ever.

شَيْطَانٌ devil.

دَقَّ u. دَقٌّ hit, pound.

شهر VIII be well known.

زول IV remove.

سَهِرَ سَهَرٌ be wakeful at night.

أرخ II date.

تَارِيخٌ history.

مُنْخُلٌ sieve.

مَسْأَلَةٌ question, problem.

غَسَلَ i. غَسْلٌ wash.

مَأْسَدَةٌ place where lions are plentiful.

مَغْرِبٌ west, sunset.

جَمِيعٌ (collected) together, all.

نظف II clean.

Exercise 61

جَلَسَ جِلْسَةَ ٱلثَّعْبَانِ ـ أَسَمِعْتَ مِثْلَ هٰذَا قَطُّ قَالَ لَا مَا
خَرَقَ مَسَامِعِي قَطُّ مِثْلُهُ ـ ضَرَبَ مُوسَى ٱلْحَجَرَ ضَرْبَةً
وَيَخْرُجُ مَاءٌ يَكْفِي ٱلْقَوْمَ جَمِيعًا ـ أَخْرَجَتْ صَاحِبَةُ
ٱلْبَيْتِ ٱللِّصَّ تَضْرِبُهُ بِٱلْمِكْنَسَةِ ـ أَسْمِعُوهُمْ كَلَامَ
ٱللّٰهِ وَأَبْلِغُوهُمْ مَأْمَنَهُمْ ـ سَافَرْنَا مَنَازِلَ وَبَلَغْنَا
مَأْسَدَةً نَخَافُ فِيهَا عَلَى خَيْلِنَا ـ فَلْنَذْكُرِ ٱلْآنَ
ٱلتَّأْرِيخَ مِنْ مَوْلِدِ رَسُولِ ٱللّٰهِ إِلَى مَبْعَثِهِ ـ جَرِّبُونِي

بِمَسَائِلَ لَمْ أَفْهَمْ مِنْهَا شَيْئًا ـ عَبَرْنَا ٱلنَّهْرَ بَعْضُنَا فِى مِعْبَرٍ وَبَعْضُنَا بِمَخَاضَةٍ ـ كَانَ أَحْفَظَ ٱلنَّاسِ لِمَا سَمِعَ وَأَقَلَّهُمْ نَوْمًا وَأَصْبَرَهُمْ عَلَى ٱلسَّهَرِ .

62

his name is famous in the east and the west — the thief came in like a lion and went out like a sheep — all his children swim like fish — as long as life remains I shall not leave the battle field — the child cut off his finger with the tailor's scissors — he washes his dog twice daily — reason is to a man a file with which he files the roughness of the heart, a broom with which he removes evil deeds, a mallet with which he bruises the head of the devil, and a sieve with which he cleans his thoughts — the Syrian boasts of the snow and fruits of his mountains and the Egyptian of the water of his river — the carpenter must not be ignorant of the qualities of the different kinds of wood.

LESSON 32

SOME VERBS

Quadriliteral roots.

Verbs from these roots have two stems like II and V of the strong verb but with two different instead of the middle radical doubled. A common type is a group of two consonants reduplicated.

perfect.	imperfect.	imperative.	infinitive.
دَحْرَجَ roll (trans.)	يُدَحْرِجُ	دَحْرِجْ	دَحْرَجَةٌ ـ دِحْرَاجٌ
تَدَحْرَجَ (intrans.)	يَتَدَحْرَجُ	تَدَحْرَجْ	تَدَحْرُجٌ

There is nothing peculiar about weak verbs :—

دَهْدَى ـ يُدَهْدِي ـ دَهْدِ ـ دَهْدَاةٌ or دِهْدَاءٌ

Impersonal expressions.

The passive cannot be used absolutely, it must be qualified by a prepositional phrase :—

سِيرَ إِلَى ٱلْعِرَاقِ there has been a going to Irak.

The result is that there seem to be a lot of superfluous prepositions and pronouns.

أُخْتُلِفَ فِيهِ there has been a difference about it.

اَلْمَسْأَلَةُ ٱلْمُخْتَلَفُ فِيهَا the question under discussion.

اَلْمَرْغُوبُ فِيهِ the thing liked;

المرغوب عَنْهُ the thing disliked.

غُشِيَ عَلَيْهِ it was covered upon him = he fainted.

غُشِيَ عَلَيْهَا she fainted.

اَلْمَغْشِيُّ عَلَيْهِ the man who fainted.

اَلْمَغْشِيُّ عَلَيْهَا the woman who fainted.

سُقِطَ فِي يَدِهِ it was fallen into his hand = he repented.

هُوَ مَسْقُوطٌ فِي يَدِهِ he is repenting.

اَلشَّجَرَةُ الْمَنْهِيُّ عَنْهَا the forbidden tree (nom.)

اَلشَّجَرَةَ الْمَنْهِيَّ عَنْهَا (acc.) اَلشَّجَرَةِ الْمَنْهِيِّ عَنْهَا (gen.)

Auxiliary verbs.

Several verbs, of which the commonest are جَعَلَ ـ أَخَذَ a. جَعَلَ 'make', are used with a following imperfect in the sense of 'begin':

جَعَلَ يَتَكَلَّمُ he began to talk.

Verbs of thought and feeling.

These may govern two accusatives; the causative may even govern three :—

أَرَاكَ أَفْعَالَكَ خَبِيثَةً

he showed you that your deeds were evil.

They may be used parenthetically; so you can say both

أَظُنُّ الْحُسَيْنَ شُجَاعًا ـ أَظُنَّ الْحُسَيْنُ شُجَاعٌ

I think Husain is brave.

With a verbal sentence following three constructions are possible :—

أَظُنُّ أَنَّ عُمَرَ يَبْنِى بَيْتًا

أظنّ يبنى عُمَرُ بيتا — أظنّ عُمَرَ يبنى بيتا

I think that Umar is building a house.

' Can.'

The imperfect alone may be used.

اِنْتَهَى ٱلْأَمْرُ إِلَى وَقْتِهِ ٱلْمَحْدُودِ ٱلَّذِى لَا يَدْفَعُهُ دَافِعٌ

the affair went on to its allotted time which no pusher can push back (postpone).

قَدِرَ ' be strong, able ' may be used or قَدَرَ u.i. قَدْرٌ

يَقْدِرُ أَنْ يَمْشِيَ — يَقْدِرُ عَلَى ٱلْمَشْيِ

he can walk.

لَنْ نَقْدِرَ عَلَيْهِ ٱلْعُقُوبَةَ we can never punish him.

اِسْتَطَاعَ X of طوع.

أَمَا تَسْتَطِيعُ أَنْ تَكْفِيَنَا هٰذَا

can you not arrange this for us ?

لَنْ يَسْتَطِيعَ مَعِى صَبْرًا

he will never be able to have patience with me.

مكن IV. The action is the subject and the agent the object :—

لَا يُمْكِنُهُ ٱلنُّهُوضُ he cannot get up.

(نهض 'stand up' as a preliminary to action.)

طوق IV and وسع can also be used :

لَمْ يُطِقْ مِنَ ٱلْوَجَعِ أَنْ يَرْكَبَ بَعِيرًا وَلَا دَابَّةً

he could ride neither camel nor horse because of the pain.

هٰذَا كَذَّابٌ أَوْ جَهُولٌ لَا يَسَعُنِى قَبُولُهُ

he is a liar or grossly ignorant, I cannot accept him.

'Must.'

لَا بُدَّ مِنْ there is no separation from (for loss of nunation see Lesson 14).

أَخْبَرَهُ بِحُضُورِ قَوْمٍ لَا بُدَّ مِنْ وُصُولِهِمْ

he told him of the presence of people, there was no escape from their arriving (were on the doorstep and must be admitted).

This phrase may be followed by a sentence introduced by أَنْ ; the من may be omitted :—

لَا بُدَّ [مِنْ] أَنْ تُحَدِّثَنِى بِمَا بَيْنَكُمَا

you must tell me what is between you two.

وجب ' be necessary ' and لزم ' stick to ' also have the meaning ' must '. The subject of both verbs may be a noun or a sentence with أَنْ :—

وَجَبَ عَلَيْهِ ٱلنُّهُوضُ he had to stand up;

لَزِمَهُ أَنْ يَصْحَبَنِى he had to accompany me;

يَلْزَمُهُ ٱلاِسْتِفْهَامُ

he must ask questions (ask to understand).

Vocabulary 32

قَضَاءٌ قَضَى judge, settle, finish.	زَمِنَ زَمَنٌ be paralysed.
بَرْءٌ بُرُوءٌ بَرِىَ بَرَأَ be cured.	II cure, acquit.
قرض IV lend.	X ask a loan.
خَلَصَ u. خُلُوصٌ be pure.	II make pure, save.
قلب II turn (trans.).	جَاعَ u. جُوعٌ be hungry.
هُدًى هَدَى lead aright.	لَطَفَ u. لُطْفٌ be kind.
شَدَّ u. شَدَّةٌ attack, tie.	نقم VIII punish.
عسر IV be poor.	طَأْطَأَ bow (the head).
وَلْوَلَ wail.	هَمٌّ (b) care, anxiety.
ثَعْلَبٌ fox.	حَرَكَةٌ movement, vowel.
طَبِيعَةٌ nature.	مَحْكَمَةٌ law court.
جَنْبٌ (b) side.	بَطِّيخٌ water melon.
وَثَاقٌ bonds.	حَيٌّ alive.
مَيِّتٌ dead.	زَلْزَلَ shake (trans.).

Exercise 63

قَضَى ٱلْقَاضِي عَلَى ٱلْمُدَّعِي وَبَرَّأَ ٱلْمُدَّعَى عَلَيْهِمْ ـ أَخَذَ يَسْتَقْرِضُ مِنِّي وَأَقْرَضْتُهُ خَمْسَمِائَةِ دِينَارٍ لِأَتَخَلَّصَ مِنْهُ ـ رَأَى ثَعْلَبًا ضَعِيفًا لَا يَسْتَطِيعُ ٱلْحَرَكَةَ فَقَالَ إِنَّ هٰذَا ٱلثَّعْلَبَ لَا بُدَّ أَنْ يَمُوتَ جُوعًا ـ اِهْدِنَا ٱلصِّرَاطَ ٱلْمُسْتَقِيمَ صِرَاطَ ٱلَّذِينَ أَنْعَمْتَ عَلَيْهِمْ غَيْرِ ٱلْمَغْضُوبِ عَلَيْهِمْ وَلَا ٱلضَّالِّينَ ـ يُرِيدُ ٱلْإِنْسَانُ طَبِيعَةً ٱلْأَشْيَاءَ ٱلْمَنْهِيَّ عَنْهَا ـ تَنَازَعَ قَوْمٌ وَطَلَبُوا مَارًّا يَقْضِي بَيْنَهُمْ وَلَمَّا سَأَلَ فِي أَمْرِ ٱلْاُخْتِلَافِ لَمْ يَصِفُوا لَهُ ٱلْمُخْتَلَفَ فِيهِ ـ ثُمَّ يُطَأْطِئُ ٱلْكَافِرُونَ رُؤُوسَهُمْ خَوْفَ مَا يَرَوْنَ وَيُوَلْوِلُونَ ـ لَا يُمْكِنُكُمُ ٱلدِّفَاعُ عَنْ نُفُوسِكُمْ فَيَلْزَمُكُمُ ٱلتَّسْلِيمُ ـ ٱلْمَصَائِبُ حَالَةٌ لَا بُدَّ مِنْهَا فَمِنْهَا مَا يَكُونُ رَحْمَةً مِنَ ٱللهِ وَلُطْفًا بِعَبْدِهِ وَمِنْهَا مَا يَكُونُ ٱنْتِقَامًا ـ كُنْ مُوسِرًا إِنْ شِئْتَ أَوْ مُعْسِرًا لَا بُدَّ فِي ٱلدُّنْيَا مِنَ ٱلْهَمِّ.

64

carry the boy who has fainted to the hospital — the defendant is in court but where is the plaintiff ? — a girl was paralysed for about 15 years ; she could not turn from side to side nor could anyone else turn her — I did not think that he could have mentioned me when there was a summons for me — as long as you had the price of this melon on you you could not hold back your desire (soul) from it — I am left with my bonds fast on me — we had to pay that to him — my own perceptions are enough for me — how is your husband ? she said, not alive that he could be hoped for and not dead that he could be forgotten — you cannot give what you have not.

LESSON 33

SOME NOUNS

Accusative as vocative.

A noun in the vocative when qualified by a genitive or a prepositional phrase is put in the accusative :—

يَا عَبْدَ اللهِ {Abdullah ! (a common name). servant of God.

يَا صَاعِدًا فِى الْجِبَالِ climber of mountains.

Note that أَيُّهَا cannot be used before a construct state because it must be followed by the definite article.

Construct state before a sentence.

A noun may govern a sentence in the genitive ; usually it is a noun of time in the adverbial accusative.

شَهَادَةُ أَنْ لَا إِلٰهَ إِلَّا ٱللهُ

the confession that there is no god but God.

هٰذَا يَوْمُ يَنْفَعُ ٱلصَّادِقِينَ صِدْقُهُمْ

this is the day when the truthful will profit by their truthfulness.

وُلِدْتُ لَيْلَةَ قُبِضَ ٱلنَّبِيُّ

I was born the night the prophet was taken (died).

فَرَّ خَوْفَ أَنْ يُعَذِّبَهُ ٱلْعَامِلُ

he fled for fear the governor would punish him.

خَوْفَ is the accusative of cause.

كَأَنَّ.

This is a compound of أَنَّ and follows the same rules, meaning 'as if'.

كَانَ ٱلنَّاسُ كَأَنَّهُمْ يُكَذِّبُونَنِي

the people were as if they did not believe me (seemed not to).

It may be a complete sentence in itself, when it must be translated 'it is as if':—

كَأَنِّي أَنْظُرُ إِلَى ٱلدِّمَاءِ بَيْنَ ٱلْعَمَائِمِ

it is as if I were looking at the blood (pl.) between the turbans (and necks).

Note the expressions :—

كَأَنِّى بِكَ تُخَادِعُنِى

it seems to me that you are deceiving me.

كَأَنِّى بِكَ قَتِيلًا I think I see you slain.

(قَتِيلًا accusative of accompanying circumstance.)

Attraction.

This occurs in a kind of relative clause. To understand the construction, it helps to think of two separate sentences of which the second consists of a noun and adjective with a pronoun referring back to the noun in the first. Instead of using a relative link, the order of the second sentence is inverted and the adjective made to agree in case with the noun of the first sentence.

رَأَيْتُ رَجُلًا ـ أَبُوهُ حَسَنٌ

I saw a man ; his father is handsome.

The combined sentence becomes :—

رَأَيْتُ رَجُلًا حَسَنًا أَبُوهُ

I saw a man whose father is handsome.

The adjective agrees in gender with its own noun and in case with the principal noun.

مَرَرْتُ بِامْرَأَةٍ حَسَنٍ أَبُوهَا

I passed a woman whose father is handsome.

سَافَرْتُ مَعَ رَجُلٍ حَسَنَةٍ أَخْلَاقُهُ

I travelled with a man whose character was good.

Is the principal noun definite, the adjective is definite also :—

نَظَرْتُ إِلَى ٱلرَّجُلِ ٱلْحَسَنِ أَبُوهُ

I looked at the man whose father is handsome.

فِى ٱلْحُلَلِ ٱلْمُضَاعَفِ نَسْجُهَا

in the garments which are double woven.

When the predicate of the subordinate sentence is a noun, inversion happens only exceptionally.

مَرَرْتُ بِحَيَّةٍ ذِرَاعٌ طُولُهَا

I passed a snake the length of which was a cubit.

لَقِيتُ رَجُلًا سَوَاءٌ عَلَيْهِ ٱلْخَيْرُ وَٱلشَّرُّ

I met a man to whom good and evil are alike.

'Enough.'

This may be expressed by the verb كَفَى or by the noun حَسْبُ which usually has a pronominal suffix :—

حَسْبُكَ مِنْ عَيْبٍ أَبُوكَ

your father is disgrace enough for you.

حَسْبُكَ جُودًا أَنْ يَكُونَ كَحَاتِمٍ

it is generosity enough for you that he should be like Hatim.

It may be used absolutely and means ' only '.

إِنَّمَا كَانَ ٱلرِّيَاسَةُ لَهُ بِبَيْتِ ٱلْمَقْدِسِ حَسْبُ لَا غَيْرَ ذَلِكَ

authority was his in Jerusalem alone and nowhere else.

Vocabulary 33

سَبَقَ u. سَبْقٌ precede, come in first.

III race.

صلو II say the ritual prayers.

ظَلَمَ i. ظُلْمٌ do wrong.

IV be dark.

قَسَا قَسْوٌ be hard.

III find hard, oppressive.

هم VIII pay attention to, think important.

بيض II whiten.

جَلَبَ u. جَلْبٌ come, bring, drive.

عَظَمَ عِظَمٌ be big.

II honour.

حَقَرَ i. حَقْرٌ and VIII despise.

بَرَكَةٌ blessing.

برك III (with على) bless.

هَدِيَّةٌ (هَدَايَا) gift.

زِرَاعَةٌ agriculture.

قُطْنٌ cotton.

زَمَانٌ (أَزْمِنَةٌ) time, period.

عَارٌ defect, disgrace.

دُعَاءٌ (أَدْعِيَةٌ) prayer, petition.

عِشَاءٌ evening.

فَجْرٌ dawn.

عشو V eat the evening meal.

غدو V eat the morning meal.

فَطَرَ u.i. فِطْرٌ break one's fast.

Exercise 65

رَأَيْتُ ٱلْفَقِيرَ مُحْتَقِرَةً حِكْمَتُهُ ـ سَأَغْسِلُ عَنِّى ٱلْعَارَ
بِٱلسَّيْفِ جَالِبًا عَلَىَّ قَضَاءُ ٱللّٰهِ مَا كَانَ جَالِبًا ـ
قَدْ عَلِمْتُ لَأَمْرُ رَسُولِ ٱللّٰهِ أَعْظَمُ بَرَكَةً مِنْ أَمْرِى ـ
كَأَنَّكَ بِٱلْحُسَيْنِ مُقْبِلًا ـ خَافَ ٱلْجَيْشُ مِنَ ٱلْمَوْتِ
حَتَّى كَأَنَّ قُلُوبَ أَكْثَرِهِمْ هَوَاءٌ ـ تَقُولُ قَوْلَ ٱلَّذِى
لَيْسَ ٱلْوَفَاءُ لَهُ خُلُقًا ـ لَقَدْ صَغُرَ عَبْدَ ٱلرَّحْمٰنِ فِى
عَيْنَيَّ عِظَمُ ٱلدُّنْيَا فِى عَيْنِهِ وَكَأَنَّهُ يَرَى ٱلسَّائِلَ إِذَا
أَتَاهُ مَلَكَ ٱلْمَوْتِ ـ لَمْ يَكُنْ هَدَايَا ٱلسُّلْطَانِ
إِلَّا لِلْفُقَرَاءِ وَٱلْمُؤَلَّفَةِ قُلُوبُهُمْ ـ أَخْرِجْنَا مِنْ هٰذِهِ
ٱلْبِلَادِ ٱلظَّالِمِ أَهْلُهَا ـ كَأَنِّى بِكَ تَتَجَاهَلُ ـ كُنْتُ
أُقَاسِى ٱلزَّمَانَ طُولَ عُمْرِى حَتَّى لَا أَرْجُو ٱلْيُسْرَ ـ
يَهْتَمُّ مَلِكُ مِصْرَ بِإِصْلَاحِ ٱلزِّرَاعَةِ لَا سِيَّمَا ٱلْقُطْنِ.

66

the worst man was born the night the best man died — you seem not to like me — if you do it again, we shall again make a lampoon on you the words of which travel

— hearer of prayer! deliver me from what my enemies devise against me — it seems to me that you are betting on a horse which will not come in first in the race — the dressmaker showed us dresses of various colours — he who teaches an old man is as if he were making a black man white — I have not seen one of the caliphs to whom bloodshed was more distasteful than Hishām — he took an evening meal and no morning meal and this was enough for him for the space of forty years.

LESSON 34

EXCLAMATIONS

Admiration and its opposite are expressed by two defective verbs نِعْمَ 'how good' (نَعِمَ u. نِعْمَةٌ be well off) and بِئْسَ 'how bad' (بَؤُسَ بُؤْسٌ be badly off). The thing approved is the subject of the verb.

1. It must be definite or a sentence.

نِعْمَ ٱلرَّجُلُ عَمْرٌو what a fine chap Amr is.

بِئْسَ مَا صَنَعَ عُمَرُ what a shocking thing Umar did.

2. The subject may be accompanied by an accusative of nearer definition.

نِعْمَ ٱلْحَسَنُ رَجُلاً how good is al-Hasan as a man.

Less general ideas are expressed by two forms of Stem IV مَا أَفْعَلَ and أَفْعِلْ بِ .

مَا أَكْرَمَ عَلِيًّا how generous Ali is.

أَعْظِمْ بِالْحَارِثِ قَدَرًا how strong al-Harith is.

When IV cannot be made from the ideas wanted, words like أَشَدَّ are used as with adjectives of defects and colours. Thus the sentence

تَسْتَقْبِحُ النُّفُوسُ الْكَرِيمَةُ الظُّلْمَ

noble souls abhor wrongdoing

becomes

مَا أَشَدَّ مَا تَسْتَقْبِحُ النفوس الكريمة الظلم

how violently the noble souls abhor wrongdoing.

The second ما with its verb is equivalent to أَن with the subjunctive and both can be replaced by an infinitive with the same meaning.

ما أشدَّ اسْتِقْبَاحَ النفوسِ الكريمةِ الظلمَ .

Admiration is also expressed by the phrase لِلّٰهِ دَرُّ with a pronoun.

دَرّ is the flow of milk from the udder and the words imply that the man and his flocks are under the special protection of God. Then the use was generalized. Two constructions are possible :—

لِلّٰهِ دَرُّهُ فَارِسًا what a fine horseman he is.

لله دره مِنْ خَطِيبٍ what a fine speaker he is.

'Beware.'

إِيَّاكُمْ وَالْكَلْبَ beware of the dog.

اياكم وَقَتْلَهُ beware of killing him.

و here is the و of accompaniment which takes the accusative, as in :

مَشَيْتُ وَالنِّيلَ I walked beside the Nile.

Prepositions used idiomatically.

هَلْ لَكَ فِى الْمَاءِ الْبَارِدِ would you like some cold water.

دُونَكَ الدَّرَاهِمَ take the dirhams ; دُونَكَهُ take it.

عَلَيْكَ حَارِثَةَ seize Haritha (a man's name).

عَلَىَّ بِهِ bring him to me.

لَا عَلَيْكَ أَنْ تَفْعَلَ

there is no (harm) to you that you do = do as you like.

بِٱللّٰهِ عَلَيْكَ I implore you by God.

Oaths.

With nouns وَ is the commonest particle; it takes the genitive :—

وَٱللّٰهِ by God; وَرَبِّ ٱلْكَعْبَةِ by the lord of the Kaaba;

وَحَيَاتِكَ by your life.

لَ is used with the nominative of عُمْرٌ (note the vocalization):

لَعَمْرُكَ by your life; لَعَمْرُ ٱللّٰهِ by the life of God.

When a verb is present, بِ is usual:

أَقْسَمْتُ بِٱللّٰهِ I swear by God; but

نَشَدْتُكَ ٱللّٰهَ I adjure you by God.

When the oath confirms a statement of fact it usually makes no change in the sentence.

When the oath confirms an intention, various things may happen.

If the intention is positive the energetic is used with لَ:

وَٱللهِ لَأَسِيرَنَّ by God, I will go.

If negative, لَا with the perfect is used:

والله لَا عَصَيْتَ رَبِّى

by God you shall not disobey my lord.

The negative may be omitted and then the imperfect is used:

قُلْتُ يَمِينَ ٱللهِ أَبْرَحُ قَاعِدًا

I said, the oath of God, I shall not cease sitting.

إِلَّا with the perfect may be used in an affirmative sense:

أَقْسَمْتُ عَلَيْكَ إِلَّا لَبِسْتَ دِرْعِى

I adjure you, put on my coat of mail.

سَأَلَهُ بِالصُّحْبَةِ إِلَّا حَدَّثَه

he besought by (their good) fellowship, tell him.

This construction may be explained from the Old Testament oath: The Lord do so to me and more also if I do not = I will do.

Verbs of fear, hindrance, etc.

When these verbs are followed by أَنْ with the subjunctive, لَا may be inserted after أَنْ without changing the sense :—

مَا مَنَعَكَ أَنْ تَسْجُدَ مَا مَنَعَكَ أَنْ لَا [أَلَّا] تَسْجُدَ	what prevented you from bowing down.

Vocabulary 34

كَسَبَ i. كَسْبٌ and VIII earn, earn a living.

عَجَزَ i. عَجْزٌ be weak, unable.

عَجِبَ عَجَبٌ and V wonder.

فَرَغَ u.a. فَرِغَ فُرُوغٌ be empty.

عَدِمَ عَدَمٌ be without, not to have.

بين II explain.

رَوِىَ رِىٌّ be satisfied with drink.

عَذَرَ i. عُذْرٌ excuse, accept an excuse.

نَصِيرٌ helper.

عَطْشَانُ thirsty.

رَائِحَةٌ scent.

عُرْيَانٌ naked.

حُمْقٌ folly.

عَطِشَ عَطَشٌ thirst.

IV weaken, incapacitate.

IV please.

II empty.

غَفَلَ u. غُفُولٌ neglect.

شَمَّ u. شَمٌّ smell.

امر VIII consult together.

حُرٌّ freeborn.

VIII excuse oneself.

مَوْلًى master, servant, freedman, cousin.

غَلِيظٌ rough, difficult.

أَحْمَقُ foolish.

فُرْصَةٌ opportunity.

Exercise 67

إِيَّاكُمْ وَمَسْأَلَةَ ٱلنَّاسِ فَإِنَّهَا آخِرُ كَسْبِ ٱلرَّجُلِ ـ
مَا أَشَدَّ مَا يَغْتَسِلُ ـ نَسْأَلُكَ بِٱللّٰهِ إِلَّا حَفِظْتَ فِينَا
وَصِيَّةَ رَسُولِ ٱللّٰهِ ـ بِئْسَ مَا ٱئْتَمَرُوا ـ اِعْلَمُوا أَنَّ
ٱللّٰهَ مَوْلَاكُمْ نِعْمَ ٱلْمَوْلَى وَنِعْمَ ٱلنَّصِيرُ ـ يَا مُصْعَبَ
ٱلْخَيْرِ ٱلْكَرِيمِ جُدُودُهُ ـ مَا أَغْفَلَهَا عَمَّا يَخُصُّ
نَفْسَهَا وَمَا أَشْغَلَهَا بِمَا يَخُصُّ غَيْرَهَا ـ مَا أَعْطَشَ
ٱلْوَلَدَ عَجَزْتُ عَنْ إِرْوَائِهِ ـ إِيَّاكُمْ وَٱلَّذِينَ يَعْتَذِرُونَ ـ
أَقْسَمْتُ أَيْمَانًا غَلِيظَةً لَا عَطِشَ مَا دُمْتُ حَيًّا ـ
أَعْجَزَنِي عَنْ إِعَانَتِهِ أَنِّي عَدِمْتُ ٱلْمَالَ وَٱلْفُرْصَةَ .

68

what a fine swimmer that boy is — what a liar he is! and the wonder is that every one believes him — how thirsty the child is! I filled three cups of milk for him and he emptied the lot — how quickly the enemy come upon us — when the waters were cut off from them they said, you have destroyed us. He said, you have reached the water, how near you are to it — you are a bad husband for a freeborn woman — by him in whose hand is my soul, he shall sleep naked in the snow — by the lord of the Kaaba, explain to me your letter — by God, the slayer of a Muslim shall not smell the scent of paradise — I must let you know that you are the fool not I.

LESSON 35

CIRCUMSTANTIAL CLAUSES, ETC.

An attendant circumstance may be expressed by one word in the accusative (Lesson 15) or by a clause (Lesson 8). This clause may refer to any part of the main sentence; the noun to which it refers is usually definite. The clause may be linked up by a pronoun, by 'and', or by both.

نَهَضَ مَحْمُودٌ لِلسَّفَرِ وَٱلْمَطَرُ وَاقِعٌ

Mahmud stood up (started) on the journey while rain was falling.

رَأَيْتُ خَالِدًا عَصَاهُ فِى يَدِهِ

I saw Khalid with his stick in his hand.

خَرَجُوا مِنْ دِيَارِهِمْ وَهُمْ أُلُوفٌ

They came out of their tents in their thousands.

Attraction can occur:

صَعِدَ مَسْلَمَةُ فِى ٱلسَّطْحِ بَاكِيًا أَبُوهُ

Maslama went up to the roof while his father was crying.

Indirect speech.

There is little indirect speech as there are no tenses. Pronouns and verbs may be put in the third person, but there is often a mixture of direct and indirect speech.

أَمَرَهُ أَنِ ٱبْنِ جِسْرًا امره أَنْ يَبْنِىَ جِسْرًا	he told him to build a bridge.

كَتَبَ إِلَى عُمَرَ أَنَّ سَعْدًا ٱسْتَعْمَلَهُ عَلَى جِبَايَةِ ٱلْخَرَاجِ وَقَدْ أَحْبَبْتُ ٱلْجِهَادَ

he wrote to Umar that Saad had appointed him (the writer) to collect the tribute but I wanted to go to the front.

There is no change in an indirect question.

أُسَائِلُكُمْ هَلْ يَقْتُلُ ٱلرَّجُلَ ٱلْحُبُّ

I ask you if love kills a man.

Alternative sentences.

أَوْ or. Used in statements and question ; it need not be repeated.

إِمَّا — إِمَّا either — or. Used in statement or question. The clauses may be treated as parts of conditional sentences.

أَمْ or. Used only in questions preceded by أَ or هَلْ .

أَخَدِيجَةُ عِنْدَكِ أَمْ فَاطِمَةُ

is Khadija with you or Faṭima?

The answer to the question must be one of the two names.

Words construed like إِنَّ.

فَإِنَّ ـ لِأَنَّ (لِئَنَّ) for, because.

لٰكِنَّ but. The shortened form لٰكِنْ makes no change in the following sentence.

لَيْتَ would that. Common is لَيْتَ شِعْرِى would that I knew.

Genitive.

رُبَّ many a . . . is followed by an indefinite noun in the genitive singular and may be continued by any sort of sentence.

رُبَّ اُمْرَأَةٍ عَارِيَةٍ فِى ٱلدُّنْيَا كَاسِيَةٌ فِى ٱلْآخِرَةِ

many a woman naked in this world is clothed in the next.

Note that an active participle is sometimes used where a passive would be expected.

وَ with the genitive is used in the same way.

Emphasis.

أَمَّا . . . . فَ أَمَّا is followed by a nominative

absolute and the sentence is introduced by فَ . It may be translated 'as for'.

أَمَّا ٱلسَّفِينَةُ فَكَانَتْ لِمَسَاكِينَ يَعْمَلُونَ فِى ٱلْبَحْرِ

as for the ship, it belonged to poor men who worked on the sea.

Subjunctive.

When the main clause says that an event may happen, a subordinate clause describing a consequence of it is introduced by فَ or وَ with the subjunctive.

لَيْتَ لِى مَالًا فَأَتَصَدَّقَ بِهِ

would that I had money so that I might give it in alms.

أَوْ 'unless,' 'until' is followed by the subjunctive.

مَا.

This can be added to a number of words without changing their meaning, e.g. بَيْنَمَا while ; أَيْنَمَا wherever.

أَنَّمَا does not govern the accusative.

It can also be added to nouns in any case to make them more indefinite.

مِنْ لَوْنٍ مَا of some colour or other.

Vocabulary 35

عَمَلَ عَمِلَ do, make, be a governor.

بَدَلَ u. بَدْلٌ change, exchange.

قَصَرَ u. قُصُورٌ be inadequate.

خَلَا u. خَلَاءٌ be empty, pass away.

شَكَلَ u. شَكْلٌ and IV be involved, difficult.

فَضَلَ u. فَضْلٌ be in excess.

حَدَاثَةٌ newness, youth.

عَهْدٌ (b) agreement, treaty, time, period.

نُورٌ (a) light.

ذَخِيرَةٌ stores, treasure.

X appoint, use.

عَمَلٌ (a) work, list.

مِنْشَفَةٌ towel.

هَضَمَ i. هَضْمٌ digest.

II make empty, leave.

مَلَكَ i. مُلْكٌ possess, be king.

نشف II make dry.

فَضِلَ u. be excellent.

دَهْرٌ epoch, age, time, fate.

صَحْرَاءُ (صَحَارٍ) desert.

عَامِلٌ workman, governor.

خَلْوَةٌ private place, privacy.

قَدَرٌ God's decree, providence.

Exercise 69

لا أَدْخُلُ وَلَا أَنْصَرِفُ أَوْ تَرْكَبَ إِلَى ٱلْمَسْجِدِ ـ إِمَّا أَنَا أَسِيرُ إِلَى ٱلشَّأْمِ فَمَا أَكْرَهُهُ وَإِمَّا أَنْ أُقِيمَ فَلِي فِيهِ أَجْرٌ ـ نَزْعَمُ أَنَّ تَفَاضُلَ ٱلنَّاسِ فِيمَا بَيْنَهُمْ لَيْسَ بِآبَائِهِمْ وَلٰكِنَّهُ بِأَفْعَالِهِمْ وَأَخْلَاقِهِمْ وَشَرَفِ نَفْسِهِمْ

وَبُعْدِ هِمَمِهِمْ ـ تَقُولُ ٱلْعَرَبُ لِمَنْ سُئِلَ وَهُوَ لَا يَقْدِرُ
فَرَدَّ بَيْتِي يَبْخَلُ لَا أَنَا ـ خَلَوْتُ بِهَا وَٱلْقَمَرُ يُرِينِيهَا
فَلَمَّا غَابَ أَرَتْنِيهِ ـ لَا تَقُلْ فِيمَا لَا تَعْلَمُ فَتُتَّهَمَ فِيمَا
تَعْلَمُ ـ لَا تَنْهَ عَنْ خُلُقٍ وَتَأْتِيَ مِثْلَهُ ـ لَا تَرْضَى
ٱلْعَرَبُ أَنْ يَسْتَعْمِلُوكَ وَأَنْتَ مِنْ غَيْرِهِمْ ـ هٰذَا ٱلشِّعْرُ
شَيْءٌ كَانَ فِي ٱلْحَدَاثَةِ قُلْتُهُ فِي زَوْجَتِي وَكُنْتُ إِلَيْهَا
مَائِلًا وَكَانَتْ لِي مَمْلُوكَةً وَلِقَلْبِي مَالِكَةً فَأَمَّا
ٱلْآنَ فَلَا عَهْدَ لِي بِمِثْلِهِ مُنْذُ سِنِينَ وَلَا عَمِلْتُ شِعْرًا
مُنْذُ دَهْرٍ طَوِيلٍ.

70

would that my mother had not borne me and I had not seen the light of day — I was in hiding in her house and she came up to me every day to ask me what I wanted — he swore that he would not change this shirt unless he had finished the business of the man who had abused him — letters came to Mahmud when he was governor of Syria to collect us in the mosque and we should stop there till he had satisfied us — many who eat gratefully have a greater reward than those who fast — he told the girl to wash the clothes and dry them thoroughly — many a desert have I crossed, many a treasure discovered, and many a difficulty solved — he asked me how old I was — would that you could go in, salute the prince, and tell him the truth of the affair so that his anger against us might cease — eat slowly so that you may digest the food thoroughly.

LESSON 36

PREPOSITIONS ; CALENDAR

مِنْ (originally a noun ' part ') from, of, than.

بَاعَ مِنْهُ he sold to him ; قَالَ مِنْهُمْ some of them said.

عَنْ from (often in the realm of ideas).

اَلْهَرَبُ عَنْ قَضَاءِ ٱللّٰهِ flight from God's decree.

قَالَ مَاقَالَ عَنْ حَسَدٍ he said what he said out of envy.

سَأَلَ عَنْهُ he asked about it.

إِلَى to, towards.

حَتَّى to, even. It cannot take suffixes.

أَكَلْتُ ٱلسَّمَكَةَ حَتَّى رَأْسِهَا

I ate the fish up to the head.

اكلت السمكة حتّى رَأْسَهَا

I ate the fish, even the head (it has no governing power).

لِ to, for, belonging to.

فِى in, concerning.

قُتِلَ كُلَيْبٌ فِى نَاقَةٍ Kulaib was killed for a she-camel.

ثَلَاثَةٌ فِى خَمْسَةٍ three multiplied by five.

بِ by, at, in, with (instrumental).

جَآءَ بِهِ he brought it.

اَلْمَعْرُوفُ بِأَبِى ٱلْحَسَنِ the man known as Abu l-Hasan.

أَرَغِبْتَ بِى عَنْهَا

do you take pleasure in me from her = do you think me too good for her?

مَعَ with (accompaniment).

عَلَى upon, on account of, in spite of, against. (In Arabic you are always on a condition.)

عَلَى ٱلْفَقْرِ in poverty.

عَلَى ٱلرِّيقِ on the spittle = on an empty stomach.

لِي عَلَيْهِ دَيْنٌ to me on him a debt = he owes me money.

مُنْذُ since, for (time). It takes the nominative, genitive, or a sentence.

مُنْذُ يَوْمَانِ ـ منذ يَوْمَيْنِ for two days.

منذ يَوْمُ ٱلْجُمُعَةِ ـ منذ يَوْمِ الجمعة since Friday.

مُنْذُ خَلِقَ since he was created (born).

The following are really nouns in the accusative ; many can be combined with مِنْ and are put in the genitive, unlike the corresponding adverbs.

نَحْوَ towards, according, about (not of place).

نَحْوَ قَوْلِهِ according to his saying (or, his ideas).

نَحْوَ عِشْرِينَ about twenty.

عِنْدَ beside, in the opinion of.

بَيْنَ between (usually repeated).

بَيْنِى وَبَيْنَهُ between me and him.

اِقْتَتَلُوا فِيمَا بَيْنَهُمْ they fought each other.

تَحْتَ under.

فَوْقَ over, above.

دُونَ below, between (as being an obstacle to the meeting of two things).

دُونَ ٱلْجَبَلِ at the foot of the mountain.

قَاتَلَ دُونَهُمْ he fought in defence of them.

هٰذَا دُونَ ذٰلِكَ this is less than that.

هٰذَا لِى دُونَكَ this is mine not yours.

قَبْلَ before (time). قُبَيْلَ a little before.

بَعْدَ after (time).

قُدَّامَ ـ أَمَامَ before (place).

وَرَاءَ behind (place).

حَوَالَى ـ حَوْلَ around (place).

قِبَلَ (usually مِنْ قِبَلِ) in possession of.

عَامِلٌ مِنْ قِبَلِ ٱلْخَلِيفَةِ

a governor representing the caliph.

مَنْ مِنْ قِبَلِكَ your subordinates.

Many prepositions can be turned into conjunctions by joining them to أَنْ ; e.g. الى ان until.

Calendar.

Days of the week.

يَوْمُ ٱلْأَحَدِ Sunday

يَوْمُ ٱلِاثْنَيْنِ Monday

يَوْمُ ٱلثَّلَاثَاءِ Tuesday

يَوْمُ ٱلْأَرْبَعَاءِ Wednesday

يَوْمُ ٱلْخَمِيسِ Thursday

يَوْمُ ٱلْجُمُعَةِ Friday

يَوْمُ السَّبْتِ Saturday

Syrian Christian months.

كَانُونُ ٱلثَّانِي	January	تَمُّوزُ	July
شُبَاطٌ	February	آبُ	August
أَذَارٌ	March	أَيْلُولٌ	September
نِيسَانٌ	April	تِشْرِينُ ٱلأَوَّلُ	October
أَيَّارٌ	May	تِشْرِينُ ٱلثَّانِي	November
حَزِيرَانٌ	June	كَانُونُ ٱلأَوَّلُ	December

The Muslim year is lunar and has twelve months of alternately 29 and 30 days. The era begins from A.D. 621, the year of the prophet's removal from Mecca — ٱلْهِجْرَةُ.

Names of the months.

1	مُحَرَّمٌ	5	جُمَادَى ٱلْأُولَى	9	رَمَضَانُ
2	صَفَرٌ	6	جُمَادَى ٱلْآخِرَةُ	10	شَوَّالٌ
3	رَبِيعُ ٱلْأَوَّلُ	7	رَجَبٌ	11	ذُو ٱلْقَعْدَةِ
4	رَبِيعُ ٱلْآخِرُ	8	شَعْبَانُ	12	ذُو ٱلْحِجَّةِ

The usual way of dating within the month is by counting the first half from the beginning and the second half from the end. Rajab has 30 days :—

on the 1st.

غُرَّةَ رَجَبٍ ـ لِغُرَّةِ رَجَبٍ ـ لِأَوَّلِ لَيْلَةٍ مِنْ رَجَبٍ ـ

لليلة خَلَتْ [مَضَتْ] مِنْ رَجَبٍ ـ لِمُسْتَهَلِّ رَجَبٍ

on the 2nd.

لِلَيْلَتَيْنِ خَلَتَا من رجب

on the 3rd.

لِثَلَاثٍ خَلَوْنَ [لِثَلَاثِ لَيَالٍ مَضَيْنَ] من رجب

on the 20th.

لِعَشْرٍ بَقِينَ من رجب

on the 30th.

لِسَلْخِ رَجَبٍ ـ لِآخِرِ لَيْلَةٍ من رجب

Note.—غُرَّةٌ blaze on a horse's forehead.

مُسْتَهَلٌّ from هِلَالٌ new moon.

سَلَخَ skin.

Vocabulary 36

حَسَبَ u. حِسَابٌ count

حَضَرَ u. حُضُورٌ be present.

جَرَى i. جَرَيَانٌ run, flow.

زَهِدَ زُهْدٌ leave, be content with little, be ascetic.

شَهَا شَهْوَةٌ and VIII desire.

نَجَا نَجَاةٌ be safe, escape.

غنى IV make rich and independent, enable one to dispense with; (with negative) be useless in the face of.

عَصَى عِصْيَانٌ disobey.

نَفَقَةٌ expenditure.

صِنَاعَةٌ handicraft, skill.

خَلَقٌ old, worn out.

ضِعْفٌ (a) equal.

دِيوَانٌ (دَوَاوِينُ) ministry of state, register, collected works of a poet.

دَخْلٌ revenue.

حَسِبَ i. حِسْبَانٌ think.

جَادَ u. جُودَةٌ be generous.

حَذِرَ حَذَرٌ be on one's guard, be cautious.

قدر II estimate, imagine.

عزو II console, condole.

نَقَصَ u. نُقْصَانٌ be diminished, imperfect.

جَوَادٌ liberal; swift horse.

حَلِيفٌ ally.

قِدْرٌ (fem.) (b) cooking pot.

مَحَبَّةٌ love.

خَرْجٌ expenditure.

Exercise 71

إِنِّى أُحِبُّكَ لِنَفْسِكَ فَوْقَ مَحَبَّتِى إِيَّاكَ لِنَفْسِى۔
كَيْفَ تَجِدُكَ قَالَ أَجِدُنِى أَجِدُ مَا لَا أَشْتَهِى وَأَشْتَهِى
مَا لَا أَجِدُ لَقَدْ أَصْبَحْتُ فِى شَرِّ زَمَانٍ وَشَرِّ نَاسٍ

مَنْ جَادَ لَمْ يَجِدْ وَمَنْ وَجَدَ لَمْ يَجُدْ ـ قَدْ أَغْنَاكَ ٱللهُ بِٱلْعُذْرِ مِنَّا عَنِ ٱلْاعْتِذَارِ وَأَغْنَانَا ٱللهُ بِٱلْمَحَبَّةِ لَكَ عَنْ سُوءِ ٱلظَّنِّ بِكَ ـ إِلَى مَنْ أَوْصَى بِكَ أَبُوكَ قَالَ أَوْصَى إِلَيَّ وَلَمْ يُوصِ بِي ـ يَا جَوَادَ ٱللِّسَانِ مِنْ غَيْرِ فِعْلٍ لَيْتَ جُودَ ٱللِّسَانِ فِي يَدَيْكَ ـ لٰكِنَّ ٱللهَ نَجَّانِي بِكَ وَمَا عَزَّانِي أَحَدٌ بِأَنْفَعَ مِنْ تَعْزِيَتِكَ ـ أَرْضِ أَخِي وَحَلِيفِي ٱلَّذَيْنِ ٱشْتَرَكَا فِي أَسْرِ ٱلْأَسِيرِ ـ أَرَادَ سُلْطَانٌ بِنَاءَ قَصْرٍ وَقَدَّرَ لِذٰلِكَ أُلُوفَ أُلُوفِ دِرْهَمٍ وَزَادَتِ ٱلنَّفَقَةُ عَلَى ٱلتَّقْدِيرِ أَضْعَافًا وَكَانَ يُطَالِبُ وَزِيرَهُ بِتَوْجِيهِ ٱلْأَمْوَالِ لِذٰلِكَ مَعَ قُصُورِ ٱلدَّخْلِ مِنَ ٱلْخَرْجِ ـ كَانَ يَعْمِدُ إِلَى مَنْ يَبِيعُ فِي ٱلْأَسْوَاقِ مِثْلَ قِدْرٍ وَقَمِيصٍ خَلَقٍ وَمَا يَغْلِبُ عَلَى ٱلظَّنِّ أَنَّ مِثْلَهُ لَا يُبَاعُ إِلَّا مِنْ ضَرٍّ شَدِيدٍ وَإِلَى ٱمْرَأَةٍ تَبِيعُ غَزْلَهَا عَجُوزٍ فَيُعْطِيهِمْ أَضْعَافَ ثَمَنِهِ وَيَدَعُهُ عَلَيْهِمْ.

72

I do not know a value for these pieces of cloth and have never seen the like of them ; had I not actually seen them I should not have believed that their like existed ; were I to say that the price of each one is 100,000 dinars I should not fear being far wrong — by God, it was not in me to give her except 200 dirhams but God sent to her by my hand 200 dinars and I shall not go back on this ; give her — the minister despised the head of the ministry of finance (tribute), and when he wanted some statement or account from the ministry, he neglected the head, summoned the clerks and asked their advice in the head's presence ; when he wanted a statement which, he knew, the head's skill was not equal to, and about which he could not speak, he discussed it with him in the presence of others to make his insufficiency plain — the prophet said of women, consult them and oppose them (do the opposite). I disobeyed him and obeyed my wife ; I bought a slave and he became a thief — caution is useless in face of (does not dispense with) providence — what is asceticism in the world ? he said that what is forbidden does not overcome your patience and what is allowed your thankfulness — teach my sons swimming before writing ; for they can find one to write for them and cannot find one to swim for them.

CONCLUSION

It is important to remember that Arabic is essentially simple however complicated it may be on the surface. When the meaning of a passage is not obvious at the first glance, make a literal translation giving each word its simplest meaning ; then this crude English will usually suggest the right sense. A chronicler writes :—

ثُمَّ دَخَلَتْ سَنَةُ ٢٤٦ وَلَمْ يَجْرِ فِيهَا شَىْءٌ يُكْتَبُ

then came in the year 246 and a thing which is written did not run in it ; this explains itself.

Some phrases have exact parallels in English; 'he came out against the government' is quite general while 'he came out in '45' is particular.

For further study Wright's grammar (two vols.) is indispensable. That is the only definite recommendation which can be made at present; the good books are out of print and too expensive or come from abroad and cannot be got. There is no satisfactory dictionary; an old copy of Hava's Arabic-English can be recommended but not one of the newer reprints which are smudged.[1] Apart from this, the two volumes by Elias, Arabic-English and English-Arabic, are the most useful. The price of each volume to-day is probably over one pound. There is a smaller edition of the Arabic-English but the type is small.

Nicholson's series of readers (Cambridge University Press) is the best introduction to classical Arabic and each of the three books has a vocabulary. In spite of its name, it is probably better to begin with the second reader. The history entitled *al-Fakhri* is a fairly easy book, but the first chapter on politics should be left to the last. There is a French translation. The beginner should avoid the *Koran* although it can be bought cheaply and translations (Rodwell, Palmer) are available. The oriental editions are lithographed and are not easy to read; the matter is often difficult because it is the record of the spoken word without the help of tone and gesture to make it intelligible. Consequently it is not typical of Arabic prose.

The *Arabian Nights* (Beirut, five vols.; volumes can be had separately) is a good stand-by; no translation corresponds exactly to this text. For modern Arabic any volume of Mahmud Taimur's stories can be recommended. *al-Ayyam* by Taha Husain, the story of the blind professor's childhood, is good reading and there is a translation, *An Egyptian Childhood* by Paxton.

Daily papers are hard to read when they have been folded. The Egyptian illustrated *al-muṣawwir* caters for various interests.

[1] A new edition is just out, clear and legible.

TABLE 1

STRONG VERB—STEM 1—ACTIVE

	Perfect	Imperfect Indicative	Imperfect Subjunctive	Imperfect Jussive	Imperfect Energetic	Imperative
sing.						
3 m.	كَتَبَ	يَكْتُبُ	يَكْتُبَ	يَكْتُبْ	يَكْتُبَنَّ	
f.	كَتَبَتْ	تَكْتُبُ	تَكْتُبَ	تَكْتُبْ	تَكْتُبَنَّ	
2 m.	كَتَبْتَ	تَكْتُبُ	تَكْتُبَ	تَكْتُبْ	تَكْتُبَنَّ	اُكْتُبْ
f.	كَتَبْتِ	تَكْتُبِينَ	تَكْتُبِي	تَكْتُبِي	تَكْتُبِنَّ	اُكْتُبِي
1 c.	كَتَبْتُ	أَكْتُبُ	أَكْتُبَ	أَكْتُبْ	أَكْتُبَنَّ	
dual						
3 m.	كَتَبَا	يَكْتُبَانِ	يَكْتُبَا	يَكْتُبَا	يَكْتُبَانِّ	

f.	كَتَبَتَا	تَكْتُبَانِ	تَكْتُبَا	تَكْتُبَا	تَكْتُبَانِّ	
2 c.	كَتَبْتُمَا	تَكْتُبَانِ	تَكْتُبَا	تَكْتُبَا	تَكْتُبَانِّ	اُكْتُبَا
pl.						
3 m.	كَتَبُوا	يَكْتُبُونَ	يَكْتُبُوا	يَكْتُبُوا	يَكْتُبُنَّ	
f.	كَتَبْنَ	يَكْتُبْنَ	يَكْتُبْنَ	يَكْتُبْنَ	يَكْتُبْنَانِّ	
2 m.	كَتَبْتُمْ	تَكْتُبُونَ	تَكْتُبُوا	تَكْتُبُوا	تَكْتُبُنَّ	اُكْتُبُوا
f.	كَتَبْتُنَّ	تَكْتُبْنَ	تَكْتُبْنَ	تَكْتُبْنَ	تَكْتُبْنَانِّ	اُكْتُبْنَ
1 c.	كَتَبْنَا	نَكْتُبُ	نَكْتُبَ	نَكْتُبْ	نَكْتُبَنَّ	

Active participle كَاتِبٌ.

TABLE 2
STRONG VERB—DERIVED STEMS

Active	II	III	IV	V	VI
Perf.	كَتَّبَ	كَاتَبَ	أَكْتَبَ	تَكَتَّبَ	تَكَاتَبَ
Imperf.	يُكَتِّبُ	يُكَاتِبُ	يُكْتِبُ	يَتَكَتَّبُ	يَتَكَاتَبُ
Imp.	كَتِّبْ	كَاتِبْ	أَكْتِبْ	تَكَتَّبْ	تَكَاتَبْ
Part.	مُكَتِّبٌ	مُكَاتِبٌ	مُكْتِبٌ	مُتَكَتِّبٌ	مُتَكَاتِبٌ
Inf.	تَكْتِيبٌ	كِتَابٌ	إِكْتَابٌ	تَكَتُّبٌ	تَكَاتُبٌ
	تَكْتِبَةٌ	مُكَاتَبَةٌ			
Passive					
Perf.	كُتِّبَ	كُوتِبَ	أُكْتِبَ	تُكُتِّبَ	تُكُوتِبَ
Imperf.	يُكَتَّبُ	يُكَاتَبُ	يُكْتَبُ	يُتَكَتَّبُ	يُتَكَاتَبُ

Part.	مُكَتَّبٌ	مُكَاتَبٌ	مُكْتَبٌ	مُتَكَتَّبٌ	مُتَكَاتَبٌ
Active	VII	VIII	IX	X	XI
Perf.	اِنْكَتَبَ	اِكْتَتَبَ	اِحْمَرَّ	اِسْتَكْتَبَ	اِحْمَارَّ
Imperf.	يَنْكَتِبُ	يَكْتَتِبُ	يَحْمَرُّ	يَسْتَكْتِبُ	يَحْمَارُّ
Imp.	اِنْكَتِبْ	اِكْتَتِبْ	اِحْمَرِرْ	اِسْتَكْتِبْ	اِحْمَارِرْ
Part.	مُنْكَتِبٌ	مُكْتَتِبٌ	مُحْمَرٌّ	مُسْتَكْتِبٌ	مُحْمَارٌّ
Inf.	اِنْكِتَابٌ	اِكْتِتَابٌ	اِحْمِرَارٌ	اِسْتِكْتَابٌ	اِحْمِيرَارٌ
Passive					
Perf.	اُنْكُتِبَ	اُكْتُتِبَ		اُسْتُكْتِبَ	
Imperf.	يُنْكَتَبُ	يُكْتَتَبُ		يُسْتَكْتَبُ	
Part.	مُنْكَتَبٌ	مُكْتَتَبٌ		مُسْتَكْتَبٌ	

TABLE 3

STRONG VERB—STEM 1—PASSIVE

	Perfect	Imperfect Indicative	Imperfect Subjunctive	Imperfect Jussive
sing.				
3 m.	كُتِبَ	يُكْتَبُ	يُكْتَبَ	يُكْتَبْ
f.	كُتِبَتْ	تُكْتَبُ	تُكْتَبَ	تُكْتَبْ
2 m.	كُتِبْتَ	تُكْتَبُ	تُكْتَبَ	تُكْتَبْ
f.	كُتِبْتِ	تُكْتَبِينَ	تُكْتَبِى	تُكْتَبِى
1 c.	كُتِبْتُ	أُكْتَبُ	أُكْتَبَ	أُكْتَبْ
dual				
3 m.	كُتِبَا	يُكْتَبَانِ	يُكْتَبَا	يُكْتَبَا

f.	كُتِبَتَا	تُكْتَبَانِ	تُكْتَبَا	تُكْتَبَا
2 c.	كُتِبْتُمَا	تُكْتَبَانِ	تُكْتَبَا	تُكْتَبَا
pl.				
3 m.	كُتِبُوا	يُكْتَبُونَ	يُكْتَبُوا	يُكْتَبُوا
f.	كُتِبْنَ	يُكْتَبْنَ	يُكْتَبْنَ	يُكْتَبْنَ
2 m.	كُتِبْتُمْ	تُكْتَبُونَ	تُكْتَبُوا	تُكْتَبُوا
f.	كُتِبْتُنَّ	تُكْتَبْنَ	تُكْتَبْنَ	تُكْتَبْنَ
1 c.	كُتِبْنَا	نُكْتَبُ	نُكْتَبَ	نُكْتَبْ

Passive participle مَكْتُوبٌ.

TABLE 4

HOLLOW VERB—MIDDLE W—STEM 1

	Perfect	Imperfect Indicative	Subjunctive	Jussive	Energetic	Imperative
sing.						
3 m.	كَانَ	يَكُونُ	يَكُونَ	يَكُنْ	يَكُونَنَّ	
f.	كَانَتْ	تَكُونُ	تَكُونَ	تَكُنْ	تَكُونَنَّ	
2 m.	كُنْتَ	تَكُونُ	تَكُونَ	تَكُنْ	تَكُونَنَّ	كُنْ
f.	كُنْتِ	تَكُونِينَ	تَكُونِي	تَكُونِي	تَكُونِنَّ	كُونِي
1 c.	كُنْتُ	أَكُونُ	أَكُونَ	أَكُنْ	أَكُونَنَّ	
dual						
3 m.	كَانَا	يَكُونَانِ	يَكُونَا	يَكُونَا	يَكُونَانِّ	

f.	كَانَتَا	تَكُونَانِ	تَكُونَا	تَكُونَا	تَكُونَانِّ	
2 c.	كُنْتُمَا	تَكُونَانِ	تَكُونَا	تَكُونَا	تَكُونَانِّ	كُونَا
pl.						
3 m.	كَانُوا	يَكُونُونَ	يَكُونُوا	يَكُونُوا	يَكُونُنَّ	
f.	كُنَّ	يَكُنَّ	يَكُنَّ	يَكُنَّ	يَكُنَّانِّ	
2 m.	كُنْتُمْ	تَكُونُونَ	تَكُونُوا	تَكُونُوا	تَكُونُنَّ	كُونُوا
f.	كُنْتُنَّ	تَكُنَّ	تَكُنَّ	تَكُنَّ	تَكُنَّانِّ	كُنَّ
1 c.	كُنَّا	نَكُونُ	نَكُونَ	نَكُنْ	نَكُونَنَّ	

Active participle كَائِنٌ.

TABLE 5

HOLLOW VERB—MIDDLE Y—STEM I

	Perfect	Imperfect: Indicative	Imperfect: Subjunctive	Imperfect: Jussive	Imperfect: Energetic	Imperative
sing.						
3 m.	سَارَ	يَسِيرُ	يَسِيرَ	يَسِرْ	يَسِيرَنَّ	
f.	سَارَتْ	تَسِيرُ	تَسِيرَ	تَسِرْ	تَسِيرَنَّ	
2 m.	سِرْتَ	تَسِيرُ	تَسِيرَ	تَسِرْ	تَسِيرَنَّ	سِرْ
f.	سِرْتِ	تَسِيرِينَ	تَسِيرِى	تَسِيرِى	تَسِيرِنَّ	سِيرِى
1 c.	سِرْتُ	أَسِيرُ	أَسِيرَ	أَسِرْ	أَسِيرَنَّ	

Active participle سَائِرٌ.

MIDDLE W OR Y—INTRANSITIVE FORM

	Perfect	Imperfect: Indicative	Subjunctive	Jussive	Energetic	Imperative
sing.						
3 m.	نَامَ	يَنَامُ	يَنَامَ	يَنَمْ	يَنَامَنَّ	
f.	نَامَتْ	تَنَامُ	تَنَامَ	تَنَمْ	تَنَامَنَّ	
2 m.	نِمْتَ	تَنَامُ	تَنَامَ	تَنَمْ	تَنَامَنَّ	نَمْ
f.	نِمْتِ	تَنَامِينَ	تَنَامِي	تَنَامِي	تَنَامِنَّ	نَامِي
1 c.	نِمْتُ	أَنَامُ	أَنَامَ	أَنَمْ	أَنَامَنَّ	

Active participle نَائِمٌ.

TABLE 6

HOLLOW VERBS W OR Y—DERIVED STEMS

Active	IV	VII	VIII	X
Perf.				
3 s. m.	أَقَامَ	اِنْقَادَ	اِخْتَارَ	اِسْتَقَامَ
2 s. m.	أَقَمْتَ	اِنْقَدْتَ	اِخْتَرْتَ	اِسْتَقَمْتَ
Imperf.	يُقِيمُ	يَنْقَادُ	يَخْتَارُ	يَسْتَقِيمُ
Imp.	أَقِمْ	اِنْقَدْ	اِخْتَرْ	اِسْتَقِمْ
Part.	مُقِيمٌ	مُنْقَادٌ	مُخْتَارٌ	مُسْتَقِيمٌ
Inf.	إِقَامَةٌ	اِنْقِيَادٌ	اِخْتِيَارٌ	اِسْتِقَامَةٌ
Passive				
Perf.	أُقِيمَ	اُنْقِيدَ	اُخْتِيرَ	اُسْتُقِيمَ

Imperf.	يُقَامُ	يُنْقَادُ	يُخْتَارُ	يُسْتَقَامُ
Part.	مُقَامٌ	مُنْقَادٌ	مُخْتَارٌ	مُسْتَقَامٌ

STEM 1—PASSIVE

	Perfect	Imperfect Indicative	Imperfect Subjunctive	Imperfect Jussive
sing.				
3 m.	قِيلَ	يُقَالُ	يُقَالَ	يُقَلْ
2 f.	قِلْتِ	تُقَالِينَ	تُقَالِى	تُقَالِى
pl.				
3 f.	قِلْنَ	يُقَلْنَ	يُقَلْنَ	يُقَلْنَ
2 m.	قِلْتُمْ	تُقَالُونَ	تُقَالُوا	تُقَالُوا

TABLE 7

VERBS FIRST W AND Y

Active	IV		VIII		X	
Perf.	أَوْعَدَ	أَيْسَرَ	اِتَّعَدَ	اِتَّسَرَ	اِسْتَوْعَدَ	اِسْتَيْسَرَ
Imperf.	يُوعِدُ	يُوسِرُ	يَتَّعِدُ	يَتَّسِرُ	يَسْتَوْعِدُ	يَسْتَيْسِرُ
Imp.	أَوْعِدْ	أَيْسِرْ	اِتَّعِدْ	اِتَّسِرْ	اِسْتَوْعِدْ	اِسْتَيْسِرْ
Part.	مُوعِدٌ	مُوسِرٌ	مُتَّعِدٌ	مُتَّسِرٌ	مُسْتَوْعِدٌ	مُسْتَيْسِرٌ
Inf.	إِيعَادٌ	إِيسَارٌ	اِتِّعَادٌ	اِتِّسَارٌ	اِسْتِيعَادٌ	اِسْتِيسَارٌ
Passive						
Perf.	أُوعِدَ	أُوسِرَ	اُتُّعِدَ	اُتُّسِرَ	اُسْتُوعِدَ	اُسْتُوسِرَ

Imperf.	يُوعَدُ	يُوسَرُ	يُتَّعَدُ	يُتَّسَرُ	يُسْتَوْعَدُ	يُسْتَيْسَرُ
Part.	مُوعَدٌ	مُوسَرٌ	مُتَّعَدٌ	مُتَّسَرٌ	مُسْتَوْعَدٌ	مُسْتَيْسَرٌ

STEM I—PASSIVE

Perf.	وُعِدَ	يُسِرَ
Imperf.	يُوعَدُ	يُوسَرُ
Part.	مَوْعُودٌ	مَيْسُورٌ

TABLE 8

DOUBLED VERBS—STEM 1—ACTIVE

	Perfect	Imperfect Indicative	Imperfect Subjunctive	Imperfect Jussive	Imperative	
sing.						
3 m.	رَدَّ	يَرُدُّ	يَرُدَّ	يَرْدُدْ		
f.	رَدَّتْ	تَرُدُّ	تَرُدَّ	تَرْدُدْ		
2 m.	رَدَدْتَ	تَرُدُّ	تَرُدَّ	تَرْدُدْ	رُدَّ	اُرْدُدْ
f.	رَدَدْتِ	تَرُدِّينَ	تَرُدِّى	تَرُدِّى	رُدِّى	اُرْدُدِى
1 c.	رَدَدْتُ	أَرُدُّ	أَرُدَّ	أَرْدُدْ		
dual						
3 m.	رَدَّا	يَرُدَّانِ	يَرُدَّا	يَرُدَّا		
f.	رَدَّتَا	تَرُدَّانِ	تَرُدَّا	تَرُدَّا		
2 c.	رَدَدْتُمَا	تَرُدَّان	تَرُدَّا	تَرُدَّا	رُدَّا	اُرْدُدَا

pl.					
3 m.	رَدُّوا	يَرُدُّونَ	يَرُدُّوا	يَرُدُّوا	
f.	رَدَدْنَ	يَرْدُدْنَ	يَرْدُدْنَ	يَرْدُدْنَ	
2 m.	رَدَدْتُمْ	تَرُدُّونَ	تَرُدُّوا	تَرُدُّوا	رُدُّوا اُرْدُدُوا
f.	رَدَدْتُنَّ	تَرْدُدْنَ	تَرْدُدْنَ	تَرْدُدْنَ	اُرْدُدْنَ
1 c.	رَدَدْنَا	نَرُدُّ	نَرُدَّ	نَرْدُدْ	Active participle رَادٌّ.

PASSIVE

sing.					
3 m.	رُدَّ	يُرَدُّ	يُرَدَّ	يُرْدَدْ	
2 f.	رُدِدْتِ	تُرَدِّينَ	تُرَدِّي	تُرَدِّي	
pl.					
3 f.	رُدِدْنَ	يُرْدَدْنَ	يُرْدَدْنَ	يُرْدَدْنَ	Passive participle مَرْدُودٌ.

TABLE 9
DOUBLED VERB—DERIVED STEMS

Active	III	IV	VI	VII	VIII	X
Perf.	رَادَدَ ـ رَادَّ	أَرَدَّ	تَرَادَدَ ـ تَرَادَّ	اِنْرَدَّ	اِرْتَدَّ	اِسْتَرَدَّ
Imperf.	يُرَادُّ	يُرِدُّ	يَتَرَادُّ	يَنْرَدُّ	يَرْتَدُّ	يَسْتَرِدُّ
Imp.	رَادِدْ	أَرِدَّ أَرْدِدْ	تَرَادَدْ	اِنْرَدِدْ	اِرْتَدِدْ	اِسْتَرْدِدْ
					اِرْتَدَّ	اِسْتَرِدَّ
Part.	مُرَادٌّ	مُرِدٌّ	مُتَرَادٌّ	مُنْرَدٌّ	مُرْتَدٌّ	مُسْتَرِدٌّ
Inf.	رِدَادٌ	إِرْدَادٌ	تَرَادٌّ	اِنْرِدَادٌ	اِرْتِدَادٌ	اِسْتِرْدَادٌ
Passive						
Perf.	رُودِدَ	أُرِدَّ	تُرُودِدَ	اُنْرُدَّ	اُرْتُدَّ	اُسْتُرِدَّ
Imperf.	يُرَادُّ	يُرَدُّ	يُتَرَادُّ	يُنْرَدُّ	يُرْتَدُّ	يُسْتَرَدُّ

Part.	مُرَادٌّ	مُرَدٌّ	مُتَرَادٌّ	مُنْرَدٌّ	مُرْتَدٌّ	مُسْتَرَدٌّ

STRONG VERB—STEM IX

	Perfect			Imperfect		
	S	D	P	S	D	P
3 m.	اِحْمَرَّ	اِحْمَرَّا	اِحْمَرُّوا	يَحْمَرُّ	يَحْمَرَّانِ	يَحْمَرُّونَ
f.	اِحْمَرَّتْ	اِحْمَرَّتَا	اِحْمَرَرْنَ	تَحْمَرُّ	تَحْمَرَّانِ	يَحْمَرِرْنَ
2 m.	اِحْمَرَرْتَ	اِحْمَرَرْتُمَا	اِحْمَرَرْتُمْ	تَحْمَرُّ	تَحْمَرَّانِ	تَحْمَرُّونَ
f.	اِحْمَرَرْتِ		اِحْمَرَرْتُنَّ	تَحْمَرِّينَ		تَحْمَرِرْنَ
1 c.	اِحْمَرَرْتُ		اِحْمَرَرْنَا	أَحْمَرُّ		نَحْمَرُّ

Participle مُحْمَرٌّ. Infinitive اِحْمِرَارٌ.

TABLE 10
VERBS FIRST HAMZA

Active	I	II	III	IV
Perf.	أَثَرَ أَسَرَ	أَثَّرَ	آثَرَ	آثَرَ
Imperf.	يَأْثُرُ يَأْسِرُ	يُؤَثِّرُ	يُؤَاثِرُ	يُؤْثِرُ
Imp.	أُوثُرْ إِيسِرْ	أَثِّرْ	آثِرْ	آثِرْ
Part.	آسِرٌ	مُؤَثِّرٌ	مُؤَاثِرٌ	مُؤْثِرٌ
Inf.		تَأْثِيرٌ	إِثَارٌ مُؤَاثَرَةٌ	إِيثَارٌ
Passive				
Perf.	أُسِرَ	أُثِّرَ	أُوثِرَ	أُوثِرَ
Imperf.	يُؤْسَرُ	يُؤَثَّرُ	يُؤَاثَرُ	يُؤْثَرُ
Part.	مَأْسُورٌ	مُؤَثَّرٌ	مُؤَاثَرٌ	مُؤْثَرٌ

Active	V	VI	VIII	X
Perf.	تَأَثَّرَ	تَآثَرَ	اِيتَثَرَ	اِسْتَأْثَرَ
Imperf.	يَتَأَثَّرُ	يَتَآثَرُ	يَأْتَثِرُ	يَسْتَأْثِرُ
Imp.	تَأَثَّرْ	تَآثَرْ	اِيتَثِرْ	اِسْتَأْثِرْ
Part.	مُتَأَثِّرٌ	مُتَآثِرٌ	مُؤْتَثِرٌ	مُسْتَأْثِرٌ
Inf.	تَأَثُّرٌ	تَآثُرٌ	اِيتِثَارٌ	اِسْتِئْثَارٌ
Passive				
Perf.	تُؤُثِّرَ	تُوُثِرَ	أُوتُثِرَ	أُسْتُؤْثِرَ
Imperf.	يُتَأَثَّرُ	يُتَآثَرُ	يُؤْتَثَرُ	يُسْتَأْثَرُ
Part.	مُتَأَثَّرٌ	مُتَآثَرٌ	مُؤْتَثَرٌ	مُسْتَأْثَرٌ

TABLE 11

VERBS MIDDLE HAMZA

Active	I			II	III	V
Perf.	سَأَلَ	سَئِرَ	بَؤُسَ	لَأَّمَ	لَاءَمَ	تَلَأَّمَ
Imperf.	يَسْأَلُ	يَسْأَرُ	يَبْؤُسُ	يُلَئِّمُ	يُلَائِمُ	يَتَلَأَّمُ
	يَسْئَلُ	يَسْئَرُ				
Imp.	اِسْأَلْ	اِسْأَرْ	اُبْؤُسْ	لَئِّمْ	لَائِمْ	تَلَأَّمْ
	اِسْئَلْ	اِسْئَرْ				

Part.	سَائِلٌ	سَائِرٌ	بَائِسٌ	مُلْئِمٌ	مُلَائِمٌ	مُتَلَئِّمٌ
Inf.	سُؤَالٌ	سُؤْرٌ	بَأْسٌ	تَلْئِيمٌ	مُلَاءَمَةٌ	تَلَؤُّمٌ
Passive						
Perf.	سُئِلَ			لُئِّمَ	لُوئِمَ	تُلُئِّمَ
Imperf.	يُسْأَلُ			يُلَأَّمُ	يُلَاءَمُ	يُتَلَأَّمُ
Part.	مَسْئُولٌ			مُلَأَّمٌ	مُلَاءَمٌ	مُتَلَأَّمٌ

TABLE 12

VERBS THIRD HAMZA

Active	I				II	III
Perf.	بَرَأَ	هَنَأَ	خَطِئَ	جَرُؤَ	بَرَّأَ	بَارَأَ
2 s. m.	بَرَأْتَ	هَنَأْتَ	خَطِئْتَ	جَرُؤْتَ	بَرَّأْتَ	بَارَأْتَ
Imperf.	يَبْرَأُ	يَهْنِئُ	يَخْطَأُ	يَجْرُؤُ	يُبَرِّئُ	يُبَارِئُ
Imp.	اِبْرَأْ	اِهْنِئْ	اِخْطَأْ	اُجْرُؤْ	بَرِّئْ	بَارِئْ
Part.	بَارِئٌ	هَانِئٌ	خَاطِئٌ	جَارِئٌ	مُبَرِّئٌ	مُبَارِئٌ

Inf.	بَرْءٌ	هَنْءٌ	خِطْءٌ	جُرْأَةٌ	تَبْرِئَةٌ	مُبَارَأَةٌ
Passive						
Perf.	بُرِئَ	هُنِئَ	خُطِئَ		بُرِّئَ	بُورِئَ
Imperf.	يُبْرَأُ	يُهْنَأُ	يُخْطَأُ		يُبَرَّأُ	يُبَارَأُ
Part.	مَبْرُوءٌ	مَهْنُوءٌ	مَخْطُوءٌ		مُبَرَّأٌ	مُبَارَأٌ

TABLE 13

VERBS THIRD W—CHARACTERISTIC A

	Perfect	Imperfect				Imperative
		Indicative	Subjunctive	Jussive	Energetic	
sing.						
3 m.	نَدَا	يَنْدُو	يَنْدُوَ	يَنْدُ	يَنْدُوَنَّ	
f.	نَدَتْ	تَنْدُو	تَنْدُوَ	تَنْدُ	تَنْدُوَنَّ	
2 m.	نَدَوْتَ	تَنْدُو	تَنْدُوَ	تَنْدُ	تَنْدُوَنَّ	اُنْدُ
f.	نَدَوْتِ	تَنْدِينَ	تَنْدِى	تَنْدِى	تَنْدِنَّ	اُنْدِى
1 c.	نَدَوْتُ	أَنْدُو	أَنْدُوَ	أَنْدُ	أَنْدُوَنَّ	
dual						
3 m.	نَدَوَا	يَنْدُوَانِ	يَنْدُوَا	يَنْدُوَا	يَنْدُوَانِّ	

f.	نَدَتَا	تَنْدُوَانِ	تَنْدُوَا	تَنْدُوَا	تَنْدُوَانِّ	
2 c.	نَدَوْتُمَا	تَنْدُوَانِ	تَنْدُوَا	تَنْدُوَا	تَنْدُوَانِّ	اُنْدُوَا
pl.						
3 m.	نَدَوْا	يَنْدُونَ	يَنْدُوا	يَنْدُوا	يَنْدُنَّ	
f.	نَدَوْنَ	يَنْدُونَ	يَنْدُونَ	يَنْدُونَ	يَنْدُونَانِّ	
2 m.	نَدَوْتُمْ	تَنْدُونَ	تَنْدُوا	تَنْدُوا	تَنْدُنَّ	اُنْدُوا
f.	نَدَوْتُنَّ	تَنْدُونَ	تَنْدُونَ	تَنْدُونَ	تَنْدُونَانِّ	اُنْدُونَ
1 c.	نَدَوْنَا	نَنْدُو	نَنْدُوَ	نَنْدُ	نَنْدُوَنَّ	

Active participle نَادٍ ـ اَلنَّادِي .　　　Passive participle مَنْدُوٌّ .

TABLE 14

VERBS THIRD Y—CHARACTERISTIC A

	Perfect	Imperfect Indicative	Subjunctive	Jussive	Energetic	Imperative
sing.						
3 m.	رَمَى	يَرْمِي	يَرْمِيَ	يَرْمِ	يَرْمِيَنَّ	
f.	رَمَتْ	تَرْمِي	تَرْمِيَ	تَرْمِ	تَرْمِيَنَّ	
2 m.	رَمَيْتَ	تَرْمِي	تَرْمِيَ	تَرْمِ	تَرْمِيَنَّ	اِرْمِ
f.	رَمَيْتِ	تَرْمِينَ	تَرْمِي	تَرْمِي	تَرْمِنَّ	اِرْمِي
1 c.	رَمَيْتُ	أَرْمِي	أَرْمِيَ	أَرْمِ	أَرْمِيَنَّ	
dual						
3 m.	رَمَيَا	يَرْمِيَانِ	يَرْمِيَا	يَرْمِيَا	يَرْمِيَانِّ	

f.	رَمَتَا	تَرْمِيَانِ	تَرْمِيَا	تَرْمِيَا	تَرْمِيَانِّ	
2 c.	رَمَيْتُمَا	تَرْمِيَانِ	تَرْمِيَا	تَرْمِيَا	تَرْمِيَانِّ	اِرْمِيَا
pl.						
3 m.	رَمَوْا	يَرْمُونَ	يَرْمُوا	يَرْمُوا	يَرْمُنَّ	
f.	رَمَيْنَ	يَرْمِينَ	يَرْمِينَ	يَرْمِينَ	يَرْمِينَانِّ	
2 m.	رَمَيْتُمْ	تَرْمُونَ	تَرْمُوا	تَرْمُوا	تَرْمُنَّ	اِرْمُوا
f.	رَمَيْتُنَّ	تَرْمِينَ	تَرْمِينَ	تَرْمِينَ	تَرْمِينَانِّ	اِرْمِينَ
1 c.	رَمَيْنَا	نَرْمِي	نَرْمِيَ	نَرْمِ	نَرْمِيَنَّ	

Active participle اَلرَّامِي ـ رَامٍ. Passive participle مَرْمِيٌّ.

TABLE 15

VERBS THIRD W OR Y—CHARACTERISTIC I

	Perfect	Imperfect				Imperative
		Indicative	Subjunctive	Jussive	Energetic	
sing.						
3 m.	رَضِيَ	يَرْضَى	يَرْضَى	يَرْضَ	يَرْضَيَنَّ	
f.	رَضِيَتْ	تَرْضَى	تَرْضَى	تَرْضَ	تَرْضَيَنَّ	
2 m.	رَضِيتَ	تَرْضَى	تَرْضَى	تَرْضَ	تَرْضَيَنَّ	اِرْضَ
f.	رَضِيتِ	تَرْضَيْنَ	تَرْضَيْ	تَرْضَيْ	تَرْضَيِنَّ	اِرْضَيْ
1 c.	رَضِيتُ	أَرْضَى	أَرْضَى	أَرْضَ	أَرْضَيَنَّ	
dual						
3 m.	رَضِيَا	يَرْضَيَانِ	يَرْضَيَا	يَرْضَيَا	يَرْضَيَانِّ	

f.	رَضِيَتَا	تَرْضَيَانِ	تَرْضَيَا	تَرْضَيَا	تَرْضَيَانِّ	
2 c.	رَضِيتُمَا	تَرْضَيَانِ	تَرْضَيَا	تَرْضَيَا	تَرْضَيَانِّ	اِرْضَيَا
pl.						
3 m.	رَضُوا	يَرْضَوْنَ	يَرْضَوْا	يَرْضَوْا	يَرْضَوُنَّ	
f.	رَضِينَ	يَرْضَيْنَ	يَرْضَيْنَ	يَرْضَيْنَ	يَرْضَيْنَانِّ	
2 m.	رَضِيتُمْ	تَرْضَوْنَ	تَرْضَوْا	تَرْضَوْا	تَرْضَوُنَّ	اِرْضَوْا
f.	رَضِيتُنَّ	تَرْضَيْنَ	تَرْضَيْنَ	تَرْضَيْنَ	تَرْضَيْنَانِّ	اِرْضَيْنَ
1 c.	رَضِينَا	نَرْضَى	نَرْضَى	نَرْضَ	نَرْضَيَنَّ	

Active participle رَاضٍ ـ اَلرَّاضِي.   Passive participle مَرْضِيٌّ.

The passive is inflected like verbs with characteristic 'i' in the perfect.

TABLE 16
VERBS THIRD W AND Y—DERIVED STEMS

Active	II	III	IV	V
Perf.	قَضَّى	قَاضَى	أَقْضَى	تَقَضَّى
Imperf.	يُقَضِّي	يُقَاضِي	يُقْضِي	يَتَقَضَّى
Imp.	قَضِّ	قَاضِ	أَقْضِ	تَقَضَّ
Part.	مُقَضٍّ	مُقَاضٍ	مُقْضٍ	مُتَقَضٍّ
Inf.	تَقْضِيَةٌ	مُقَاضَاةٌ	إِقْضَاءٌ	تَقَضٍّ
Passive Perf.	قُضِّيَ	قُوضِيَ	أُقْضِيَ	تُقُضِّيَ
Imperf.	يُقَضَّى	يُقَاضَى	يُقْضَى	يُتَقَضَّى
Part. m.	مُقَضًّى	مُقَاضًى	مُقْضًى	مُتَقَضًّى
f.	مُقَضَّاةٌ	مُقَاضَاةٌ	مُقْضَاةٌ	مُتَقَضَّاةٌ

Active	VI	VII	VIII	X
Perf.	تَقَاضَى	اِنْقَضَى	اِقْتَضَى	اِسْتَقْضَى
Imperf.	يَتَقَاضَى	يَنْقَضِي	يَقْتَضِي	يَسْتَقْضِي
Imp.	تَقَاضَ	اِنْقَضِ	اِقْتَضِ	اِسْتَقْضِ
Part.	مُتَقَاضٍ	مُنْقَضٍ	مُقْتَضٍ	مُسْتَقْضٍ
Inf.	تَقَاضٍ	اِنْقِضَاءٌ	اِقْتِضَاءٌ	اِسْتِقْضَاءٌ
Passive				
Perf.	تُقُوضِيَ	اُنْقُضِيَ	اُقْتُضِيَ	اُسْتُقْضِيَ
Imperf.	يُتَقَاضَى	يُنْقَضَى	يُقْتَضَى	يُسْتَقْضَى
Part. m.	مُتَقَاضًى	مُنْقَضًى	مُقْتَضًى	مُسْتَقْضًى
f.	مُتَقَاضَاةٌ	مُنْقَضَاةٌ	مُقْتَضَاةٌ	مُسْتَقْضَاةٌ

KEY

Most English sentences can be translated into Arabic in several ways, all equally right.

1

a big river — the gracious king — the house is clean — a beautiful garden — good bread — the poor man — an ugly man — the meat is good — the street is spacious — I am rich — a dirty boy — is he beloved ? — an old castle — are you speaking the truth ?

2

بَيْتٌ صَغِيرٌ ـ اَلْبَيْتُ صَغِيرٌ ـ رَجُلٌ فَقِيرٌ ـ اَلْحَبِيبُ صَادِقٌ ـ هُوَ قَبِيحٌ ـ أَنَا رَجُلٌ ـ أَنْتَ لَطِيفٌ ـ اَلْبُسْتَانُ اَلْوَاسِعُ ـ نَهْرٌ عَرِيضٌ ـ اَلْبَحْرُ حَسَنٌ ـ اَلشَّارِعُ اَلْقَبِيحُ ـ اَلْوَلَدُ اَلصَّغِيرُ وَسِخٌ ـ اَلْخُبْزُ طَيِّبٌ.

3

a little girl — a big (elder) sister — the town is clean — the mother is beautiful — a new house — the wind is strong — a truthful old woman — the tall chief (old man) — the market is far off — the tree is small — an extensive island — is the girl (daughter) beloved ? — oh boy ! — oh mighty queen ! — a neighbouring land — are you (fem. sing.) rich ?

4

اَلشَّمْسُ اَلْحَارَةُ ـ اَلْجَزِيرَةُ بَعِيدَةٌ ـ أُمٌّ طَوِيلَةٌ ـ اَلْأُخْتُ اَلْكَبِيرَةُ ـ اَلْعَجُوزُ لَطِيفَةٌ ـ اَلنَّارُ حَارَّةٌ ـ

اَلشَّيْخُ ٱلْعَزِيزُ ـ اَلْبَيْتُ جَدِيدٌ (اَلدَّارُ جَدِيدَةٌ) ـ
اَلْقَصْرُ ٱلْقَدِيمُ ـ أَهِيَ فَقِيرَةٌ ـ أَنْتِ لَطِيفَةٌ.

5

a door of a house — the door of the garden — the window of the house is open — the land is extensive — the tribe is rich — does the book belong to the daughter of the chief? — no, it belongs to the sister of the merchant — the street of the town is wide — the big courtyard of the house of the king — the key of the door is in the lock — the costume of the chief is clean — the girl's face is beautiful — the safety of man is in the guarding of the tongue — the neighbour before the house and the companion before the road (journey) — power belongs to God — the head (beginning) of wisdom is the fear of God— the caliph is the shadow of God on the earth.

6

بُسْتَانُ مَلِكٍ ـ عِزُّ ٱلْإِنْسَانِ فِى ٱللِّسَانِ ـ وَجْهُ
ٱلْبِنْتِ ٱلْحَسَنَةِ ٱلْحَسَنُ ـ مِفْتَاحُ ٱلْبَابِ ثَقِيلٌ ـ
اَلْبَيْتُ ٱلصَّغِيرُ فِى ظِلِّ شَجَرَةٍ كَبِيرَةٍ ـ اَلرَّفِيقُ
ٱلْحَسَنُ رَأْسُ ٱلسَّلَامَةِ عَلَى ٱلطَّرِيقِ ـ اَلتَّاجِرُ عِزُّ
ٱلْأَرْضِ ـ إِنَّ ٱلْكِتَابَ ٱلصَّغِيرَ لَخَفِيفٌ ـ لِلْبِنْتِ
كِسَاءٌ خَفِيفٌ وَلِلْعَجُوزِ كِسَاءٌ ثَقِيلٌ.

7

is the baker rich ?— no, he is poor — the bakers and the carpenters are busy — there are many bakers and carpenters in the town — the two eyes and the two ears are in the head — the two boys (children) are playing — two playing girls — the two hands of the boy are dirty — the old man and the old woman are sitting beside a short and shady tree — two horses and two donkeys — the two sisters of the merchant are in the little room — are you two speaking the truth ? — yes, we are speaking the truth — the few sheep belong to the owner of the little house.

8

بَابَا ٱلْبَيْتِ مَفْتُوحَانِ ـ هُوَ صَاحِبُ فَرَسَيْنِ ـ هِيَ صَاحِبَةُ بَيْتٍ وَبُسْتَانٍ فِي ٱلْمَدِينَةِ ـ اَلْحِمَارُ فَرَسُ ٱلْفَقِيرِ ـ فِي ٱلْمَدِينَةِ طَبِيبَانِ ـ لِكُلِّ حُجْرَةٍ فِي ٱلْبَيْتِ شُبَّاكَانِ ـ أَأَنْتُمْ فَرَّاشُونَ ـ لَا نَحْنُ طَبَّاخُونَ ـ إِنَّ فِي ٱلْبَيْتِ قِطْعَتَيْ لَحْمٍ وَخُبْزًا كَثِيرًا ـ [قِطْعَتَا لَحْمٍ وَخُبْزٌ كَثِيرٌ فِي ٱلْبَيْتِ] ـ اَلْبُسْتَانُ لِصَاحِبَيِ ٱلْمَلِكِ ـ هُنَّ خَيَّاطَاتٌ مَشْغُولَةٌ [مَشْغُولَاتٌ].

9

relatives are scorpions — the learned are the heirs of the prophets — the carpenter has partners — the cook has the eatables in the kitchen — the windows of the great house are many — there are many schools in the town — has the watchman the keys of the town? — no, the governor has them — the old men and the old women are sitting in the shade of the trees — an Arab tribe has many dogs — the vices of the elect are the virtues of the mob — the loaves are from the shops of the bakers — the nobles are the associates of the governors in guarding the towns — the shops of the greengrocers are in a special market.

10

اَلْفَلَّاحُونَ وَٱلتُّجَّارُ أَعْمِدَةُ ٱلْأَرْضِ ـ أَصَابِعُ ٱلْوَلَدِ
وَسِخَةٌ ـ اَلْعَبِيدُ عِبَادٌ ـ اَلْحِنْطَةُ طَعَامُ ٱلْأَشْرَافِ
وَٱلشَّعِيرُ طَعَامُ ٱلْفُقَرَاءِ ـ أَصْحَابُ ٱلْكِسَاءِ ٱلْحَسَنِ
فِي بُيُوتِ ٱلْمُلُوكِ ـ فَوَاكِهُ ٱلشَّأْمِ طَيِّبَةٌ ـ أَوْلَادُ
ٱلْأَشْرَافِ فِي مَدَارِسَ خَاصَّةٍ ـ إِنَّ أَظْفَارَ ٱلْبِنْتِ
نَظِيفَةٌ وَأَظْفَارَ ٱلْوَلَدِ وَسِخَةٌ ـ اَلْكِلَابُ حُرَّاسُ
ٱلْعَرَبِ ـ إِنَّ ٱلرِّيَاحَ عَلَى ٱلْجَزَائِرِ بَارِدَةٌ ـ قُلُوبُ
ٱلنَّاسِ بَيْنَ أَصَابِعِ ٱللّٰهِ.

11

my hand is clean — your two hands are clean — his fine horses are swift — Zayd, his daughter is beautiful — his cattle have much milk — my weight (worth) in his opinion is as the weight of a dog — the strength of a man is in his intelligence and his tongue — the poets and knights of the Arabs are many — he has two boys, the elder of the two is short and the younger of the two is tall — the honour of a man is his sons and his care his house and his neighbour — your graceful poems are known among men, all of them — my poor friend has two donkeys and your woman friend has many horses — your big box is light and her little box is heavy.

12

إِنَّ حِنْطَتِى وَشَعِيرِى فِى صَنَادِيقِى ٱلْكَبِيرَةِ ـ يَدَيْهَا لَنَظِيفَتَانِ ـ وَطَنُنَا حَبِيبٌ إِلَيْنَا ـ يَا أَوْلَادُ أَعِنْدَكُم كُتُبُكُمْ ـ رَسَائِلُكَ ٱللَّطِيفَةُ فِى حِفْظِ صَاحِبِى [رَسَائِلُكُمُ ٱللَّطِيفَةُ] ـ يَدَاىَ وَرِجْلَاىَ ـ أُخْتُكَ وَخَادِمَاتُهَا جَالِسَةٌ عِنْدَ طَبَّاخِى ـ شُيُوخُهُمْ أَصْحَابُ ٱلْحِكْمَةِ ـ يَدَا ٱلْعَجُوزِ وَعَيْنَاهَا ضَعِيفَتَانِ ـ وَزْنُ ٱلْإِنْسَانِ وَزْنُ عَقْلِهِ ـ حِكْمَةُ ٱلشَّيْخِ مِنْ كَثْرَةِ تَجَارِبِهِ .

13

the old man hit the boy's head — the old woman understood the girl's words — did you seek food from the kitchen? — I fetched meat from the butcher's shop — the boys came out from the mosque and went into the school — the sempstresses went away from our town and returned to their native land — girls, have you drunk water? — no, we drank milk — did you two hear the voices (song) of the birds on the trees? — I cut the meat into small pieces — my mother sent me to you — the men came down from the top of the mountain and captured the town.

14

أَكَتَبْتَ ٱلرَّسَائِلَ ـ هَلْ كَتَبْتُمُ ٱلرَّسَائِلَ ـ كَسَرَ
ٱلْوَلَدُ قَدَمَ ٱلْكَلْبِ بِحَجَرَةٍ ـ سَمِعُوا كَلَامَ ٱلْأَمِيرِ
وَرَجَعُوا إِلَى بُيُوتِهِمْ ـ دَخَلَ ٱلْمُلُوكُ ٱلْأَرْضَ وَفَتَحُوهَا ـ
فَتَحْتُ ٱلشُّبَّاكَ وَدَخَلَ كَلْبٌ ـ صَرَخَ حُرَّاسُ ٱلْبَقَرِ
هَلْ سَمِعْتُمُوهُمْ ـ قَطَعَ ٱلْأَطِبَّاءُ يَدَ ٱلرَّجُلِ وَرِجْلَهُ ـ
أَدَخَلْتُمُ ٱلْحُجْرَةَ ـ يَا بَنَاتُ هَلْ لَعِبْتُنَّ مَعَ ٱلْكَلْبِ
ٱلْكَبِيرِ ـ قَطَعَ رِجَالٌ قَبِيحَةٌ آذَانَ ٱلْبَقَرِ ـ يَا بِنْتَانِ
أَبَعَثْتُمَا تُحْفَةً إِلَى أُخْتِكُمَا .

15

the boys went into the sea to swim — the carpenter sent to me to ask for wood — we sat by the spring drinking and laughing — the commander of the army came out, went up the mountain and looked at the ranks of the enemy — the companions went from Syria to Jerusalem stopping every night in a village — men in summer go away from the hot towns and put up in towns near the sea

— the merchant progressed to the king's city collecting the dinars from his clients — you will hear the sound of the drums.

16

سَيَفْتَحُ ٱللّٰهُ ٱلْمَدِينَةَ عَلَى يَدِ نَبِيِّهِ ـ خَرَجَ ٱلْكِلَابُ
يَنْبَحُونَ [تَنْبَحُ] ـ يَلْبَسُ ٱلنَّاسُ [ٱلْإِنْسَانُ] ثِيَابًا
ثَقِيلَةً فِى ٱلشِّتَاءِ ـ جَلَسْتُمْ تَسْمَعُونَ كَلَامَ ٱلشَّاعِرِ ـ
أَتَصْنَعُ ٱلْبَنَاتُ ثِيَابَهُنَّ [ثِيَابَهَا] ـ يَضْرِبُ ٱلْمَلِكُ
دَنَانِيرَ طَيِّبَةً ـ خَرَجَ ٱلْأَوْلَادُ يَلْعَبُونَ ـ قَدِمَ ٱلْجَيْشُ
يَضْرِبُونَ طُبُولَهُمْ ـ صَنَعَ لَنَا ٱلنَّجَّارُ كُؤُوسًا مِنْ
خَشَبٍ نَشْرَبُ مِنْهَا ـ سَمِعْنَا ٱلْحُرَّاسَ يَصْرُخُونَ عَلَى
ٱلْعَدُوِّ ـ نَظَرْتُ إِلَيْهِ وَهُوَ يَغْضَبُ عَلَى كَلَامِى.

17

these two men are the two chiefs of the tribe — this is the truthful slave girl — this estate of mine is renowned in the country — these girls are playing in the court of the school — those men have camped at the entry of the town — I heard that dog of yours barking — this is your bed — whose are these jewels ? — they belong to the agent of the owner of this estate — those are slave girls from the household of the chief — who made those cups and dishes of yours ? — whom did you send to me ? — from whose statement is this ?

18

ٱلْأَشْعَارُ ٱلْقَصِيرَةُ هِيَ ٱلْمَشْهُورَةُ ـ أَغْضَبُ [أَنَا]
عَلَى مَا فَعَلْتَ ـ لِذٰلِكَ ٱلْوَكِيلِ فِضَّةٌ كَثِيرَةٌ وَذَهَبٌ
كَثِيرٌ ـ لِمَنْ تِلْكَ ٱلضَّيْعَةُ ـ صَعِدَ ٱلْحَارِسُ فِي مَنَارَةِ
ٱلْمَسْجِدِ ذٰلِكَ يَصْرُخُ ـ سَيَكْتُبُ ٱلْأَوْلَادُ عَلَى
تِلْكَ ٱلْأَوْرَاقِ بِهٰذِهِ ٱلْأَقْلَامِ ـ ذَهَبَ صَاحِبُكَ
ٱلْفَقِيرُ ذٰلِكَ يَطْلُبُ ٱلْقُوتَ ـ جَمَعَ وَكِيلُكَ هٰذَا مَالًا
كَثِيرًا ـ أَوْرَاقُ ٱلشَّجَرِ هٰذِهِ قُوتٌ لِلْغَنَمِ ـ ٱلْمَخْرَجُ
مِنْ جَهْلِهِ عَسِيرٌ عَلَى ٱلْجَاهِلِ ـ مَالِي هُوَ سَيْفِي
وَكُتُبِي.

19

that dog of yours is white — this horse is black — the black slave is in the red room — this tree is green in summer — the two eyes of the girl are blue — the Path is sharper than a sword and thinner than a hair — the colour of this flower, what is it ? — it has two colours, blue and yellow — the leaves of the trees are brown and red in autumn — gold is heavier than silver — prayer is better than sleep — best of gifts is understanding and the worst of calamities ignorance — a dumb slave girl is the best — my daughter is taller than I.

20

لَهُ إِمَاءٌ طُرْشٌ وَسُودٌ ـ جَيْشُنَا أَقَلُّ مِنْ جَيْشِ
أَعْدَائِنَا ـ اَلْغَنَمُ فِي بِلَادِ ٱلْعَرَبِ سُودٌ [سَوْدَاءُ] ـ
اَلْقُوتُ ٱلْأَحَبُّ إِلَى ٱلْعَرَبِ ٱلْأَسْوَدَانِ ٱللَّحْمُ وَٱلتَّمْرُ ـ
اَلنَّخْلُ أَطْوَلُ مِنَ ٱلزَّيْتُونِ ـ ضَيْعَتُكَ أَصْغَرُ مِنْ ضَيْعَتِي ـ
إِنَّ لِهٰذَا ٱلطَّائِرِ صَدْرًا أَصْفَرَ وَجَنَاحَيْنِ أَحْمَرَيْنِ ـ
بَعَثَ إِلَيَّ أَصْدِقَائِي مَوَاهِبَ كَثِيرَةً وَمَوْهِبَتُكَ هِيَ
ٱلْحُسْنَى ـ بَعَثَ ٱللّٰهُ نَبِيَّهُ لِكُلِّ ٱلنَّاسِ ٱلسُّودِ
وَٱلْبِيضِ وَٱلْحُمْرِ ـ إِنَّ أُخْتَكَ ٱلصُّغْرَى هِيَ أَلْطَفُهُنَّ.

21

my father and your brother heard the noises of the riding beasts — the daughter looked for her father in the market — the old man gathered his sons round his bed before his death — the greengrocer's daughter took the white papers away from her brother's hand — the woman with her sons went into the presence (between the hands) of the caliph — boys, do you know the names of the flowers? — yes, we know the name of every flower in the garden — I followed your brother in the road writing his name on the wall of every house — your parents rejoice at your success — a man is in the two smallest (parts) of him, his heart and his tongue — the beauty of a man lies in his tongue and the beauty of a woman in her understanding.

22

أَفَهِمْتُمَا أَنْتَ وَأَخُوكَ كَلَامِي ـ يَلْعَبُ أَخَوَايَ
وَأُخْتَايَ مَعَ إِخْوَانِكَ وَأَخَوَاتِكَ ـ أَبَعَثَ أَبُوكَ أَخَاكَ
إِلَيَّ ـ بَعَثَتِ ٱلْمَرْأَةُ أَبْنَاءَهَا يَطْلُبُونَ ٱلْمَالَ فِي
بُلْدَانٍ بَعِيدَةٍ ـ مَا ٱسْمُكَ ـ اِسْمِي مَشْهُورٌ هُوَ
أَشْهَرُ أَسْمَاءِ ٱلْعَرَبِ ـ يَا ٱمْرَأَةُ أَلَكِ أَوْلَادٌ ـ نَعَمْ
إِنَّ لِي ٱبْنًا وَٱبْنَتَيْنِ ـ لِهٰذَا ٱلرَّجُلِ أَبَوَانِ أَبُو
جِسْمِهِ وَأَبُو عَقْلِهِ ـ هَلْ نَزَلْتَ عِنْدَ أَبِي صَدِيقِي ـ
ذَوُو ٱلْعِلْمِ وَٱلْمَالِ هُمْ أَقَلُّ ٱلنَّاسِ.

23

women, listen to the noise of your infants — the going into this business is easier than the coming out from it — maid, go to the market and ask for my new clothes from the dressmaker — the hider of a secret is a faithful friend — self conquest is the greatest conquest — general, dismount from your horse and enter my house ; this will be a great honour to me — what is required from you is to return from the far country to the house of your parents — he who is served, in your opinion, is the servant of you all — we belong to God and to him we return — a man's serving his brother is honour.

24

يَا ٱبْنَتِي ٱسْمَعِي قَوْلِي ـ اُطْلُبِ ٱلْعِلْمَ مِنَ ٱلْكُلِّ
ٱلرِّجَالِ وَٱلنِّسَاءِ ـ دُخُولُ ٱلْمَالِ عَسِيرٌ وَٱلْخُرُوجُ
مِنْهُ يَسِيرٌ ـ مَعْرِفَةُ نَفْسِكَ ٱلْمَعْرِفَةُ ٱلْكُبْرَى
وَٱلْعُسْرَى ـ فَرِحَ ٱلْمَلِكُ بِرُجُوعِ جَيْشِهِ بَعْدَ فَتْحِهِ
أَعْدَاءَهُ ـ قَطْعُ ٱلْيَدِ عَذَابُ ٱلسَّارِقِ ـ يَفْرَحُ ٱلْكَرِيمُ
بِقُدُومِ ٱلْأَضْيَافِ ـ حَفْظُكَ ٱللِّسَانَ مِنَ ٱلْقَبِيحِ
مَخَافَةُ ٱللّٰهِ ـ مَطْلُوبُ بَعْثِي هَذَا ٱلْغُلَامَ إِلَيْكَ دُخُولُهُ
فِي خِدْمَتِكَ.

25

he who hurries repents — the government sent its servants to measure the fields — the doctor wanted me to drink much milk — had you been at the war, you would know which of the two armies was the braver — let him take its prey from the mouth of the lion that we may know his strength and courage — I do not like that you should look on the faults of your neighbours — the caliph wrote to the commander of his army; do not kill old men and infants and do not cut down trees — if you get out of this affair, you will be glad all your life — it is part of courage to put up with calamities and the unpleasant — the father called for two doctors to find out his son's illness.

26

لَا تَلْعَبْ بِذَلِكَ ٱلسَّيْفِ ٱلْحَدِيدِ ـ لَأَكْشِفَنَّ عَنْ
سِرِّهِ ـ لِيَسْكُتِ ٱلْغُلَامُ بَيْنَ يَدَىْ أَكْبَرَ مِنْهُ ـ
لِأَدْخُلْ دَارَكَ لِأَنْظُرَ إِلَى فُرُشِكَ ـ كَسَرُوا ٱلْكَأْسَ
لِيَسْقُطَ ٱلسُّمُّ فِيهَا عَلَى ٱلْأَرْضِ ـ اِبْعَثِ ٱلْغُلَامَ
لِيَجْمَعَ ٱلتَّمْرَ ٱلسَّاقِطَ عَلَى ٱلْأَرْضِ ـ تَخْرُجُ نِسَاءُ
ٱلْقَبِيلَةِ كُلَّ يَوْمٍ لِيَجْمَعْنَ حَطَبًا [لِجَمْعِ ٱلْحَطَبِ] ـ
لَا تَغْضَبْ عَلَى ٱلصَّدِيقِ ـ مِنَ ٱلشَّرَفِ أَنْ تَكْرَهَ
عُيُوبَ نَفْسِكَ .

27

do not beat your children — my father did not send me to look for a book for you (a book of yours) — he will never be noble who does not hide secrets — we have never heard the like of this story — God is one, nothing is like him — we do not return from our work in the fields while the sun is in the sky — we were not glad at this news and not sorry — there is no poverty and no trial like greed graspingness and no wealth like contentment — there is no intelligence like good management, no piety like self control and no beauty like the beauty of character — running away in the time for it is better than holding on when it is not the time for it — two are not satisfied, the seeker after knowledge and the seeker after wealth.

28

إِنَّ أَعْدَاءَنَا لَا رَحِمَهُمُ ٱللّٰهُ كَثِيرَةٌ ـ لَا تَفْزَعْ مِنَ
ٱلشُّغْلِ ـ لَمْ يَشْبَعِ ٱلنَّبِيُّ لَحْمًا فِي حَيَاتِهِ ـ لَا تَقْنَعْ
بِقَلِيلٍ مِنَ ٱلْعِلْمِ ـ لَنْ يَرْجِعَ ٱلْأَيَّامُ ٱلذَّاهِبَةُ ـ مَا
أَطْلُبُ تُحَفًا مِنَ ٱلْحُكُومَةِ ٱلْيَوْمَ ـ لَا تَفْزَعْ إِلَى
غَيْرِ ٱللّٰهِ ـ يَا بِنْتِي لَا تَضْحَكِي عَلَى مُصِيبَةِ ٱلْفَقِيرِ
وَلَا تَغْضَبِي عَلَى نَجَاحِ ذِي مَالٍ ـ هُوَ ذُو مَالٍ
وَضِيَاعٍ وَبُيُوتٍ وَلَا يَقْنَعُ ـ لَسْتَ ذَا حِكْمَةٍ [بِذِي
حِكْمَةٍ].

29

it is yellow in colour (he is fair of complexion) — Zayd is stupid but Umar is more stupid than he — the wind to-day is stronger than it was yesterday — he fled from the country for fear of the wrath of the sultan — he went right and left looking for food — they waited for no long time — I stayed away from the war out of cowardice — the peasants planted their fields with barley — I am more afraid of him than he of me — I aimed at (entering) the service of some great man for the sake of getting rich — I was glad but hid my feelings in sorrow for the sick man — I bowed down to God for joy at his sending the prophet.

30

فَزِعَتْ فَزَعًا عَظِيمًا ـ لَمْ يَهْرُبْ أَحَدٌ هَرَبِى ـ
سَكَنْتُ فِى تِلْكَ ٱلْمَدِينَةِ سِنِينَ كَثِيرَةً ـ إِنَّ لَهُ
مَالًا قَلِيلًا وَيَقْنَعُ بِفَقْرِهِ [هُوَ ذُو مَالٍ قَلِيلٍ] ـ اَلْحَرُّ
اَلْيَوْمَ أَشَدُّ مِنْهُ ٱلْبَارِحَ ـ شَجَاعَتُهُ شَجَاعَةُ ٱلْأَسَدِ ـ
إِنَّهُ أَشْجَعُ مِنَ ٱلْأَسَدِ ـ سَكَتَ طَوِيلًا ـ لَا أَذْهَبُ
إِلَى ٱلْبُلْدَانِ ٱلْحَارَّةِ خَوْفًا مِنَ ٱلْمَرَضِ ـ لَبِسَ ثِيَابَ
ٱلْحَرِيرِ فَرَحًا فِى جَمْعِهِ مَالًا كَثِيرًا ـ هُوَ قَوِىٌّ
ذِرَاعًا وَضَعِيفٌ قَدَمًا.

31

whose argument is short, his tongue is long (much verbiage instead of a good case) — stand up, my boy, and go to your grandfather — the children were playing in the street — the girl feared the violence of the wind — the caravan came back through fear of brigands — my daughter, be not afraid; you will not go alone — let him say what he thinks — I was the son of my father then I became the father of my son — the colour of the snake is dark (a darkness) inclining to blackness — the bedouin were selling the skins of sheep and goats to the peasants — the army will have overcome its enemies before sunset.

32

قَامَ مِنْ فِرَاشِهِ وَٱلشَّمْسُ قَدْ مَالَتْ لِغُرُوبِهَا ـ إِنْ
مَاتَ شَيْخٌ مِنْ قَوْمِنَا قَامَ شَيْخٌ [يَمُتْ . . . يَقُمْ] ـ
يَكُونُ ٱلْقَافِلَةُ سَارَتْ أَيَّامًا كَثِيرَةً ـ قَدْ سَمِعَ
ٱلْجَمَاعَةُ كُلُّهَا مَا أَقُولُ ـ يَقِيلُ كُلُّ ٱلنَّاسِ فِي
أَيَّامِ ٱلصَّيْفِ ٱلْحَارَّةِ ـ يَقُولُ كَثِيرٌ غَيْرَ مَا فِي
قَلْبِهِ ـ لَا تَخَفْ مَكَارِيهَ ٱلطَّرِيقِ ـ قَدْ كَانَتِ
ٱلْمَرْأَةُ تَصْنَعُ ثِيَابًا لِأَوْلَادِهَا ـ لَا يَكُونُ ٱلْأَضْيَافُ
قَامُوا مِنْ فُرُشِهِمْ قَبْلَ ذَهَابِكِ ـ يَا جَدَّتِي هَلْ
تَسِيرِينَ مَعَ ٱلنِّسَاءِ ٱلْأُخَرِ إِلَى ٱلْقُدْسِ.

33

I spoke to him and did not speak to any other — the rich man fed many poor men so they went away grateful — boys, do not oppose your parents — we were following the peasant and got separated from our fellows — wait for me in the market and do not go away — the inhabitants of the town were perturbed on the arrival of the news of the defeat of the army — all you approve in a dog, demand it in a horse — the woman were crowding round the gate of the palace to receive the queen's gifts — the brigands overpowered the town and destroyed all that was in it — I asked my farm labourers to store up the snow in chambers under ground — I do not wish you to compare my boasts with my acts — the leader surrendered the fortress to the besiegers.

34

اِسْتَغْفَرْتُ ٱللّٰهَ فَيَغْفِرُ لِى - أَنْظِرْنِى إِلَى قُدُومِ
ٱلْأَضْيَافِ لِأَسْمَعَ أَخْبَارَهُمْ - سَأَنْتَظِرُكَ بَعْدَ غُرُوبِ
ٱلشَّمْسِ - قَدْ يُنَازِعُ ٱلْإِخْوَانُ أَخَوَاتِهِمْ - سَأُعَذِّبُ
ٱللُّصُوصَ وَكُلَّ فَاعِلِى ٱلشَّرِّ - غَالَبَنِى وَغَلَبْتُهُ - لَا
يَسْتَقْبِحُ وَلَدٌ أُمَّهُ - اِخْتَلَفَ ٱلْجَمَاعَةُ فِى مَا يَفْعَلُونَ -
اِسْتَخْلَفَ ٱلْأَمِيرُ ٱبْنَهُ فِى غُيُوبِهِ - يُلْبِسُ كُلُّ
ٱلنَّاسِ أَوْلَادَهُمْ ثِيَابًا جَدِيدَةً عَلَى ٱلْعِيدَيْنِ
ٱلْكَبِيرَيْنِ - أَبُوكَ أَقَدْ يُدْخِلُ فَقِيرًا ٱلْبَيْتَ وَيُطْعِمُهُ.

35

that coin was struck in Stamboul — a man is known by his companions — it was gone two miles (two miles were traversed) — if you are killed, being killed is the noblest mode of death — I was burdened with the care of my younger brothers after our father's death — he was doubted about his pedigree, attacked for it (the genuineness of his descent was suspected and attacked) — he, who has been forbidden kindness, has been forbidden all good — this is a matter wherein there is difference (of opinion) — Ramadan was fasted (the fast of Ramadan was kept) — the caliph died and the youngest son of his uncle succeeded — entry is forbidden — he was carried on government horses to Egypt — have you learnt engineering? yes, the teacher taught it to us — the fields were sown with flowers.

36

يُنْشَدُ شِعْرُهُ بَيْنَ يَدَيْ كِبَارِ ٱلْبِلَادِ ـ زُرِعَ ٱلْمَزَارِعُ
حِنْطَةً وَشَعِيرًا وَذُرَةً ـ دُخُولُ ٱلْمَسَاجِدِ مَمْنُوعٌ ـ
قُتِلَ ٱلرَّئِيسُ وَٱنْهَزَمَ ٱلْجَيْشُ ـ صُنِعَتِ ٱلْأَرْضُ فِرَاشًا
لَكُمْ ـ صُرِفَ وَجْهُهُ عَنْ قَصْدِهِ ـ فَخْرُهُ مَشْكُوكٌ
فِيهِ ـ قُتِلَ أَبُوهُ قَتَلَهُ رَجُلٌ مِنْ مِصْرَ ـ يَقْدَمُ قُدُومَ
ٱلْجَمَلِ ٱلْمَحْمُولِ عَلَيْهِ ـ لِمَ (كَانَ يُلَامُ) عَلَى صَوْمِهِ
ٱلْكَثِيرِ ـ سَيُكْشَفُ عَنْ سِرِّهِ .

37

do you want to go away? — let a writer not be unwilling to write — get down out of paradise for it is not for you to act proudly in it — we did not busy ourselves with mentioning that, that the book might not be too long — I do not believe that anyone is superior to Zayd in learning and manners — the beautiful forgiveness is that you do not blame him whom you pardon — your blood is tabu to you (murder is an unholy act) till you stand before your lord — someone asked a woman in marriage and she said, No, until you divorce your wife — I do not fear for you that you should be afraid; I only fear for you that you should not be afraid — the child is so heavy that its mother cannot carry it — a bedouin heard a man say: I testify that Muhammad the apostle of God; so he said, does what?

38

طَالَ خُطْبَتُهُ حَتَّى يَنَامَ ٱلسَّامِعُونَ ـ نَعْتَقِدُ أَنَّ ٱللّٰهَ
أَحَدٌ وَأَنْ يَغْفِرَ لِلنَّادِمِينَ ـ كَرِهَ ٱلزَّوْجُ أَنْ يُطَلِّقَ
زَوْجَتَهُ ٱلْعَجُوزَ رَحْمَةً عَلَيْهَا ـ اِسْتَمَعْتُ كُلَّ ٱلسَّمْعِ
خَوْفًا أَنْ يَسْقُطَ عَنِّي شَيْءٌ مِمَّا يَقُولُ ـ مَا مَنَعَكَ
أَنْ تَسْجُدَ [مَا مَنَعَكَ مِنَ ٱلسُّجُودِ] ـ يَبْعَثُ غِلْمَانَهُ
لِيُنْزِلُوا ٱلثَّلْجَ مِنَ ٱلْجِبَالِ لِحِفْظِ طَعَامِهِ فِي ٱلْأَيَّامِ
ٱلْحَارَّةِ ـ نَخَافُ أَنْ يُنَازِعَ ٱلْجَمَاعَتَانِ بَعْضُهُمَا
بَعْضًا ـ أَخْبِرْهُ أَنِّي صَنَعْتُ هٰذَا ٱلصَّوْتَ لَهُ.

39

he will soon come back from his journey — the sick man scarcely moves on his bed — you always benefited me by your advice and example — if he talked to us, he talked well; if we talked to him, he listened attentively — can a man like this compose poetry or make good poetry — a number of nights befell us when we did not sleep from the cold and almost died — the shop-keeper was in the morning and people crowding in front of his shop (the shop-keeper woke to find, etc.) — learn knowledge for if you are unimportant in one people perhaps you may become important in another — if he marries you to her, perhaps you may be granted a child like me — I am almost afraid of the noise of the wind.

40

كِدْتُ أَعْتَقِدُ مَا يَقُولُ ـ هَرَبُوا هَرَبًا سَرِيعًا ـ أَسْرَعُوا ٱلْهَرَبَ ـ لَمْ يَلْبَثْ أَنْ يَدْخُلَ ـ عَسَى أَنْ يَرْجِعُوا غَدًا ـ لَعَلَّهُمْ يَرْجِعُونَ غَدًا ـ لَمْ تَكَدْ تَلُومُ ٱبْنَهَا عَلَى أَنْ يَسْبَحَ فِي ٱلنَّهْرِ ٱلْكَبِيرِ وَهُوَ لَا يُحْسِنُ ٱلسِّبَاحَةَ ـ يُوشِكُ ٱلْمُتَكَبِّرُونَ أَنْ يَنْدَمُوا عَلَى تَكَبُّرِهِمْ ـ إِنَّ ذٰلِكَ ٱلْغُلَامَ كَادَ يَعْكِسُ ٱلدُّنْيَا ـ هَزَمُونَا مَرَّةً وَلَا يَعُودُونَ يَهْزِمُونَنَا ـ حَرَّكَ رَجُلَانِ ذَوَا قُوَّةٍ عَظِيمَةٍ ٱلْحَجَرَ وَلَمْ يَكَدْ يَتَحَرَّكُ ـ لَا تَعُدْ تَفْعَلُ هٰذَا [تفعل].

41

God is one; he does not beget and is not begotten — he is a man, his description cannot be described (supremely ordinary) — he did not let his younger son inherit with the elder — leave excuses alone for most of them are sins (lies) — God's knowledge embraces the acts and thoughts of his servants (of men) — justice is that you should put things in their places — who is the worst of men as to position? he said: he whose knowledge is wide, his power narrow, and his ambition far-reaching — they suspected him of unbelief for his studying the books of the philosophers — it is necessary for the learner that he should seek the truth — I expected the arrival of the news and it has not yet come — the two doctors will soon agree on the treatment of the invalid.

42

صِفْ أَحْوَالَ مَرَضِكَ (صِفِي أَحْوَالَ دَائِكِ) ـ كَانَ
أَخْبَارٌ جَدِيدَةٌ تَصِلُ كُلَّ سَاعَةٍ ـ ضَاقَتْ عَلَيْهِ
ٱلْأَرْضُ وَقَدْ كَانَتْ وَسِعَتْ ـ وَجَّهْتُهُ إِلَيْكَ وَلَمْ يَتَوَجَّهْ ـ
سَمِعْنَاكُمْ تَصِفُونَ مَا فَعَلْتُمْ ـ سَنَجِدُهُمْ يَقِفُونَ فِي
ٱلشَّارِعِ ـ لَا يُوجَدُ كُفْرَانٌ [لَا كُفْرَانَ] كَكُفْرَانِ
ٱلْوَلَدِ ٱلْكَافِرِ ـ سَمِعْتُ أَصْدِقَاءَهُ يُوَدِّعُونَهُ ـ أَوْجَبَ
عَلَيْكَ أَنْ تَكِلَ هٰذَا ٱلْأَمْرَ لِغَيْرِكَ ـ ضَعْ يَدَكَ عَلَى
كِتَابِ ٱللّٰهِ وَٱحْلِفْ.

43

he had cousins who inherited from him — you are not those who run away from the truth (duty) — what a man sows to-day he will reap to-morrow — I got down from the couch on which I had been thrown — that was the seal (last) of his good deeds which surpass description — how are you not pleased with a plan which will combine for you health of body, acuteness of mind, and much wealth ? — the two girls, whom I sent to the girls' school, have turned out learned and cultured — be to them as a doctor who does not hurry with a remedy before knowing the disease — did you sell the two slaves with whom you were displeased ? — describe to me (the man) who spoke to you.

44

وَكَّلْتُ أَحَدًا أَتَّكِلُ عَلَيْهِ ـ يَزْعَمُ أَنَّ مَا نَزَلَ بِهِ لَمْ يَنْزِلْ عَلَى غَيْرِهِ ـ مَنْ لَا يَعْرِفُ الدَّاءَ لَا يَعْرِفُ الدَّوَاءَ ـ لَا يُرِيدُونَ أَنْ يَبِيعُوا الْكِتَابَيْنِ الَّذَيْنِ وَرِثُوهُمَا مِنْ عَمِّهِمْ ـ زَرَعْنَا الْمَزَارِعَ الَّتِي وَجَدْنَاهَا غَيْرَ مَزْرُوعَةٍ ـ هٰذَانِ هُمَا الِاثْنَانِ اللَّذَانِ وَجَدَا الْمَجْرُوحَ وَحَمَلَاهُ إِلَى مَنْزِلِي ـ خَرَجْتُ مِنَ الْبَابِ الَّذِي دَخَلْتُ فِيهِ ـ إِنَّ الْحُقُوقَ الَّتِي وَجَبَتْ عَلَيَّ جَاوَزَتْ قُوَّتِي ـ وَدَّعْتُ الشُّغْلَ الَّذِي أَرْغَبُ فِيهِ وَتَوَجَّهْتُ إِلَى شُغْلٍ أَرْغَبُ عَنْهُ.

45

I love her, she loves me, and my camel loves her she-camel — I thought that he was preparing to climb mountains — do not think that I oppose you — he who is moderate, the meeting with him is light on his friend; the man of (many) requests, his face is loathed — a different story is told about Musaab and his brother's dismissing him from Basra and sending him back to it — the quickest to (take part in) civil strife are the least of them as to shame at running away — I perceived the noise of the passing of a snake; did you not perceive it? — stretch out your hand to the rope of God and he will help you — count the sick and get ready the medicines for treating them — he passed by the boys telling them the stories of the prophet.

46

دُلَّنِي لِمَا يَسُرُّنِي ـ ظَنَنْتُ أَنَّكَ تَدُلُّنِي وَأَضْلَلْتَنِي ـ
كَانَ ٱلْوَلَدُ يَسْتَمِدُّ ٱلْمُعَلِّمَ وَيُمِدُّهُ ـ تُحِبُّ أَنْ تَصِيرَ
شَيْخَ ٱلْقَوْمِ فَٱسْتَخِفَّ مَا يَقُولُ ٱلنَّاسُ ـ ظَنَنَّا
ٱلنِّسَاءَ يَفْرِرْنَ خَوْفًا وَهُنَّ يُسْرِعْنَ لِلِقَاءِ أَزْوَاجِهِنَّ ـ
لَا نَعْرِفُ مَا نَظُنُّ ـ ضَلَّ ٱلْكَافِرُونَ وَيُضِلُّونَ
غَيْرَهُمْ ـ سَلَّمْتُ عَلَى ٱلْجَمَاعَةِ وَرَدُّوا سَلَامِي ـ
أَتَظُنُّهُمْ سَيُقِرُّونَ بِحُقُوقِي ـ لَا رَادَّ لِمَا يَفْعَلُ ٱللهُ.

47

the noble's promise is cash down, the ignoble's is postponement — we went hunting and made a bag — my sister did not wish to obey the orders of her teacher — why do you not wish to leave your work ? — bats hide in the daytime for fear lest they should be hunted for their beauty — my father wanted to buy what his family needed — some one heard a man asking God's help for his mother. He said to him, What about your father ? He said, He is a man and can fend for himself — Did your father give you any choice in your marriage ? — No, my mother chose a wife for me — we heard a Jew threatening his servant — you must answer (obey) the call of the government — greed led those women to incline from the path of kindness and they let themselves be led.

48

سَكَتَ وَأَطَالَ ٱلسُّكُوتَ ـ يُمِيلُ ٱلْبُخْلُ ٱلنَّاسَ
عَنِ ٱلصِّرَاطِ ٱلْمُسْتَقِيمِ ـ اِسْتَعَنَّاهُ وَأَعَانَنَا ـ أَقَامَ
حَجَرًا كَبِيرًا ذِكْرًا لِمَا أَصَابَ ٱلْقَوْمَ مِنَ ٱلشَّرِّ ـ
أَخَافَ ٱللُّصُوصُ سُكَّانَ ٱلْبُيُوتِ ٱلْبَعِيدَةِ ـ يُمِيتُنِى
عَنَايَةُ أَهْلِى وَبَيْتِى ـ يَفْعَلُ ذٰلِكَ ٱلْيَهُودِىُّ مَا يُرِيدُ
وَيُصَوِّبُهُ ٱلْيَهُودُ وَٱلنَّصَارَى ـ يَتَعَلَّمُ ٱلْحَكِيمُ مِمَّا
يُصِيبُ غَيْرَهُ مِنَ ٱلشَّرِّ ـ اِحْتَاجَتْ إِلَى ٱلْعَوْنِ وَلَمْ
تَجِدْ مُعِينًا ـ اِحْتَلْتُ كُلَّ ٱلِاحْتِيَالِ لِأَخْرُجَ مِنَ

أَلْحِصْنِ ٱلَّذِى أَنَا أَسِيرٌ فِيهِ وَلَمْ أَجِدْ مَخْرَجًا ـ اِبْتَاعَتِ ٱمْرَأَتِى ثِيَابًا مِنَ ٱلْحَرِيرِ وَٱلصُّوفِ.

49

who trains his child when young will find pleasure in him when grown up — I believe in God, in his angels, in his apostles, in his books, and in the last day — does the commander allow me to question the prisoners ? — I rented my house from a merchant and paid him the rent for it every month — they began the festival with the reading of the noble Koran ; then one of the women preached telling the story of the apostle — the old man was friendly with the beggars and refugees — he earned a great reward by composing a book in defence of the religion of the Christians — people congratulated him on his return safe from the war — greet him (from me) and inform him that I will meet him to-morrow — I am not the man to prefer anyone with my share from you (I will not give up to any what you have given me) — is anyone safe from misfortune ?

50

آكِلِ هٰذَا ٱلسَّائِلَ وَأْمُرْهُ بِٱلذَّهَابِ ـ لَمْ يَأْمَنْ مَا يَحْتَالُ ٱلْحَاسِدُ ـ أَسْتَأْجَرْتَ رِجَالًا يَحْصُدُونَ مَزَارِعَكَ [هَلِ ٱسْتَأْجَرْتَ رِجَالًا أَنْ يَحْصُدُوا] ـ آنَسْتُ هٰذَا ٱلْقَوْمَ فَيُكَافِئُونَنِى مُكَافَأَةً عَظِيمَةً ـ

سَيُؤَاكِلُنِي أَصْدِقَاؤُكَ وَيُشَارِبُونَنِي ـ سَأُوكِلُهُ
خُبْزًا وَتَمْرًا ـ ثُمَّ يَسْتَأْذِنُ ٱلشُّعَرَاءُ ٱلْأَمِيرَ أَنْ يَبْتَدِئُوا
إِنْشَادَ أَشْعَارِهِمْ ـ أَثَّرَ ٱلشَّمْسُ فِي وَجْهِ ٱلْفَلَّاحِ
وَلَمْ يَتَأَثَّرْ قُوَّةُ جِسْمِهِ ـ تَأَخَّرَتِ ٱلْقَافِلَةُ أَخَّرَهَا
ٱلْمَطَرُ.

51

when you do a man a good turn, forget it — there is no good in kindness when it is counted — a man hid what (kindness) he did and published what was done to him — the Arabs say, a turbaned chief, meaning that every crime one of his tribe commits is bound on his head (he takes the responsibility for it) — why do you not make lampoons long ? he said, what goes round the neck is enough of a necklace for you — what I like does not come to me, and what comes to me I do not like — make me independent by my need of you and do not make me poor by my being able to do without you — what is little and sufficient is better than what is much and distracts — why do you not go to war ? he said, I hate cordially death in my bed, how can I go to it with a run ? — buy dates from Mosul and carry them to Basra ; that will destroy your fortune.

52

سَأَكْفِيكَهُ ـ مَا أَنْسَ لَا أَنْسَ مُؤَانَسَتَكَ ـ
أَشْتَرَيْتَ مَا تَحْتَاجُ إِلَيْهِ [هَلِ ٱشْتَرَيْتَ] ـ يَا ٱبْنَتِي

خُذِي مَا أُعْطِيكِ وَٱشْتَرِي مَا تُرِيدِينَ - بَكَتِ
ٱلنِّسَاءُ عَلَى ٱلْمَقْتُولِينَ [ٱلْقَتْلَى] - مَنْ يَبْكِي ٱلْآنَ
سَيَضْحَكُ - أَظُنُّ أَنَّهُمْ سَيَبْقَوْنَ عَلَى مَا هُمُ ٱلْآنَ
عَلَيْهِ - لَا يُلْهِكَ لَعِبٌ عَنْ دُرُوسِكَ - نَهَيْتُهَا
وَٱنْتَهَتْ - أُلْهُوا عَمَّا يَصْنَعُونَ - أُلْهِينَ عَمَّا يَصْنَعْنَ -
إِنَّ ٱلْخَلِيفَةَ أَبْقَاهُ ٱللهُ لَا يَنْسَى مُكَافَأَةَ مَنْ
يَسْتَحِقُّهَا .

53

he said, let me make my will, and he said, make it — they held the views of the philosophers — are you not ashamed that this should be the measure of your kindness to your son ? — when you feel no shame (at it) then act as you please — why do you hear and not understand ? — they made him rich and he made them little return — may God let you see in your sons what he let your father see in you and may God let your sons see in you what he let you see in your father — when he promised something good, he performed ; when he threatened, he did not perform and forgave — prefer what you will meet to-morrow to what you will never see — I used to find those who promise and perform, those who promise and do not perform wearied me — I was ashamed (of my treatment) of him and sent (one) to him with the jewels — we have what you want ; go to your house and it will come to you — let one of you guard his face from the Fire — the caliph appoints whom he will.

54

أَمَرَهُمْ أَنْ يَأْتُوا بِكُتُبِهِمْ ـ كَيْفَ رَأَيْتَ مِصْرَ ـ هَاؤُلَاءِ ٱلنِّسَاءُ هَلْ تَفِينَ مَا وَعَدْنَ ـ اِتَّقُوا ٱلاتِّهَامَ ـ حَيَّوْنَا تَحِيَّةَ ٱلْكَرِيمِ ـ أَرِنِي كَيْفَ ذٰلِكَ يَنْفَعُنِي ـ سَلِ ٱلْحَافِظَ أَنْ يُرِيَكَ مَا فِي ٱلصَّنَادِيقِ ـ اِتَّقُوا ٱللّٰهَ وَأَكْرِمُوا ٱلْمَلِكَ ـ أُوثِرُ أَنْ يَخَافَنِي ٱلنَّاسُ مِنْ أَنْ يَتَّقُوا ٱللّٰهَ ـ اِيتِنِي سَهْمِي مِنَ ٱلطَّعَامِ فَأَكَلَهُ عِنْدَ ٱلنَّهْرِ ـ أَلَمْ تَرَوْا كُلُّكُمْ مَا كَتَبَتْ عَمَّتُكُمْ ـ إِنَّ ٱلدَّرْسَ ٱلْكَثِيرَ يُعْيِي ٱلصِّغَارَ.

55

if you do not kill him, I shall certainly marry him; then he will have killed your father and married your mother; so he killed him — had avarice been a shirt, I would not have put it on; had it been a road, I would not have travelled it — if what keeps me alive is in heaven, send it down; if it is in the earth, bring it out; if it is far off, bring it near; and if it is near, make it easy — if you sit with the learned, be more eager to hear than to speak — were it not that his deeds do not make necessary (make impossible) the forgiving of him, he would deserve to be left alive for this excellence — there is no strength except under the garment of hard work — why do you not compose long lampoons? I have not found a poem (longer) than one verse to travel — he deposited this money with several men ; they made off with it, except one Jew — I have come only on business which concerns the minister and myself alone ; discussion of it is useful only in strict privacy — there is a remedy for every disease except death — you are nothing but a thing to which nobody pays any attention — they are infidels ; they shall be asked to repent ; if they repent (well and good) ; if not, their heads shall be cut off.

56

مَنْ لَمْ يَخْطِئْ لَمْ يَصْنَعْ شَيْئًا ـ جَاءَ كُلُّ ٱلسُّكَّانِ
إِلَّا أَبَاكَ ـ إِنْ صَوَّبْتُمُوهُ فَاتَّبِعُوا أُسْوَتَهُ ـ إِنْ وَجَدْتَ
أَنِّي جِئْتُ فِي أَمْرٍ يَخُصُّنِي وَلَا يَعُمُّ ٱلْقَوْمَ جَمِيعًا
فَأَذْهِبْنِي ـ مَا أَيْقَظَنِي إِلَّا حَرُّ ٱلشَّمْسِ عَلَى
ظَهْرِي [لَمْ يُوقِظْنِي] ـ أَيْنَمَا سَكَنْتَ لَقِيتَ أَصْدِقَاءَ ـ
لَا يُشَابِهُ مِنَ ٱلْأَوْلَادِ أَبَاهُمْ إِلَّا مُحَمَّدٌ ـ إِنْ صَدَّقْتُمْ
مَا يَقُولُ وَجَبَ عَلَيْكُمْ أَنْ تَفْعَلُوا عَلَيْهِ ـ لَمْ يَدَعْ
مِنَ ٱلْبِرِّ شَيْئًا إِلَّا فَعَلَهُ ـ إِنْ أَبْطَأْتَ ٱلْأَكْلَ أَطَلْتَ
ٱلْعُمْرَ ـ إِذَا مَاتَ تَقَاتَلَ وَرَثَتُهُ عَلَى ٱلْوِرَاثَةِ ـ لَوْلَاهُ
لَهَلَكَ ٱلْجَيْشُ.

57

he knew that when he refused them civil strife would flare up, from the consequences of which he would not be safe, and that the (right) policy made gentleness to them necessary — while we were burying him another body was carried — I felt acute pain and when it was in the night it became quiet and I slept — when your fathers made mistakes no one did right except you — when the illness grew strong upon him he kept his bed — there did not pass over this except less than a month until (less than a month after this) the caliph summoned his cousin and invested him with the ministry — I was talking to him when some young men appeared; he called the eldest of them and whispered to him something apart from me and his fellows (which we could not hear) — he went with him until they reached the house like horses racing — his friends had evil forebodings and feared for him, yet the first thing they knew was that he was there driving the camels and they two drove them with him — he stayed in the town till, when the heat of summer fatigued him, he went to his estate.

58

لَمَّا ٱشْتَرَكُوا فِي ٱلشُّغْلِ ٱشْتَرَكُوا فِي ٱلرِّبْحِ ـ لَمَّا
أَقْبَلْ سَهْمِي مِنَ ٱلْأَجْرِ ـ مَتَى رَأَيْتُمْ أَحَدًا يُشَابِهُهُ
وَجْهًا ـ أَشْرَكَنِي مَعَ نَفْسِهِ فِي طَلَبِهِ مِنَ ٱلْحُكُومَةِ ـ
إِذَا ذَهَبْتَ إِلَى بِلَادٍ غَرِيبَةٍ فَٱتَّخِذْ عَادَاتِهَا ـ لَمَّا
أَعْطَوْنِي سَهْمِي لَمْ أَرْضَ عَنْهُ ـ أَصَابَهُ ٱلْفَقْرُ وَإِذَا

أَصْدِقَاؤُهُ مَعَهُ [يُسَاعِدُونَهُ] ـ لَمَّا رَأَتِ ٱلنَّهْيَ غَيْرَ نَافِعٍ بَكَتْ ـ كَانَ يَشْتَغِلُ بِٱلْكِتَابَةِ حَتَّى إِذَا قَدْ كَتَبَ أَوْرَاقًا كَثِيرَةً أَعْيَا بَيَاضُ ٱلْوَرَقِ عَيْنَيْهِ ـ إِنَّ ٱلْوَعْدَ إِذَا لَمْ يَصْحَبْهُ إِنْجَازٌ يُحَقِّقُهُ كَكَلَامٍ لَا مَعْنَى لَهُ .

59

I stayed in the land of polytheism 4 months and 11 days — she bought one cock and 15 hens — his caravan consisted of 100 camels and 25 donkeys — he was born in the year 1932 — the war lasted two years and a half — the government takes one-tenth of all the goods of the merchants who come into its country from outside — I have not eaten anything for three nights (days) and I want you to stay with me that we may eat and talk — his death was two years before the great earthquake — he is 65 years old — a kind act is only perfected by 3 qualities, doing it quickly, making light of it, and keeping it secret.

60

إِنَّ أَنْوَاعَ ٱلتَّمْرِ هِيَ ٱثْنَانِ وَسَبْعُونَ نَوْعًا ـ هِيَ بِنْتُ سَبْعَ وَعَشْرَةَ سَنَةً ـ كَانَ ذَلِكَ ٱلشَّيْخُ أَبَا قَوْمِهِ كَانَ لَهُ سِتَّةَ عَشَرَ ٱبْنًا وَٱثْنَتَا عَشْرَةَ ٱبْنَةً ـ قَطَعَتِ ٱللَّحْمَ ٱثْنَى عَشَرَ سَهْمًا ـ ٱنْصَرَفَ ٱلْأَضْيَافُ ٱثْنَيْنِ

اُثْنَيْنِ ـ سَافَرَ تِسْعَةَ عَشَرَ يَوْمًا يَعْبُرُ ثَلَاثَةَ أَنْهَارٍ
وَيَصْعَدُ فِي سَعْبَةِ جِبَالٍ ـ أَعْفُ عَنْهُ سَبْعِينَ مَرَّةً ـ
وَصَلَ رَسُولِي بَعْدَ وُصُولِي بِثَلَاث سَاعَاتٍ ـ وَرِثَتِ
اُبْنَتُهُ رُبْعَ رُبْعِ مَالِهِ ـ هُوَ اُلِابْنُ اُلسَّابِعُ لِاُبْنٍ
سَابِعٍ.

61

he sat like a tired man — have you ever heard the like of this? he said, no, the like of it has never torn my ears — Moses hit the stone once and water came out enough for all the people — the woman of the house drove out the thief, hitting him with the broom — cause them to hear the word of God and bring them to their place of safety — we journeyed some stages and reached a place where lions were numerous where we feared for our horses — let us now mention the history from the birth of the apostle of God to (the time of) his mission — they tried me with questions of which I understood nothing — we crossed the river, some by a ferry and some by a ford — he was the most remembering of men for what he heard, the least of them in (need of) sleep, and the most enduring of wakefulness.

62

اِشْتَهَرَ اُسْمُهُ فِي اُلْمَشْرِقِ وَاُلْمَغْرِبِ ـ دَخَلَ اُللِّصُّ
دِخْلَةَ اُلْأَسَدِ وَخَرَجَ خِرْجَةَ اُلشَّاةِ ـ يَسْبَحُ أَوْلَادُهُ
جَمِيعًا سِبْحَةَ اُلسَّمَكِ ـ مَا دَامَتِ اُلْحَيَاةُ لَا أَتْرُكُ

الْمُقَاتَلَ - قَطَعَ الطِّفْلُ إِصْبَعَهُ بِمِقَصِّ الْخَيَّاطِ - يَغْسِلُ كَلْبَهُ كُلَّ يَوْمٍ غَسْلَتَيْنِ - إِنَّ الْعَقْلَ لِلْإِنْسَانِ مِبْرَدٌ يَبْرُدُ بِهِ خُشُونَةَ الْقَلْبِ وَمِكْنَسَةٌ يُزِيلُ بِهَا أَعْمَالَ السُّوْءِ وَمِدَقٌّ يَدُقُّ بِهِ رَأْسَ الشَّيْطَانِ وَمُنْخُلٌ يُنَظِّفُ بِهِ أَفْكَارَهُ - يَفْتَخِرُ الشَّامِيُّ بِثَلْجِ جِبَالِهِ وَفَوَاكِهِهَا وَالْمِصْرِيُّ بِمَاءِ نَهْرِهِ - مَا كَانَ لِلنَّجَّارِ أَنْ يَجْهَلَ كَيْفِيَّاتِ أَنْوَاعِ الْخَشَبِ الْمُخْتَلِفَةِ .

63

the judge decided against the plaintiff and acquitted the defendant — he began asking a loan of me and I lent him 500 dinars to get quit of him — he saw a sick fox which could not move and said, this fox must die of hunger — lead us in the straight path, the path of those to whom you have given bounty, who were not the object of your anger and have not gone astray — man wants by nature the things forbidden — some people fell into an argument and looked for a passer-by to decide between them ; when he asked about the matter in dispute they could not explain the point of difference — then the unbelievers will drop their heads in fear of what they may see and will wail — you cannot defend yourselves, you must submit — misfortunes happen inevitably ; some of them are mercy and grace from God to his servant and others are punishment (vengeance) — be rich if you will or poor, care is unavoidable in the world.

64

اِحْمِلُوا ٱلْوَلَدَ ٱلْمَغْشِيَّ عَلَيْهِ إِلَى ٱلْمُسْتَشْفَى – إِنَّ
ٱلْمُدَّعَى عَلَيْهِ فِي ٱلْمَحْكَمَةِ وَأَيْنَ ٱلْمُدَّعِي – كَانَتْ
بِنْتٌ زَمِنَتْ نَحْوَ خَمْسَ عَشْرَةَ سَنَةً لَا يُمْكِنُهَا أَنْ
تَتَقَلَّبَ مِنْ جَنْبٍ إِلَى جَنْبٍ أَوْ يُقَلِّبَهَا غَيْرُهَا – مَا
ظَنَنْتُ أَنَّهُ أَمْكَنَهُ أَنْ يَذْكُرَنِي حَتَّى دُعِيَ بِي –
مَا كَانَ مَعَكَ ثَمَنُ هٰذَا ٱلْبَطِّيخِ مَا قَدَرْتَ تَمْنَعُ
نَفْسَكَ مِنْهُ – أَتْرُكُ مَشْدُودًا عَلَيَّ وَثَاقِي – لَمْ نَجِدْ
مِنْ دَفْعِ ذٰلِكَ إِلَيْهِ بُدًّا – حَسْبِي ٱلَّذِي بِي – كَيْفَ
أَصْبَحَ زَوْجُكِ قَالَتْ لَا حَيًّا فَيُرْجَى وَلَا مَيِّتًا
فَيُنْسَى – لَا تُعْطِي مَا لَيْسَ عِنْدَكَ.

65

I saw (thought) the wisdom of the poor despised — I shall wash disgrace off me with the sword though God's providence brings on me what it may — I know, the command (business) of the apostle of God is more blessed than mine — it is as if al-Husain was advancing towards you — the army feared death till the hearts of most of them were as air — you speak the words of one whose character it is not to keep truth — the importance of the world in the eye of Abd al-Rahman and that he thought the beggar who came to him the angel of death made him small in my sight — the gifts of the sultan were only for the poor and those whose hearts had been won over — take us out of this land the people of which are evil-doers — I seem to see you pretending to be ignorant — I have suffered from time (fate) all my life till I cannot hope for prosperity — the king of Egypt devotes his attention to the improvement of agriculture especially cotton.

66

وُلِدَ ٱلرَّجُلُ ٱلشَّرُّ لَيْلَةَ مَاتَ فِيهَا ٱلرَّجُلُ ٱلْخَيْرُ –
كَأَنِّي بِكُمْ تَكْرَهُونَنِي – إِنْ تُعِيدُوهَا نُعِدْ لَكُمْ
مِنْ هِجَاءٍ سَائِرٍ كَلَامُهُ – يَا سَامِعَ ٱلدُّعَاءِ
خَلِّصْنِي مِمَّا يَحْتَالُونَ عَلَيَّ أَعْدَائِي – كَأَنِّي بِكُمْ
تُرَاهِنُونَ عَلَى فَرَسٍ لَا يَسْبِقُ فِي ٱلسِّبَاقِ – أَرْتِنَا
ٱلْخَيَّاطَةُ ثِيَابًا مُخْتَلِفَةً أَلْوَانُهَا – مَنْ عَلَّمَ شَيْخًا
فَكَأَنَّهُ يَبَّضَ أَسْوَدَ – مَا رَأَيْتُ أَحَدًا مِنَ ٱلْخُلَفَاءِ
أَكْرَهَ إِلَيْهِ ٱلدِّمَاءُ مِنْ هِشَامٍ – كَانَ يَتَعَشَّى وَلَا
يَتَغَدَّى فَحَسْبُهُ ذٰلِكَ أَرْبَعِينَ سَنَةً.

67

beware of begging from men, for it is man's last way of earning — how vigorously he is washing himself — we ask you by God to observe towards us the testament of the apostle of God — what a bad decision they have arrived at — know that God is your lord, what a lord, what a helper — worthy Musaab! whose ancestors are noble — how careless she is in her own affairs, how busy about those of others — how thirsty the boy is, I cannot satisfy him — beware of those who make excuses — I swore extravagant oaths, he shall not thirst so long as I live — lack of money and opportunity made me unable to help him.

68

نِعْمَ ذٰلِكَ ٱلْوَلَدُ سَابِحًا ـ أَكْذِبْ بِهِ وَٱلْعَجَبُ أَنَّ
كُلَّ وَاحِدٍ يُصَدِّقُهُ ـ مَا أَعْطَشَ ٱلطِّفْلَ مَلَأْتُ لَهُ
ثَلَاثَ كُؤُوسٍ لَبَنًا وَيُفَرِّغُهَا جَمِيعًا ـ مَا أَسْرَعَ
مَا يَأْتِيكُمُ ٱلْعَدُوُّ ـ إِذِ ٱنْقَطَعَ عَنْهُمُ ٱلْمِيَاهُ قَالُوا
أَهْلَكْتَنَا قَالَ قَدْ بَلَغْتُمُ ٱلْمَاءَ مَا أَقْرَبَكُمْ بِهِ ـ
بِئْسَ زَوْجُ ٱلْمَرْأَةِ ٱلْحُرَّةِ أَنْتَ ـ وَٱلَّذِى نَفْسِى بِيَدِهِ
لَيَنَامَنَّ عُرْيَانًا فِى ٱلثَّلْجِ ـ وَرَبِّ ٱلْكَعْبَةِ إِلَّا
بَيَّنْتَ لِى رِسَالَتَكَ ـ وَٱللّٰهِ لَا شَمَّ قَاتِلُ مُسْلِمٍ رَائِحَةَ
ٱلْجَنَّةِ ـ يَجِبُ أَنْ أُعَرِّفَكَ أَنَّكَ أَنْتَ ٱلْأَحْمَقُ لَا أَنَا.

69

I shall not come in and not go away until you ride to the mosque — either I go to Syria, and how unpleasant that will be, or I stay ; and therein is a reward for me — we claim that men are graded in excellence not by their fathers but by their acts, their characters, their magnanimity, and their high ambitions — the Arabs say of one who is asked to give and cannot and refuses, my house is stingy not I — I was alone with her and the moon showed her to me ; when it disappeared she showed it to me — do not speak of what you do not know lest you be suspected in what you do know — do not forbid a quality (mode of behaviour) and come to (do) something like it — the Arabs will not consent to put you in authority as you are not one of them — this poem is something which happened in youth ; I made it about my wife. I was inclined to (in love with) her, she was my slave and ruled my heart ; but now, I have had no truck with such things for years and have not made poetry for a long time.

70

لَيْتَنِي لَمْ تَلِدْنِي أُمِّي وَلَمْ أَرَ نُورَ ٱلنَّهَارِ ـ كُنْتُ أَسْتَتِرُ فِي بَيْتِهَا وَهِيَ تَصْعَدُ إِلَيَّ كُلَّ يَوْمٍ تَسْأَلُ مَا أَحْتَاجُ إِلَيْهِ ـ حَلَفَ أَلَّا يَبْدُلَ هٰذَا ٱلْقَمِيصَ أَوْ يَفْرَغَ مِنْ أَمْرِ مَنْ شَتَمَهُ ـ وَرَدَتِ ٱلْكُتُبُ إِلَى مَحْمُودٍ وَهُوَ عَامِلُ ٱلشَّأْمِ أَنْ يَجْمَعَ بَيْنَنَا فِي ٱلْمَسْجِدِ وَلَا نَبْرَحَ أَوْ يُرْضِيَنَا ـ رُبَّ آكِلٍ شَاكِرٍ أَعْظَمُ

أَجْرًا مِنْ صَائِمٍ ـ أَمَرَ ٱلْأَمَةَ بِغَسْلِ ٱلثِّيَابِ وَتَنْشِيفِهَا
تَنْشِيفًا تَامًّا ـ رُبَّ صَحْرَاءَ قَطَعْتُهَا وَذَخِيرَةٍ وَجَدْتُهَا
وَمُشْكِلَةٍ حَلَلْتُهَا ـ سَأَلَنِي ٱبْنُ كَمْ أَنْتَ [كَمْ عُمْرُكَ
ـ كَمْ سَنَةً لَكَ] ـ لَيْتَكَ تَدْخُلُ فَتُسَلِّمُ عَلَى ٱلْأَمِيرِ
وَتُخْبِرُهُ بِحَقِيقَةِ ٱلْأَمْرِ فَيَسْكُنَ غَضَبُهُ عَنَّا ـ أَبْطِئِ
ٱلْأَكْلَ فَتَهْضِمَ ٱلطَّعَامَ هَضْمًا كَامِلًا.

71

I love you for yourself more than my loving you for myself (profit) — how do you find yourself? I find myself not finding what I desire and desiring what I do not find. I am in a very bad age among very bad men; he who is generous does not find (anything to give) and he who does find is not generous — by the excuse we make God has enabled you to dispense with excusing yourself and by our love to you God has enabled us to dispense with thinking badly of you — to whom did your father give his dying charge about you? he gave his charge to me, not about me — liberal of tongue without action! would that the liberality of the tongue was in your hands — but God has saved me by you; no one has consoled me with a more useful than your consolation — satisfy my brother and my ally who between them took the captive — a sultan wanted to build a palace and estimated for this millions of dirhams; the expenditure was above the estimate several times and he required the minister to send money for this although the income (of the country) came short of the outgoings — he picked out those who sold in the markets things like cooking pots and old shirts and what one would be compelled to think unsaleable except from dire distress and old women who sold what they had spun and gave them several times the price of it (the goods) and left it (the goods) with them.

72

مَا أَعْرِفُ لِهٰذِهِ ٱلثِّيَابِ ثَمَنًا وَلَا رَأَيْتُ مِثْلَهَا قَطُّ
وَلَوْلَا أَنِّي شَهِدْتُهَا لَكَذَّبْتُ بِوُجُودِ مِثْلِهَا وَلَوْ
قُلْتُ أَنَّ ثَمَنَ كُلِّ وَاحِدٍ مِائَةُ أَلْفِ دِينَارٍ مَا خِفْتُ
ٱلْبُعْدَ ـ وَٱللهِ مَا كَانَ فِي نَفْسِي أَنْ أُعْطِيَهَا إِلَّا
مِائَتَيْ دِرْهَمٍ وَلٰكِنَّ ٱللهَ أَجْرَى لَهَا عَلَى يَدِي
مِائَتَيْ دِينَارٍ فَلَا أَرْجِعُ فِي ذٰلِكَ أَعْطِهَا ـ كَانَ
ٱلْوَزِيرُ يَسْتَخِفُّ صَاحِبَ دِيوَانِ ٱلْخَرَاجِ وَإِذَا أَرَادَ
عَمَلًا مِنَ ٱلدِّيوَانِ أَوْ حِسَابًا غَفَلَ عَنِ ٱلصَّاحِبِ
وَٱسْتَدْعَى ٱلْكُتَّابَ وَٱسْتَشَارَهُمْ وَٱلصَّاحِبُ حَاضِرٌ
فَإِذَا أَرَادَ عَمَلًا يَعْلَمُ أَنَّ صِنَاعَةَ ٱلصَّاحِبِ لَا تَفِي
بِهِ وَلَا يُمْكِنُهُ ٱلْكَلَامُ فِيهِ شَاوَرَهُ بَيْنَ يَدَيِ ٱلنَّاسِ

لِيُبَيِّنَ نَقْصَهُ ـ قَالَ ٱلنَّبِيُّ فِي ٱلنِّسَاءِ شَاوِرْهُنَّ
وَخَالِفُوهُنَّ وَإِنِّي عَصَيْتُهُ وَأَطَعْتُ صَاحِبَتِي فَٱشْتَرَيْتُ
غُلَامًا فَسَرَقَ ـ لَا يُغْنِي حَذَرٌ مِنْ قَدَرٍ ـ مَا ٱلزُّهْدُ
فِي ٱلدُّنْيَا قَالَ أَنْ لَا يَغْلِبَ ٱلْحَرَامُ صَبْرَكَ وَلَا
ٱلْحَلَالُ شُكْرَكَ ـ عَلِّمْ أَوْلَادِي ٱلسِّبَاحَةَ قَبْلَ
ٱلْكِتَابَةِ فَإِنَّهُمْ يُصِيبُونَ مِنْ يَكْتُبُ عَنْهُمْ وَلَا
يُصِيبُونَ مَنْ يَسْبَحُ عَنْهُمْ.

INDEX

(Supplementary to the Table of Contents)